MARRIED IN MOSCOW

A RED-HOT MEMOIR IN COLD WAR TIMES

JOANN AND JIM MEAD

Married in Moscow: A Red-Hot Memoir in Cold War Times
Copyright © 2024 Joann and Jim Mead

Produced and printed by Stillwater River Publications. All rights reserved. Written and produced in the United States of America. This book may not be reproduced or sold in any form without the expressed, written permission of the author(s) and publisher.

Visit our website at www.StillwaterPress.com for more information.

First Stillwater River Publications Edition

ISBN: 978-1-963296-91-4

Library of Congress Control Number: 2024919347

Names: Mead, Joann, author. | Mead, Jim (James Valda), author.
Title: Married in Moscow : a red-hot memoir in Cold War times / Joann and Jim Mead.
Description: First Stillwater River Publications edition. | West Warwick, RI, USA : Stillwater River Publications, [2024]
Identifiers: ISBN: 978-1-963296-91-4 | LCCN: 2024919347
Subjects: LCSH: Mead, Joann. | Mead, Jim. | Americans--Soviet Union--Biography. | Teachers--Russia (Federation)--Moscow--Biography. | Married people--Russia (Federation)--Moscow-- Biography. | Soviet Union--Politics and government--1945-1991. | Soviet Union--Foreign relations. | Cold War. | Diplomacy. | Spies. | LCGFT: Autobiographies.
Classification: LCC: DK34.A45 M43 2024 | DDC: 947.004130092--dc23

1 2 3 4 5 6 7 8 9 10

Written by Joann and Jim Mead.
Cover and interior design by Elisha Gillette.
Published by Stillwater River Publications, West Warwick, RI, USA.

The views and opinions expressed in this book are solely those of the author(s) and do not necessarily reflect the views and opinions of the publisher.

To Gina Anne
Conceived in Moscow
Back in the USSR

TABLE OF CONTENTS

Authors' Note and Acknowledgments   vii

Moscow Arrival and British Vetting   1
My Arrival and the Matchmaker   7
Tin Foil Hats and Diplomats   17
Accidental Kindergarten Teacher   25
Red Square and Rockets' Red Glare   33
Driving in the Soviet Union   41
Collections, Attachés, and Correspondents   51
Dissidents, Artists, and Refuseniks   61
Soviet Leadership and Books Changing History   75
Shopping for Anything, Everything, and Art   85
Fun and Games in Moscow   101
Ladies Play Broomball and Bob Hope   109
Diplomacy, Right?   117
Trains, Planes, and Trucks?   127
Kiev (now Kyiv) and Kompromat   137
Propaganda   147
Kids in the Caucasus   159
Komsomol Kids   173
Dinner with U.S. Ambassador Watson   181
Olympic Dreams and Nakhodka Nightmares   187
Journey to Japan   195
Misha Bear Meets Mickey Mouse   203
Big Bird and Baba Yaga   213
Married in Moscow?   225
Goodbyes and Baby Arrivals   235

Afterword   249
About the Authors   252

AUTHORS' NOTE AND ACKNOWLEDGMENTS

WHEN YOU THINK ABOUT YOUR LIFE, IS THERE AN INFLEC-tion point where something happens that redirects your future? During our time in Moscow, 1979-1981, our lives changed as did the world around us. Today, Moscow is a very different place. But back in the USSR, we had fun. And that is what most of this memoir is about. We tell our story in two very different voices. It was the best of times for some, it was the worst of times for others. And sometimes, things could go horribly wrong for us. Living in the Soviet Union during the Cold War did not come without risk.

We were teachers at the Anglo-American School in Moscow. We had diplomatic status and were under the protective umbrellas of our embassies—Jim, the British embassy, and Joann, the U.S. Embassy in Moscow. Today, the Anglo-American School (AAS) no longer exists. The school was originally founded in 1949 as the Children's Center. In 1955 the American and British Ambassadors changed the name to the Anglo-American School. In 2021, the school was no longer a diplomatic school when history teacher, Marc Fogel, was detained for smuggling medical marijuana in his luggage. He did not have diplomatic immunity, as did we, and was sentenced to fourteen years in a Russian penal colony. In 2023, the Russian Ministry of Justice designated the Anglo-American School as a "foreign agent" and the school was permanently closed.

So, what inspired us to write our memoir? Plenty. We both like to write and have published articles and books. Joann wrote a short story about our wedding in Moscow that sparked the idea to write a memoir. During the pandemic, Jim digitized hundreds of slides that Joann had hidden away for over forty years. Some of the best are photographs in our book. Another hidden treasure was buried in a large poster tube—twenty Soviet communist propaganda and satire posters from the 1970s and early 1980s. We restored and framed our collection. Drawings and paintings from our friend Sasha, a dissident artist, contrast starkly with the Socialist Realism posters. All these images bring life to our memories and stories. Many are humorous, some are risky, and a few are not funny at all. Most bring laughter while others might make you cry. We hope to open windows for you to see life under the Soviet Union, the remote places we traveled to, and the people we came to know. We want to share with you our understanding of the suppression of dissidents, journalists, and political prisoners. The tradition of harsh suppression of political dissenters stretches back to the czar and forward to the present day. Russia today is shaped by its past. Present-day Putin is a product of the Soviet Union under which we lived.

Are the people in our memoir real? Yes, but sometimes we change their names, for various reasons. Many other people willingly came along for the ride. More than forty years later, we agree that our time in Moscow was an incredible adventure. But it's the warmth and kindness of the teachers, the diplomats, the correspondents, and Russian friends, that left an indelible mark.

We have since reconnected with Moscow friends who shared their memories. We thank Marcia Morris who, with her seamless translations, allowed us to "talk" and make friends with Russians—mostly dissidents and artists. Marcia, the Russian teacher at the Anglo-American School (AAS), is now professor emerita of Slavic languages at Georgetown University. On a trip to three Caucasus countries with six teachers and thirty rambunctious middle school kids, she reluctantly took on the role of fearless leader. Her stories pepper our memoir, adding more spice to the red-hot flavor.

Other colleagues from AAS contributed more stories and added photos to our personal collection. Anne (Gray) Higgins lives in Scotland. She was Maid of Honor at our Moscow wedding. Our Canadian friend, Ken Blogg, shook Bob Hope's hand. Both show up in so many stories that you will feel like you know them.

Denise Williams contributed her memories from her two visits to Moscow. Dody Vendrick showed up in Moscow with her family, and Russell Piti critiqued and parsed our every word. Our friend Jan Kreutziger listened patiently to our continuing Soviet sagas over the years. There are way too many friends to mention who encouraged us to write this memoir. You know who you are. Thank you all.

ОДИН ONE

MOSCOW ARRIVAL AND BRITISH VETTING

JIM: IN 1979 I WAS NOT BY ANY STRETCH OF THE IMAGination a veteran international traveler. My overseas experience was three short vacations in Portugal and Italy and one French day trip. The letter confirming my job in the Soviet Union filled me with excitement and trepidation. I believe the letter said, "Welcome to the Red Star Express." I spent some time conjuring up images of living in Russia, most of which were wrong.

Just a couple of my pre-arrival fantasies. I worried I knew no Russian so how would I speak with my Russian neighbors in my apartment block? Wrong! Foreigners didn't live with Russians, we had separate apartment complexes that most Russians would avoid like the plague. A stern *militsiya* (police) was on guard twenty-four hours to keep regular Russians out and log our coming and going. Another fantasy, I would purchase a motorcycle and sidecar as I had never driven a car—Wrong.

Imagine my relief when I got a letter inviting me to the British Foreign and Commonwealth office. At last! Someone would give me useful information about living in the Soviet Union—Wrong. The dingy office on an upper floor in London would not look out of place in a Dickens novel. The slightly portly office denizen conjured up Mr. Bumble from Dicken's Oliver Twist. His glasses perched well down his nose. When I was seated, he started to ask about various details of my life. As Bumble asked questions, he occasionally glanced at a file on his desk and took a few notes.

"Okay old boy, you were a leader in student unions and a representative in the UK teaching union. How would you describe your political affiliations?" I have a problem, what is in that file? I was always on the election slate that included left-wing Labour Party members, unaligned socialists, and gulp—Communists. My answer is still in my memory. "I canvassed for Labour Party candidates and was labeled as an unaligned socialist and a Fabian. I can see my new job disappearing, but I have given him a multiple-choice answer that excludes the word communist. "Let's put you down as Labour Party." Mr. Bumble makes a careful note. Yes, I think to myself let's do that. The new job is coming back in reach.

"This is only a formality; would you be willing to sign the Official Secrets Act?" This is no formality in my mind, it is a big deal. I am going to teach kindergarten kids. I don't think the average five-year-old provides information important to MI6 spies. Mr. Bumble does say that this will give me some protection if things get tricky. He fails to embellish on what "tricky" means. All I can think about is shipping you off to Siberia permanently. Or "enjoying" a treason trial with a long British prison sentence for something I did or said in the Soviet Union. I sign on the dotted line.

We have spent about thirty minutes in our "old boy" chat, and I have learned precisely nothing about life in the Soviet Union. Mr. Bumble sounded like a product of Oxford or Cambridge, maybe with a first-class degree. He was not one of our infamous English upper-class twits. He steered our talk with deft skill. Finally, I get a nugget of information. I must go to the Soviet Embassy to get my visa. Why was this useful? It gave me a first-impression view of Soviet bureaucracy at its finest. "You need to fill out this form and send it to the Russian embassy here in London with the listed supporting documents. If I were you, old chap, I would plan to spend a day at the Russian embassy when they send you confirmation of an appointment." Thank you I say bemused and not much informed on any of the questions I had floating in my head.

As I didn't drive, my local Labour London councilor, fellow Fabian, and a friend drove me to the Russian Embassy. Mr. Bumble was wrong, I only spent about four hours sitting in a waiting room to get my visa. I only remember lots of dark wood paneling, pictures of people I didn't know, and liberal amounts of red. At least the lowly functionary who gave me my visa did not call me "old boy" or its near Russian equivalent Comrade. His face was as solemn as the Soviet dignitaries on the walls as he stamped my visa.

I finally got some information that might help me adapt to the diplomatic community. My father was a bank manager with a client who was a tailor. The tailor had an office in the famous London Saville Row and a shop in Broadstairs, Kent. He had outfitted diplomatic gentlemen in overseas posts. We purchased a tailor-made three-piece pinstripe suit, a velvet dinner jacket with bow tie and dress shirt, and a heavy sheepskin coat with beaver collar. The coat still sits in my closet, rarely used. The red velvet dinner jacket was my choice. I had no intention of looking like a penguin in a regular black dinner jacket at some embassy function.

My worldly goods have been shipped and I board a British Airways plane at Heathrow. My suitcase is in the aircraft's hold, and I only have my guitar and the coat. It is early September, and I don't know what to do with my heavy sheepskin coat. There is no room in my suitcase. Early morning at Heathrow airport the weather was not warm, so I think wearing the said coat is still a good idea—Wrong. Upon arrival at Sheremetyevo airport, the heat greets me with a furnace-like blast. Damn, I think how do I carry my heavy suitcase, guitar, and coat? With my English stiff upper lip set and beads of sweat beading on my brow, I walk into the airport buildings with the coat on.

I am standing in line to present my passport and visa. I have five or so in front of me. Panic is setting in. Will this uniformed officer with an unreadable face ask me questions in Russian? Will he think I have something to hide because I am now sweating profusely in this damn coat? The other military types I can see have automatic weapons. I don't think the USSR specializes in warm welcomes. Nobody offered me the traditional Russian welcome of salt and bread. No questions from the stone-faced official. He looks me up and down a few times probably thinking who is this perspiring idiot? The mad dogs and Englishmen go out in the midday sun song sneaks unwanted into my brain. In his elevated booth designed to stop you from seeing what the man is doing, I hear a quick stamp sound, and my passport is returned.

I was told that someone would meet me at the airport. I cannot wait to take off this bloody coat. We are ushered into the customs hall where I retrieve my baggage. This is going to be okay I think to myself—Wrong. As my suitcase is emptied all the contents are given a minute inspection. Is the customs officer fascinated with my new socks and underwear? The whole process takes time. My guitar is looked at and seems to pass muster. Then the customs officer brandishes my guitar sheet music. My songbooks by Jimmy Hendrix, Pink Floyd, and The Who have captured

Jim in Red Square with Lenin, Engels, and Marx

the customs officer's interest. Suddenly, lucky sweaty me has two customs officers paying close personal attention to me. Who would think a kindergarten teacher sweating bullets and overdressed for the ninety-degree heat would be so fascinating? No Russian remember, so how do I explain myself? I point to the guitar and then open one of the music books. Please, oh please, I think, do not ask me to perform a quick medley. My pointing seems to have got across. To this day I cannot play more than one song out of each of the three song books but who cares? My five-year-old kindergartners think I am a cross of Jimmy Hendrix and Pete Townsend with my three chords. I am left to re-pack my case.

    I stagger out of customs, and I see people who are waiting for me. I have the guitar in one hand and the suitcase in the other. I wonder what impression my new boss has gained. I am so overheated in this coat, I am passed caring. For my two years in Moscow, I would be reminded at various times of my arrival in late summer and that sheepskin coat with the beaver collar. Jim has arrived. Look out Mother Russia.

ДВА TWO

MY ARRIVAL AND THE MATCHMAKER

JOANN: IT WASN'T MY FIRST POSTING IN AN INTERnational school. The Anglo-American School in Moscow, USSR, would be night and day compared to my four years teaching in an American School in London. The Principal, Gene, had interviewed me in snowbound New York City the previous winter. I'd flown from Los Angeles to New York to interview for a big oil company school on a Venezuelan peninsula. They covered my travel expenses and paid big buck salaries. One week before, I'd been offered a teaching job with an international school in Tel Aviv. So, I now have three choices. But why, of all places, would I choose the snowy winters of Moscow, Russia during a Cold War when relationships with the West were decidedly frigid? Well, it wasn't for the money. Deep pockets never tempted me. And it wasn't for the sunshine. I wanted adventure, and the intrigue and mystique of Moscow, a place shrouded in mystery, lured me in.

Odd things happened in the months after I accepted the Moscow job. More than once, a yellow note appeared taped to my apartment door. It read something like "Sorry we missed you. Please call for the U.S. Census survey." Of course, I didn't. A second note was left. On the third try an elderly gentleman in a casual suit appeared at my door with a clipboard and papers asking if he could ask some survey questions. He looked pretty harmless, so I asked him to sit on a sofa. I was in my usual attire, my bathrobe. I only dressed in my airline uniform or pajamas. Shift work left me perpetually jet-lagged and tired without having the joy of traveling somewhere exciting. He asked questions like, where did you live last year? London. Where will you live next year? Moscow. He followed with Why questions. His demeanor was in no way threatening. He seemed pleasant and almost grandfatherly. But it all struck me as weird.

Another odd thing happened. I was at work on a grueling job with twelve-hour shifts selling airline tickets to London for the now-defunct Freddie Laker as I waited for my next overseas adventure. During a welcome lull at my desk, I was trying to learn Cyrillic from a Russian textbook when two young guys appeared and asked, "Why are you reading that?" I said something about leaving for a job in Moscow. I was excited and usually talkative and gregarious. They kept asking questions, as if it were a test, about what I knew about the USSR, which was virtually nothing. I assumed they were customers, but they didn't buy tickets and never asked about the flights. Weird. Double weird.

In retrospect, it was pretty transparent. I hoped those weird interviews by a secretive organization found what they wanted to know. They were likely low-level or near-retirement foreign service office people vetting me for a security clearance.

In the summer of 1979, I would meet up with Gene again on a hot, humid summer day at Sheremetyevo airport. I wanted to explore Moscow before school started so I arrived earlier than the other teachers. As Gene drove to my apartment, his assistant Donna chatted with her obvious Canadian accent. We arrived at an enormous Soviet-style apartment block where they were also housed along with their spouses. My neighbors were embassy staff from just about everywhere. A Bangladeshi family lived next door.

A Russian military guard at the entrance waved to us from his sentry box. Nicknamed the "Mili-Man" by expats, he'd watch over my safety, and my comings and goings. All housing blocks designated for foreigners had guards whose real task was to keep Russians out. They also reported any suspicious activities or unusual visitors. Fraternizing with Soviet natives was not encouraged.

My two-bedroom apartment is not far from Moscow State University (MGU). You can't miss MGU and its mammoth Stalin-era "wedding cake" building. My not-so-humble abode, unusually lavish by Soviet standards, is fully furnished with American appliances, Swedish furniture, and Finnish dinnerware. The American Embassy supplied everything I could possibly need, and the Soviets supplied their listening devices. The first thing you must remember when you arrive in Moscow is that Big Brother is real in the Soviet Union.

Once left on my own, I talk to the walls. "Hello. Hello, are you there? I know you're listening to me." I chuckle at my insanity. "Hello there. Where are you, my little friends?" I bantered as if the walls were my audience (well, the walls did have ears). I'd always imagined myself a comedian.

On my second day, to get acquainted with this exotic capital of the Soviet Union, I set out on my own and rode the Moscow underground to Gorky Park. I thought navigating Moscow would be easy, having taken a two-week crash course in Russian. I could now phonetically read the Russian alphabet, Cyrillic, quite an accomplishment in my estimation. I wanted to ride the Gorky Park Ferris Wheel, alleged at that time to be the biggest of its kind, like everything else in the USSR! As luck would have it, it wasn't operating that day.

Gorky Park is enormous. I could easily get lost walking on its vast network of trails, but I'm getting hungry. Maybe, I think, there's a fast-food kiosk or café? A hamburger or even a hotdog on a stick would do. But Gorky Park is not Coney Island. I found a wooden snack shack, but on entering I saw no written menus, not even a chalkboard with scribbles. The patrons, a homogenous group of scruffy men, looked up at me, a Western woman in new jeans. My clothes didn't quite fit in with the usual clientele. The men, I presume, are workers on their lunch break. They sit at a long table eating bowls of overboiled mushy grey-green peas topped off with a slimy mix of fatty sausage. I passed my first test of reading Cyrillic in the Moscow Metro and now I've passed on eating lunch.

Gorky Park soon became famous in Martin Cruz Smith's crime and espionage novel. His classic book was followed by a movie and his depiction of Gorky Park, and the Cold War still rings true. Most memorable were his three dead bodies found when the snow melted, their faces and fingertips surgically removed. Those dismembered bodies and crime novels followed me later in life. I would end up curating lab cadavers and writing crime thrillers.

I'd barely been in Moscow a few days when someone from the American Embassy called. She had compiled a "who's who" guide to who's new in Moscow. Not just Americans, but all sorts of people. She arranged tours and outings for newcomers to Moscow.

When I first met Jim, we were the only two people who showed up for a tour of the Moscow Metro. We entered the underground and arrived in another place in time. Built in 1935, the "palaces of the people" were majestic and ornate. Quite breathtaking with marble walls, statues, paintings, stained glass mosaics, and chandeliers, it was incredibly opulent and kept very clean. Don't think about dropping a gum wrapper or an officious grandma (babushka) will descend upon you with all her wrath. In a country that lost so many millions during the Great Patriotic War (World War II), there were far fewer *dedushkas* (grandfathers) than babushkas.

As I walked by Jim's side, his arm brushed lightly against mine. Like electricity, the shock from his skin made my hair stand up on end. I felt a distinct tingling, but make no mistake, it was not one of those tingling feelings like "falling in love". He was, like me, another teacher—someone I'd be working with at the Anglo-American School. And, as a rule, I would never date another teacher. Oh no.

Jim said, self-mocking, that his sweat made his watch run backward. "It's got something to do with the salt content of my skin." I couldn't help but think that this guy was a bit weird. A pleasant, kind-of-cute long-haired nerd, what the British would call a "boffin". I wondered why this boffin would admit to a quirk of body chemistry that could somehow reverse time. No, he was not my type. I still hadn't figured out what that type was or even if there was such a thing.

Our guide took us to all the best Metro stations, including some she hadn't seen before. You could ride the underground all day for five kopeks, about a nickel. It was one way to keep warm on a freezing day, of which there are many, during the harsh Moscow winters. Those grand ballrooms hidden below contrasted wildly with the stark, monolithic structures above on street level. Moscow above ground couldn't be more mundane with its brutalist Stalin-era buildings. But it was those huge "wedding cake" buildings above that might have prophesied our future. Parting ways at the end of the tour, we knew we'd run into each other again during teacher orientation at the school.

Just a day or two later, I got a phone call. No, not from Jim, the Englishman.

"Hi, I'm the Ambassador's Aide. There's a party at the American dacha. Would you like to go?" I hesitate. "How did you get my number?"

"I'm new to Moscow. An American Embassy staffer gave me your number. Would you like to go to the dacha?" So, the embassy lady was at it again. Was she the official matchmaker? Was this the American Embassy Grindr service? Dating apps on smartphones did not exist back in 1979. Later, I'd come to find out that she'd shown him photos of single women, both embassy staff and teachers. So, I somehow beat out the competition. He must have had some pretty poor pickings.

I discovered that a dacha is a get-away country home for vacations or simply an

Moscow State University MGU

escape from the big city. They're often modest cottages used for summer outings. The American Embassy dacha, a rustic wood-paneled house, was set in the woods about a thirty-minute drive from Moscow. I was not impressed when we got there, it seemed somewhat ramshackle to me.

My new friend is absorbed in a conversation I couldn't follow so I grabbed a beer and wandered the rooms. I find two young men playing Mahjong or trying to learn how to play Mahjong. They'd lined up domino-like white tiles with circles, bamboo, and Chinese characters. I asked to join in a game that I didn't have a clue how to play. But they didn't either. So, I made up the rules as I went along, my usual modus operandi. I knew you could pick and discard tiles by throwing the dice. But how to win was a mystery to me. Time passed and they reckoned I'd beaten them at a game of my invention. "You won." They nod in agreement. But how could that be? "Really?" I couldn't see how. I thought, are they just putting me on, pulling my leg? Or maybe they're spies in training. Could they be practicing the art of deception? In Moscow, nothing is ever what it seems.

The Ambassador's Aide called again. "Guess what? I have two tickets for the Moscow premiere of the Francis Ford Coppola movie, 'Apocalypse Now'." Yes, I knew who Coppola was, the cinematic genius known for "The Godfather" movies. He'd recently released his new 1979 epic Vietnam War film. I'm thinking, now this should be interesting. "Wow, I'd love to go." It certainly beat playing Mahjong in an old wooden Boy Scout hut.

On August 24, 1979, just nine days after the U.S. release of "Apocalypse Now", the movie premiered at the Moscow Film Festival. People stopped us as we walked toward the cinema theater, they were hoping to buy our tickets. We shake our heads, no way. *Nyet*! We're shown to our seats. For over three hours, I was mesmerized, baffled, and mystified by what I'd seen. Overwhelmed, it was just too much for my tiny brain to take in.

I love the big screen. As a kid, I grew up not far from the heart of Hollywood. I was born in Santa Monica, California at St John's Hospital, known as the "Hospital of the Stars". There's a long list of celebrities who were born or died there. It was more than just fate that I'd be drawn to Hollywood. MGM was just a few miles away from home, and our neighborhood boys starred in Rin Tin Tin and Circus Boy. My favorite pastime on Saturday afternoons would be a double feature at the Art Deco-styled Loyola Theatre near Los Angeles Airport. And if there was a major studio preview all the better. We'd keep our eyes peeled for movie stars. Are they sitting in the front row?

So, I'm at a premiere in Moscow of an American film just released in New York

City, Toronto, and my hometown, Los Angeles. I walk out of the theatre and join a parade of people on the red-carpeted hallway but for some reason, the focus seems to be on me. Wait, maybe this is all in my imagination? No, they're not looking at me but above my head, just to my right at a towering figure who from my diminutive perspective seems like a striking hairy giant. The dark-haired full-bearded face I immediately recognize is the icon of cinema, Francis Ford Coppola. And now I'm starstruck, in awe of the creator of the spectacle I've just seen. On that night in Moscow, Soviet culture collided with another, Hollywood. There's a mutual obsession between East and West. We are always fascinated by each other. It's a passionate love-hate relationship.

But I'd come to Moscow to teach, not to paint the town red. The Soviets already commandeered the color red for its propaganda campaigns. So, getting down to business, it's off to work I go. Hi ho! It's orientation day for teachers at the Anglo-American School (AAS). Everyone is brought together for a meet-and-greet of curious teachers and staff excited about the upcoming year. The kids would soon arrive, and we await their first day.

AAS had about two hundred and fifty kindergarten to ninth-grade students from over thirty countries. Many of the kids had lived overseas and were, yet again, displaced to another foreign country. Moscow would have its challenges for all of us, but we were all in it together. Strangers in a strange land, I would teach science to kids in middle school.

The school's Principal was always an American. At that time, five full-time embassy-affiliated teachers hailed from the United States, four from the United Kingdom, and two from Canada. We teachers were considered technical staff of our embassies. Other teachers and assistants were hired from the local community—wives of diplomats and embassy staff from Australia, New Zealand, and other Western embassies. Spouses of foreign correspondents, TV, radio, and newspaper journalists also joined the school staff. The infusion of those groups made the teachers' break room an exciting place to be. It was where all the "breaking news" was shared. Along with my coffee, I'd get a daily dose of what was happening in Moscow and other parts of the Communist world. In the break room, I learned people's different points of view, but usually pro-western. I also heard great gossip. Who was doing what, when, how, why, and where—sometimes even more savory bits.

One afternoon, the NBC correspondent's wife gathered eleven U.S., U.K., and Canadian teachers into the break room. "The 1980 Moscow Summer Olympic Games are just around the corner and NBC is bringing in its production crew of seven hundred, and…" OK, now we are curious. "You teachers all have Soviet driver's licenses and cars." We all owned either a Lada Zhiguli or Niva. "Would you be interested in driving the NBC film crews around Moscow to the different venues?" Now, she has my attention. She gave us a map of the upcoming Moscow Olympics with the locations of press centers, the Sports Palace, sporting events, stadiums, arenas, pools, gyms, other landmarks, and the Olympic Village.

I didn't need money to motivate me. But it would take me a while to learn to navigate Moscow's two Ring roads and figure out the odd system of no left turns. But it's nine months until the opening ceremonies, so plenty of time for practice runs.

"And NBC will pay you one hundred dollars a day, plus gas (petrol) and all other expenses." In 1980 this sounded good enough for us teachers, especially having the bonus of enjoying some of the games up front and personal. I could only anticipate that the film crew might be fun people. So, life in Moscow might not be the hardship I had imagined.

ТРИ
THREE

TIN FOIL HATS AND DIPLOMATS

JOANN: IT WAS LATE SEPTEMBER 1979 WHEN I MET up at the U.S. Embassy with two other new teachers (I'll call them Kate and Tommy). By this time, we teachers had get-togethers with food and drinks, so our stories had poured out. The Iranian revolution led to the fall of the Shah. Kate and Tommy escaped from the country in January of 1979. I remember how they described their harrowing journey in a convoy of cars out of Isfahan. Their lurid details of an amorous goat herder, I cannot repeat here.

Already friends, Kate and I had the same silly sense of humor. Amused and excited, we elbowed each other as we ascended a secret stairway. A security officer took us to a small room not much bigger than an American bathroom. It was somewhere on an upper floor of the embassy chancery. Offices in the building were minuscule. It was snug as a bug in the embassy, a little too cozy to say the least.

While living in Moscow, you always assume that everything has bugs, not as in cockroaches or spiders, but hidden microphones or other gizmos of the surveillance trade. It was well known that the U.S. embassy had more bugs than a swamp, making it vulnerable to surveillance and espionage. Devices had been discovered in multiple nooks and crannies. Bugs were even found hidden in typewriters, there were no computers with cameras in 1979. Microphones were strategically placed so that conversations could be transmitted to the KGB. To get around the problem, the Soviet employees of the U.S. Embassy were limited to the first few floors. All diplomats and higher-ups were higher up on the top floors. But that territory came with other risks. We were told that the upper floors of the chancery were impenetrable and proven to be free of bugs or any surveillance equipment. So, we were told, but the aluminum foil covering the windows in the tiny room did not inspire much confidence. Nor did the security officer complain of a bad headache. He didn't look well. But I couldn't help but wonder if KGB spies could hear us. If this was true, why were the windows covered in aluminum foil? There was a good reason. Microwaves.

Microwaves, low-level at first, were detected long before embassy staff were ever told. Despite their complaints of headaches and other ailments, the radiation was ignored. But over the years, the microwave radiation became more intense and so did the mysterious symptoms. But whose idea was it to kitchen-foil the windows? It seemed like a band-aid on a bullet hole to me. Perhaps mandatory tin foil hats would have better protected the embassy employees. Many of them over the years suffered health consequences, leukemia, and other medical problems. In retrospect, the more I read now about the "Moscow Syndrome" (cousin of the "Havana Syndrome"), the more I wonder.

It's hard to pinpoint the effects of microwaves on people's health. Besides, microwave beams sound too much like sci-fi weapons. Did the electromagnetic waves disturb the electrical activities in my brain? My embassy briefing suggests that something weird might be happening. What else would explain my subsequent naughtiness? Bad Joann.

Officious and grouchy, the security officer sat us at a small wooden table with four chairs. Again, he grimaced with pain and mumbled, "Headache." Was it too much champagne and caviar at an embassy reception last night? Or perhaps he was just feeling annoyed. He went on to tell us what we needed to know. I can't remember his exact words, but whose memory isn't clouded by decades of assaults on our aging brain cells? I'll blame the microwaves.

Our briefing started with the services provided by four Soviet ladies on the ground floor. The Intourist ladies arranged our American apartments in compounds guarded by the Soviet military. I wondered how closely the Miliman watched my comings and goings. The guard was there for my safety and security, right? Protection against thugs and criminals? I doubt it. Over time, I would understand their real purpose—to keep Russians out of our American homes, lest they be tainted by our liberal Western values, freedoms, and relatively opulent lifestyles. The Intourist ladies arranged our cars, travel plans, tickets to the Bolshoi ballet, opera, Moscow circus, cultural and sporting events like hockey or soccer…and lousy restaurants. The Aragvi restaurant, an exception, was always packed. It served up edible Georgian delicacies, great wines, lots of dancing, and fun. But ordinary Russians didn't have the money or the connections, so it was frequented mostly by Soviet elites, gangsters, and foreigners. One other restaurant, the Kiev, served decent Chicken Kiev. We always ordered chicken.

Russian staff operated the embassy switchboard, supposedly to make sure our conversations were kept private. Yeah, right! The Soviets trusted their KGB operatives to watch over us. Our guardian angels, the lovely ladies and gentlemen, monitored everything we Americans did, where we went, and who we went with. They even assigned our seats at events we attended. You always had to assume you might be surrounded by KGB spies who may try to compromise you.

Mr. Headache went over the rules of the U.S. Embassy. First were the rules about the diplomatic pouch. I wondered if it was a leather pouch like the ones used on stagecoaches in the late 1800s. Or was it a bag, a box, or a container? I was never sure what the pouch looked like. It was meant for diplomatic documents and had legal protection. We embassy staff could use the pouch for mailing letters, small boxes, and mailing tubes. It was sealed, tracked, and monitored during transit. I mostly used the pouch to send letters home and my photo film for processing. My slides were a good idea, we finally digitized them forty years later. What a treasure trove that would become. The diplomatic pouch must not be used for anything "illegal". But people will be naughty, right? Contraband and smuggling tempted a few to send illegal art, bibles, and the occasional Alice B Toklas (marijuana) brownies. What else was transported you can only imagine?

"There are also the rules of the Soviet government. You must abide by both American and Soviet rules." Probably not his exact words, but it doesn't matter. You get the gist of it. Right? The Soviet rules are not the "Moscow Rules" as in James Bond or John le Carré spy novels. The "Legal Status of Foreigners in USSR 1975" are the laws of the Supreme Soviet. These laws are meant to keep you under control and out of mischief. Supreme, as in the jumbo-sized group of people who made the laws. Sort of like our American Congress? No, I don't think so. More a giant rubber stamp committee!

But "the head of the diplomatic mission and members of the mission's diplomatic staff enjoy immunity from the criminal, civil, and administrative jurisdiction of the

U.S.S.R." Ahh great! Diplomatic staff enjoy immunity. Moreover, they have personal immunity and cannot be detained or placed under arrest. Phew! I'm considered technical staff, so I must also be protected by the U.S. umbrella, tight? I didn't think much more about it. After all, I'm not a criminal, not by any American standard rule of law. Occasional parking tickets were my biggest infractions.

Simply put, diplomats can't be arrested. I had heard of PNG, *persona non grata*. If you do something or say something your host country disapproves of, you, the foreigner, can be expelled or ordered to leave the country. But they still can't lock you up and throw away the key. I think.

There are other rules, referred to as the Rules of Nonengagement. Engaging with Soviet citizens is not encouraged. Perhaps that means it's not discouraged either. I'd like to get to know some Russian people. I'd heard they can be quite friendly and generous with their vodka.

Mr. Headache handed out two types of maps, one in English, supposedly drawn up by the American CIA. It dates to 1953 but has been edited over the years. My version goes back a few years—it shows the old location of the Anglo-American School before it was relocated in 1976. The other map shows Moscow in two colors. Pink and white. The map says Moscow: Areas Closed to Foreigners, 4 January 1978. Pink means no-go. I am curious (Pink)!

"You must stay within a twenty-five-mile radius of Moscow. Going beyond that on your own is not permitted unless arranged and approved by the Soviet travel bureau." Mr. Headache was adamant. If we travel, we must make arrangements through the travel office on the first floor. "Only and exclusively through our Russian staff on the embassy's first floor. Otherwise, bad things could happen." Mr. Headache warns us.

"What do you think might happen if you bought your own train ticket and ended up in a sleeper car with five big Russian men?" He stares directly at me. Too quick off the mark, loose cannon that I am, I fire away. "You might have some fun?" I shrug and stupidly grin. My unfiltered sense of humor caught everyone off guard. I even surprised myself. Kate's big eyes widened as we glanced at each other. She repeatedly kicks me under the table.

Looking even more annoyed, Mr. Headache didn't think I was funny. He scribbles a note, maybe something about the nutcase teacher who thinks she's a comedian. I get the message; this briefing is not a laughing matter. His headache must now be getting worse.

Then, he says, "There are cities and regions in the U.S.S.R. that are closed to foreigners. Remember all those no-go pink areas. Any violation of these rules is punishable by administrative measures or in a court of law. This is the Soviet law."

"Closed cities" sounds so mysterious to me. What exotic things might be in those cities contained in a sealed box? What intrigue might be found there? Oh, the temptation. Now, those would be fun places to visit, to explore the back alleys, the nooks and crannies, the spooks and spies. I'm daydreaming again about Spy vs Spy in the Mad magazines I devoured as a kid. Those wordless cartoons are full of espionage. Two pointy-nosed agents hide around corners and try to assassinate each other. Each one holds fused bombs that are ready to explode!

Mr. Headache drones on, "When you travel, you become suspect. Whether you're a diplomat or a teacher, you might become useful to them. You can be compromised." He warned. Uh oh, I thought. I'm intrigued but not sure what he meant by "compromised". It didn't mean anything to me at the time. But I would later find out the meaning of the Russian word Kompromat.

There are more Soviet rules, plenty of travel restrictions, and no-go areas. That second map, "Western USSR: Areas Closed to Foreigners, 4 January 1978", had huge splotches of pink and white, as if the USSR had some exotic skin rash. I had never been limited in my travels; I already had a dozen countries under my travel fanny pack. My passport was so full, it needed pages added. Still a California wild child at heart, I had little knowledge or understanding of repressive regimes.

Mr. Headache glares at me as he speaks. "Remember, the women on the first floor work for Intourist. They will assist you. Other people will keep track of you. Someone might make note of who you talk to, they might even listen in on your conversations, bug your telephone, and your home. If you travel, someone will be 'attached' to you. They'll watch over you, follow you, and they might end up in the seats around you at the Bolshoi ballet or the Hockey game." Later, Jim and I found out at a Hockey match, that we low-level, technical staff were left on our own with empty seats all around us. We weren't important enough to bother with, just quasi-diplomats of little concern.

Mr. Headache tells us that there are limits on photography and Soviet rules against taking certain images. The underlying message is to leave the spying to us professionals! The rules are: No boats, no trains, no airplanes. No amber waves of grain. That means no photos of the vast wheat fields for agriculture spies to estimate the harvest. And we must not photograph anything that might put the Soviet Union

Oops! Bad Joann

in a bad light. Nor reveal their technological or military prowess. No military men, no missiles, no munitions, and certainly no MIGs. My antennae go up. I love taking photos.

ЧЕТЫРЕ FOUR

ACCIDENTAL KINDERGARTEN TEACHER

JIM: MY FATHER ALWAYS OFFERED HIS OPINION THAT education was a waste of time. He would back this up by telling me about his departure at fourteen from school. My mother's education was equally short. I followed in Mum and Dad's footsteps and "left" when I was sixteen. My mother had a conference with the headmaster. "Mead needs to apply to a *looser* educational institution; the restrictions of a grammar (selective and exclusive) education do not suit him." My lack of attendance may have influenced the headmaster's conclusion. When we got home my parents made it clear I should look for a job, no loose education institution for me! I drifted into a bank job. At twenty-one I entered teaching college to be a primary school teacher. You can guess how that was received on the home front.

I signed up to teach in London schools before I graduated. This guaranteed me a job. The catch was that the schools I would teach in were in deprived areas. That is the polite teacher code for schools where many kids have learning and behavioral difficulties. In some cases, family situations were where the social services and the police were frequent visitors. I loved the school and the kids I taught. But this environment put a heavy burden on the teachers, including me.

On Fridays, I read an education supplement with teaching job advertisements in the UK and abroad. I thought an international school job might be interesting and a major change in my career. "Teach in the Soviet Union at the Anglo-American School Moscow." For reasons I cannot recall I decided to apply. Moscow sounded exotic compared with jobs in Europe or ones that offered suitcases of cash in the Middle East. I thought about it over the weekend. My current headmaster offered to give me a good confidential reference. I was on good terms with his secretary who said she would type up my application letter. After several rewrites, I handed her the letter to be typed. To save postage she put my application letter, unseen by me, and the reference in the same envelope. Keep this little detail in mind, it has major consequences.

A few weeks later I had an interview with the Moscow principal. I took some time off work and walked across a bridge over the Thames to an office on the opposite riverbank. I introduced myself. I am offered a seat. Gene, the school principal, is from Chicago and managed a mid-west mumble with an immobile top lip. I listen intently to figure out what he's saying as he mumbles.

"It is great to find a male kindergarten teacher."

I smile but I am feeling a little confused. I only took kindergartners for gym classes. I was never their full-time classroom teacher. How on earth did he get this idea? I am in a state of panic.

The mystery is solved as Gene quotes from my application letter. The secretary had decided to change the British "Infants 1 and 2 and primary grades" into American "kindergarten through fifth grade". Gene has read this to mean that I was a kindergarten teacher. I want the job, so I do my best to demonstrate my teaching. From watching and talking with our school's Infant teachers, I describe my limited knowledge of kindergarten teaching. I walked back over the bridge. I am pessimistic despite the cordial way Gene and I finished the interview. A few weeks later a letter arrives from the school. Welcome to the Red Star Express, it reads, with the steps I should take before I arrive in Russia.

One evening in Moscow Gene told me, "I knew something was not right. You looked surprised but I thought you would do your best. You were a good teacher so you could handle things, especially if I gave you a good aide." Those first months I had a wonderful Australian aide, Annie. She was a kindergarten teacher but didn't have the required years of teaching wanted by the Moscow school.

We had a few days to prepare before the students turned up. There are two kindergarten classes. My Canadian colleague, Judy, was a veteran teacher. I quickly discovered a difference in what we would teach. British teachers teach reading in kindergarten. Americans and Canadians don't. My class list showed that most of my kids were used to the English system except for one American. The storeroom had several different reading series. My Canadian colleague didn't need them, so I took them. The more the merrier I thought, if a kid didn't like one series, they could try another. The goal in my mind is to get kids to read. We used phonetic spelling. The child could break the new words they didn't know into their letter sounds. Phonic pronunciation means you don't mind sounding like a gorilla or exotic animal in heat. But for many kids, it works.

The aide and I started to put words on objects in the classroom that we would use for *I Spy* and singing songs. It takes a long time to organize all those pencils, crayons, glue sticks, scissors, and containers to put them in. Plus, we ensure every kid has folders for their work and their names on their storage shelf and coat hook. I found classroom preparation for the school year is always intense. Any lesson you prepared could take hours, but the kids would often finish in a few minutes!

The storeroom also had American textbooks for different subjects. I was fascinated with the Teacher Guide edition that accompanied some children's textbooks. These special editions were written for American consumption. I crack one open and find out this is behaviorism at its best. For example, the book tells the teacher about teaching addition. The script says you should do and say this. Then the teacher points to what is on the board and asks written questions, all in minute detail. As I read, I think only a mindless robot would use this stuff. I quizzed a friendly British teacher.

"Are we supposed to use these things? All I got was a smile. I concluded by paraphrasing a popular primer reading series. "See Jim", "See Teacher Guide", "Run Jim Run."

When I did my doctorate several years later at Michigan State I attended a speech by the Dean of Education, a former primary teacher. She talked about boots and mittens in the cold mid-west. This reminded me of my kindergarten class in Moscow. A big part of the day is spent undressing the kids' winter clothing on arrival. Then at morning break or lunch recess, you dress them in snowsuits, hats, boots, and mittens to go out to play. At the end of the break, you undress the outer clothing again. Finally, at the day's end, you dress the kids to leave. It is exhausting! I laughed at the Dean's boots and mittens ritual based on my memories of Moscow's kindergarten.

Regardless of the temperature, my five-year-olds went out to play. There is a buzz of excitement as they move in a single file down the stairs. Outside the door is the playground where they scatter in all directions. Mittens and hats come off. Luckily, the mittens were on elastic thread that went through the sleeves. My aide and I did not want to spend time finding lost mittens in the snow. Those discarded mittens hung forlornly on their elastic tethers. Coats we had carefully buttoned and zipped would be opened--those small bodies didn't feel the cold. It was a good job that parents didn't see them. Their favorite activity was sliding down the icy snow incline of about fifteen feet at great speed. Another fun activity was playing with the snow in hands sans mittens.

I have taught everything from kindergarten to graduate school, but I have a special feeling about teaching a five-year-old to read. For young primary children, every day is full of wonders. Their enthusiasm is infectious. In Moscow, Edward was the son of the Kenyan embassy driver. He had trouble sitting anywhere for more than a few seconds. He would adopt serious teacher-like postures and tell me who was not doing their work. He always wanted to know what everyone in the class was doing. He was not the fastest reader, but it kept him in his seat for a few minutes. He loved the "pirate series" of early readers. British readers would identify these pirates as "Captain Pugwash" a TV series for the young. There is no walking the plank or scary Long John Silver from the book Treasure Island. Pugwash was for five-year-olds. There was "Argh, avast there she blows", with Polly the parrot perched on his shoulder. The captain's mate was ten times cleverer than Pugwash. The pirate books came in different colors with blue being the top reading level. Edward says with a flourish, "The blue pirate sailed away in the sunset on his ship." This final sentence meant he finished the whole book. There was an emphasis on the word "blooo p-i-r-it" carefully sounded out in a Kenyan phonetic tone. Then he looked at me with a huge grin, "Look, Mr. Mead, I did it." "Yes, you certainly did."

Not all was "plain sailing" to keep the nautical theme. A parent wanted to come and talk to me about a concern. Years of experience tell me this is not "What a wonderful teacher you are." More a, "How did you allow this awful thing to happen to my child?" In general, teachers communicate well with children. Talking to their adult parents is more likely to cause teacher stress. I wracked my brains and so did Annie the aide, "Whatever could have upset Belle's dad?" After the other children left, Belle and Dad turned up in my classroom. Dad is something in security at the American embassy. His tone tells me he is not a happy camper.

"How could you let the children cut their hair?"

Well, at least I now have some idea what this is about.

"Look at her bangs, it is so uneven, and Belle says Alice did it."

The light is there at the end of the tunnel, the question is whether I can lead this man to a reasonable explanation. First thing, I drop down to Belle's level. It is a good idea not to tower over this diminutive creature who looks ready to burst into tears because of Dad's aggressive tone.

"Belle, how did you get your hair cut? Were you playing with Alice?"

Belle and Alice, a British girl, were always together and best friends.

"Mr. Mead, we played beauty parlor in the bathroom." Belle's lips twitch and her eyes fill with unshed tears. "We took a pair of scissors from the classroom."

Dad is ready to pounce, "How could you or your aide allow the kids to have scissors? The points on the scissors are dangerous."

I strode over to the scissors in a storage pot on one of the tables.

"These are the scissors, please take a good look, they are blunt, not pointed. Here is a piece of thick paper, please try, it is difficult to cut paper with them." I guess Belle's fine hair was cuttable. "Belle and Alice were playing. Maybe a few snips will make that fringe straight. It will grow out fast." I agree with Dad that I will talk with Belle and Alice tomorrow, so we don't have a repeat performance. Plus taking scissors out of the classroom is not something we want to happen again.

Belle looks more than ready to agree to the scissor rules. Dad seems satisfied as he leaves with a relieved child.

The following day Alice and Belle are sitting with me in the criminal court for five-year-olds, instead of going to recess.

"Alice, Belle tells me you were playing hairdressers in the toilets, Is that right."

"Yes, Mr. Mead."

Belle is looking puzzled. I learned quickly you had to speak British and American, so all understood.

"Belle, beauty parlor is the hairdresser in England and toilet is the English word for bathroom."

The young ladies solemnly swear they will not take scissors out of the classroom. Any creative haircuts are best left to hair professionals, all in five-year-old language.

This dual language performance is interesting. Try standing in front of a mixed American and British group and ask them to take out their "rubbers" in British and "erasers" in American. My authority with five-year-olds required an icy stare for any sniggers the first few times I said this. In class, we would have some interesting talks about the different words in the two types of English.

Young people have accidents. You might call it "spill and spew" time. Major clean-up required a Custodian (Janitor) armed with a mop, bucket, and cleaning materials. The problem is this Russian staff member is down in the basement, and I don't have the required language skills to ask him to come to the class. Mark is five years old, a British student who speaks pretty fluent Russian. Mark would march down the stairs feeling very important in his task. A few moments later Mark would rush back "he's on his way." A few minutes passed and the Russian clean-up crew appeared at my door.

One of the best opportunities for a "spill" was during lunch. We had no catering, so the kids brought packed lunches to eat at their desks. There are several pitfalls that an unsuspecting teacher can fall into.

"Would you like one of my sandwiches, Mr. Mead?" That sandwich I could swear was last seen being hastily picked up off the floor a few minutes before. "Thank you, but I have already eaten, but it is good to share." Five-year-olds like to "trade". Especially stuff they either dislike or are bored with getting the same thing each day in their lunch box. My aide and I had to monitor trading. We got in the habit of saying "sharing" your lunch is good, but handing over everything is a bad idea. Belle and Alice were constant sharers. Belle got to sample half of an English cheese and Branston pickle sandwich. Alice got to like the American staple, peanut butter, and jelly.

All special days are celebrated in Moscow's kindergarten class. It depended on which nationalities were in the class. Halloween (American), Guy Fawkes Night (a British ritual where you set off fireworks and burn an effigy of a Guy, yes, his name was Guido Fawkes) who tried with others to blow up Parliament. It is all good clean English fun. Older grades hear about how Guy was hung, drawn, and quartered. Who said British people were staid and had little fun in the seventeenth century? Public executions were a good excuse for a nice family picnic. American Thanksgiving, luckily, I didn't have any Canadians because their Thanksgiving is a different day. Easter for kindergarten is all bunnies and Easter eggs, painted or chocolate. Kindergarten and the Catholic Church share a crowded calendar marking significant days and festivals.

The lead-up to Christmas was time for me to bring in the guitar I had brought to Moscow. My playlist was limited but I could fake my way strumming Twinkle-Twinkle Little Star and Rudolf the Red Nose Reindeer. Kindergarten classrooms always have a carpeted section in one corner with bookshelves and a chair for me to sit on for story time or singing.

The only other time I sang in public was when I was forced to play and sing in a UK primary school concert. I struggled through a Pink Floyd song. Then I did a duet of The House of the Rising Sun. I will admit it was one of my least shining moments. Especially when the school board president suggested a gambling song about drinking in a house of prostitution was not suitable for this audience.

Five-year-olds have different ideas about musical appreciation. On hearing their comments on my "brilliant" chords you would think I was Eric Clapton and Jimi Hendrix all wrapped up together. We sang the two songs several times and then had a story.

The Anglo-American school had a full-day kindergarten to accommodate working parents. It is 3:15 in the afternoon and several of my students see "story time" on the carpet as an excellent chance for a nap. I swear my stories were riveting but five-year-old fiction is not great literature. It was not unknown for me to find one of my young ladies or gentlemen using my foot as a pillow.

Kindergartners love visitors. Joann has always taught middle and secondary science. I persuaded her to come down from her classroom and teach a little science to the class. There was an air of excitement that the "big kids" teacher would talk science to us. I preview and make sure we are all in the mood. I build up the excitement and explain how lucky we are that our visitor has time to be with us. Joann learns that kindergarten is like herding cats. A five-year-old has a different learning style compared with older kids who will sit and listen for at least a few minutes. "How do you teach them anything?" Joann told me afterwards. "After a minute into my presentation chaos reigned. It was like I had left the room. They ignored me, chattered amongst themselves, and constantly played with the equipment." She retreated to her Science Lab and never made another offer to visit us.

I will confess that the accident that led me to be a kindergarten teacher for a year was a memory I hold fondly. I have taught kindergartners a few times as a substitute in America. But, like first love, I remember those eager smiling young faces in Moscow. If only kindergartners dressed and undressed quickly, the world would be perfect!

FIVE

RED SQUARE AND ROCKETS' RED GLARE

Red Square, October Revolution parade, Nov 7, 1979

JOANN: MY LITTLE ROLLEI CAMERA ISN'T FANCY, but its clarity and bright colors are best on a sunny day—especially the reds, how apropos in this setting. I was on a mission that gray morning, Wednesday, Nov 7, 1979, as I headed to Red Square. It was the sixty-second-anniversary parade of the 1917 October Revolution. But why, you might ask, is the revolution celebrated on November 7th? There are two different calendars, the Gregorian and Julian. In the Gregorian calendar, October 24th, is November 7th (in the Julian). Vladimir Ilyich Lenin led his comrades in the Bolshevik political party in a coup d'état—a literal "blow to the state" where they overthrew the existing government. They seized power in Petrograd, called Leningrad when I lived in Moscow. Today it is St. Petersburg. I wish they'd make up their mind. But enough of the confusion.

Any visitor to Moscow would visit Red Square, the huge landmark with its famous buildings, the Lenin Mausoleum, and the GUM department store. The most visually stunning is Saint Basil's Cathedral. Built during the reign of Ivan the Terrible, his violent outbursts and rage somehow coexisted with his passion for beauty. The vibrant colors also symbolize Ivan's obsession with power. Legend had it that after the builder constructed the cathedral, he was blinded so that he could never create such a thing of beauty again.

I would gaze at Saint Basil's on many occasions, it reminded me of a fairy tale castle. My first memory growing up was the Cinderella castle in Disney's fantasyland—those teal blue turrets and beige-toned domes seem drab by comparison. But Saint Basil's garish, colorful nine domes, some striped, others mottled, look as if it has sprouted flower buds. Its sculpted swirling towers might have sprung out of the earth.

Saint Basil's Cathedral, an Orthodox church, was confiscated a hundred years ago as part of the Soviet anti-religion campaign. Atheism, the state's official dogma during Communist rule, led to persecution in its attempt to eliminate all religions.

A central piece of the Kremlin is the fortified fortress within the city. The word Kremlin refers to the government of the Soviet Union. Within its defensive walls are churches and palaces and nineteen towers. Since the 13th century, the Kremlin was the official residence of the supreme power. A symbol of authority, today, the Kremlin is not just Vladimir Putin's home, the Kremlin is Putin himself.

Red, in Russian, is *krasny* or *krasnaya*, but the words have double meanings.

GUM Department Store in Red Square

Red is a color, but it also means beautiful. Within the U.S.S.R., everything red was beautiful. Also red means glorious, splendid, magnificent, and any other words you could find in a thesaurus of superlatives. A red flag with a gold hammer and sickle, topped with a gold star was once the national flag of the Soviet Union. The Red Star symbolizes the Red Army. The *Kransnaya Strela* or Red Arrow is the overnight train from Moscow to Leningrad (now St Petersburg). I would have reason to ride the Red Arrow on a future adventure.

But, more than anything, red, the color, symbolizes power. Why? Because red represents communism, it embodies all its beliefs and dogmas. People must tow the party line to show they are good communists. Consequently, Communists are often referred to as "Reds". Reds are glorified as pillars of society, honorable and good. The Komsomol Youth and Young Pioneers, young Communists in training, wear red scarves. I think you've got the picture.

Today, I have the day off! The journey would involve buses and the underground metro, I was warned not to go by car. I set off too late and it took me forever to get there. Snow is on the ground, it's a gray drizzly day, but at least it's not snowing as I navigate the buses and metro. After my challenging adventure, I eventually arrive at

The Power of Red

the entrance to Red Square and file in alongside other pedestrians. At five foot tall, dressed in baggie cords, a plain coat, and a brown woolen hat, I could have been somebody's child. I hear in the distance the drums, trumpets, and marching bands. I'd missed the arrival of the dignitaries and top Communist Party members. The ministers now sit above Lenin's tomb ready to inspect the Red Army parade formations.

Red Square is in its full regalia with ginormous propaganda banners and posters. Can you guess what color they are? The three-story figure of Lenin in proletarian dress and a worker's cap looms over the crowd. It's imposing, impossible to miss. I can see oversized banners, one with the date 1917 and comrade Vlad Lenin looking to the left. A symbol of his ideals, perhaps? Another with Leonid Brezhnev, the Chairman of the Supreme Soviet, his arm is raised in a salute, maybe to his Red Army. During his eighteen years at the top, this Supreme Being invested heavily in military power.

I got lucky and found a spot behind a crowd of spectators, only four or five people deep. My small stature again works against me, I'm unable to see anything at ground level. But I could hear marching and the rumble of vehicles getting louder. My trusty Rollei and my little arms, unseen or unnoticed, go into automatic action and I snap shots of what I cannot see. Just minutes later, I see the tips of red and silver pointed

Rockets Red Glare

objects as they pass by above the woolen caps, fur hats, and brown Soviet military hats. I know the best of the parading spectacle has arrived. Those illegal guns and tanks and missiles, Oh My! Almost a reflex, and mostly by intuition, I lift my camera, aim blindly, and click. Lift arms, click. Lift arms, click again.

Somewhere around thirty-six clicks later the parade is coming to an end. And I get lucky again, nearing the end of my roll of film, my final few snaps coincided with the well-choreographed grand finale. Great puffs of smoke arise as the trucks carrying those long-pointed missiles abruptly circle (doing wheelies?) as they exit stage left and the curtains come down. Just imagine my excitement! The show's now over. But what I had captured on film would remain a surprise. I had no idea if the exercise would result in a sea of hats, the dark sky above, or just firmly toned arm muscles. And I wouldn't find out for a few weeks until that film would travel to and from America via the U.S. Embassy diplomatic pouch.

The closest I'd ever come to a big parade was when I lived in Pasadena, California in the early 1970s. It was an easy ten-minute walk from my home to Colorado Boulevard to watch the Rose Bowl parade. The floats and flowers provided little excitement to me. Parades in America are as boring as they come. There's the occasional 4th of

July parade with some military guns and cannons fired. But a mass shooter event in a Chicago suburb put an end to those displays. There were many military parades at the end of World War II, but the last U.S. military parade with troops and tanks on the street was in 1991 to celebrate the end of the Gulf War. There's been nothing much since then so let's hope it stays that way.

A lot was going on in the world. Just three days before Moscow's November 7, 1979, October Revolution parade, Iranian students seized the U.S. Embassy in Tehran. The Iranian Revolution led to the eventual overthrow of the Shah of Iran, leaving Tehran's American embassy a vulnerable target. After the embassy seizure, more than fifty American embassy staff from the Chargé d' Affaires to junior member staff would be held hostage for four hundred and forty-four days. Remember, what happens in one part of the world will change what happens elsewhere, leaving others vulnerable too, even if on a smaller scale. So how might the Hostage Crisis impact us expats in Moscow? That will remain to be seen.

ШЕСТЬ SIX

DRIVING IN THE SOVIET UNION

JIM: **LIVING AND WORKING IN A FOREIGN COUNTRY WAS** a first for me. Much of what I believed before coming to Moscow was quickly revised on arrival. For example, since I only had a British motorcycle license, I needed to buy a trusty Ural motorcycle with a sidecar. I reasoned that Russia with all its snow and ice meant a regular motorbike was not a good option. The first suspicion I get that my brilliant idea may not be so brilliant is the look on people's faces at work. They seem doubtful when I tell them my cunning plan. This would often be followed by, "Jim, you do know winters here are extreme?" The few Russians who own cars put them in storage during the cold winter. Plus, I don't see many motorcycles on Moscow streets. I am in a quandary.

Everyone else at school is excited about buying a car. However, first, you need a Russian driver's license. All our foreign licenses, including my UK license with no photograph, are sent somewhere so we can be issued with a Russian one. Like many things in the USSR, bureaucracy with magic is available in plentiful supply. I magically got this small red canvas-covered driver's permit (surely the only color it could be?). There was twofold magic. First, the Russian license now has a picture of me. Where did that come from? Second, some unknown Russian bureaucrat transforms my British motorcycle license into a Russian automobile permit. Maybe the bureaucrat did not see many British driver permits. In 1979 your UK license had numbers that said what type of vehicle you could drive. My motorcycle number was magically transformed into a car-driving number. Regardless of how the magic happened, I abandoned Plan A of sliding around Moscow on my Ural sidecar. I confess I was sad my sidecar plan was not to be. On reflection, the Russian below-freezing "cool" I would have on Moscow's streets, was not the exhilarating "cool" feeling, of driving motorcycles elsewhere.

Plan B buy a car, but now I have a new challenge, I have never driven a car!

I learned the USSR is not England. Living and working overseas will always surprise you. It certainly surprised me. The start of school and my brand-new license means I need a car fast. I have about a week to learn how to drive before school starts. An additional problem is the only road map I have was produced by the CIA in 1953, over twenty years ago. I am expected to believe that the roads and buildings on the map still exist. For example, I learned the school is no longer where it appears on my circa 1953 map. Luckily someone helpfully marked the new location so I could see the route from my apartment to the school. I will do several dry runs when I get my car.

I could have picked a new car with the other new teachers. The vehicles "grow" in a field somewhere in the Moscow area. It is lots of fun. You get to try several until you find one that looks like you can drive it off the lot. Half of the cars do not start. Put a bottle of whisky on the back seat, and by magic, your battery, spark plugs, and distributor leads transform into supposedly reliable Yugoslav parts instead of the standard Russian issue. See more Soviet magic!

I forgo this school 'field' trip to the "new" car lot. Instead, a British embassy employee is about to leave, and he is keen to sell me their car. A few British pounds sealed the deal. I was now the proud owner of a tasteful pea green soup Zhiguli. It lacked good looks but turned out to be reliable. In addition, the car seller gave me a bonus of a Siberian long-haired cat. I was told a sad story about how they could not take this feline back home with them. The cat is another tale I write about elsewhere. I should have asked why the sellers were keen to sell this whiskered bonus to an unsuspecting British countryman. We all know the Soviet Union is full of spies and other pitfalls for the unwary. It took me some time to work out my bargain car paid for in pounds allowed the departing family extra hard currency for their trip home. Unlike some other embassies, the British did not have a magic slush fund to exchange Russian rubles for a currency you could use outside the country. This currency fun fact about rubles and dollars will come up later in Finland.

My used car is waiting for me in the British embassy parking lot plus cat and feline equipment (carrier, litter box, and feeding bowls). I share my problem with a colleague who takes pity on me. She agrees to accompany me on my first drive. My goal is modest, take the car from the British embassy to my apartment block. We spend a little time in the parking lot seeing if I can select a gear. It is manual so like my motorbike I know about the clutch. Four gears forward, like my bike, but the reverse gear is new. We are facing a brick wall, so I had better learn how to reverse.

Sweaty palms as I try to get into reverse. My colleague, Margaret, makes encouraging noises probably to cover the grinding sound as I try to find the reverse gear. Gently I allow out the clutch and we ease out of the parking space. First gear, no problem for a couple of yards we go forward in gentle kangaroo hops and stall the car. I stall twice inching forward as I find out how fast to lift my foot on the clutch. There are more soothing noises from my colleague who is probably wondering if her medical insurance is paid up. Eventually, we are on the city roads. I have managed to get through three out of four forward gears, so we are speeding at about twenty mph down the street. We take back routes and eventually arrive at my apartment car park. Passenger and driver breathe a sigh of relief. Curiously, I do not recall my friend ever taking another drive with me in my two years there.

Over the next few days, I will drive around the apartment's parking lot. I can now use all four forward gears and reverse without hitting anything. The next day I think it is good to try and drive to school, I hope the car and I will arrive in one piece. I have got better with the gears and clutch. There are fewer stalls and fewer kangaroo hops. There are no seat belts, so I take a firm grip on the steering wheel, and stiffening my spine is required should I stall. This stops me during hops and unplanned stops from sailing towards the dashboard and windshield. In a few days, I feel I could join a world rally car team.

I learned two other odd things in my early Moscow driving days. My windshield wipers are in the glove compartment. Why? you might ask. Well, at least I did. Left in the usual place on the windshield they can disappear. This was not more Soviet magic but more a case of Soviet supply and demand problems. When it rains in Moscow you see everyone parking on the side of the road and hastily fitting said wipers. The second thing I learned is that vodka is used as windshield washer fluid. Why? you ask. It is cheap and readily available. Plain water freezes in the winter. The Moscow joke was you had to beware of a desperate Russian climbing on your hood for a quick drink.

Remember, people told me Russian winters could be brutal. They were right, especially for vehicles. Russian folklore says that diesel fuel is less flammable than gasoline. Truck drivers test this by lighting a small wood fire under the engine to warm up the engine block. There is an added advantage to setting a fire under the engine. For most common trucks, Gaz or Zis, the cab is on top of the engine and that fire is below. The driver can keep warm in their cab while they wait for the engine to warm up. I guess the Russian folk tale about diesel flammability was true. On frigid nights some drivers leave the truck's engine running for hours.

My petrol-driven Zhiguli needs a different winter starting method. I would start thirty minutes before I had to leave to ensure a prompt departure. First step, brush off the snow that has accumulated during the night. The icy outside windows may need a scrape. The second step, open the car door. I never locked my car because freezing locks are an unwanted time-wasting feature. Diplomatic car parks have guards who ensure thieves do not enter the premises. So my car is safe. The door may still need some heavy pulling to open if some water has frozen overnight around the door hinges. Step three, fumble with the ignition key in heavy Winter gloves. If the engine starts you, are a winner! Jump to step five. However, when it doesn't start, curse mentally. The interior of your windshield will ice up with heavy breath from cursing out loud. Then you will have more scraping. Move to step four, put your foot on the accelerator pedal. Pump the gas pedal many times and retry the ignition key. Step four may need to be repeated a few times. I had difficulty keeping a straight face as I looked along the line of parked cars. Several of your neighbors take part in the gas pedal ballet. It looks like the Grand Prix grid drivers, but they are hopping like crazed frogs at the starting line, with an up-and-down movement in their seats. Suddenly the car bursts into life. Fifth step, sit and wait for the vehicle to approach the take-off temperature. Look at the temperature gauge to ensure the engine is warm enough before I can turn on the car heater. Otherwise, haste will get the windshield iced over requiring more cursing and scraping. Following this protocol, I would be good to go, maybe just a little wheel spin as I exit the parking lot.

The whole performance makes me tired. I turn on the car radio once I exit the parking lot. The English-speaking Russian station, Radio Moscow, gave me the latest and greatest propaganda. Plus, you got to hear the official Russian point of view on world events. You learn interesting facts about the Soviet Union. For example, I am told there was no pollution in the USSR. The large truck in front of me that belches thick blue smoke and dense clouds of particulates is a fantasy of my fevered Western imagination. There was no invasion in Afghanistan, simply willing Russians helping a poor Marxist neighbor. It is always good to get those diverse points of view!

My grandmother told me you shouldn't get too clever because Lady Luck is bound to bring you down a peg or two when the luck runs out. My car works, I have improved my driving skills, and a rudimentary knowledge of Moscow streets.

Then came basketball. I confess I hate playing basketball because I am pathetic at it. I cannot score baskets, I rarely hit the backboard or dribble. I stopped dribbling when I was two years old. This accounts for why I am no good at basketball. As I stagger toward the basket, I have another air ball aimed vaguely toward the backboard. On my vain journey to the basket, I left a student sprawled on the court. He was okay but my glasses flew off and lay broken on the floor. This is a problem that will take about six weeks to repair. As a kid, I used to break my glasses regularly playing different sports. My mother always gave me cheap National Health frames. However, my only spare pair in Moscow is very dark prescription sunglasses.

What does this have to do with driving? Not only is it cold but the winter daylight is very short. I must drive to and from work in the dark. Russian law decrees that you can only use dim side lights, not the headlights. Magical Soviet thinking says the street lighting is perfect, just like the lack of pollution! Headlight use is only permitted in the countryside. The additional challenge is that most Russian pedestrians wear dark winter clothes. Muscovite ideas of road safety say they can cross streets whenever and wherever they feel like it. The poor street lighting and my dark sunglasses considerably decreased my night vision. I endured a troubled six weeks of driving. It has been made abundantly clear that mowing down the local populace guarantees a fast ticket out of the country or an unpleasant brush with Russian law. My semi-diplomatic status as a humble teacher makes me think about avoiding car meets human encounters. Consider me brought down a peg or two, thanks for the thought, Grandma. I drive with extreme snail-like caution until my regular glasses reappear several weeks later.

Russian driving law prohibited left turns or U-turns at most road junctions at the time. Instead, you use a *razvorot* (*raz* for short) to turn left. A *raz* is where you can cross the median center line and return in the opposite direction, a U-turn. I had to do a *raz* every morning to get to the small side street where the school was. It was easier to do than it is to describe. Main roads are kept clear of snow but there could be snow in the *raz* turn. Scandinavian rally drivers use the handbrake to turn. After two years of trying, I got pretty good at pulling up the handbrake at the right moment, and locking the back wheels, to make the U-turn. This just livened up my trip to work!

Some foreigners import snow tires either with or without small metal studs. You can tell someone has studded winter tires as they click and clack past you. I never had winter tires. Instead, I lowered the tire pressures in Winter to get more traction. This is not something I recommend as it damages the tires over time. Whatever you do, don't try to sneak a U-turn or left-turn at a junction. Every junction has traffic cops on foot or parked in a police car.

It is just part of daily driving in the Soviet Union that you would be stopped by a traffic cop a few times. Maybe I had done something wrong, he wanted a bribe, or he was bored with no Russian donuts that morning. I would pull over to the side of the road and crack the window open no more than an inch. This meant the cop had to bend down a bit so that he could talk to me. I kept a slight smile on my face to show I was friendly. The stream of Russian from the cop would eventually stop. At that point I would say "*Ya diplomatiski*," and then in English, "I am very sorry, but I do not understand Russian." It was close to the truth in my case. My limited Russian only extended to asking for a beer or the price of a loaf of bread. I also learned a phrase that suggests you go and have intercourse with your mother. But with the cop looking frustrated this was probably not a good place to display one's colloquial Russian. At this point, it would depend on how bored or upset the cop was. Most of the traffic cops knew this was all part of the performance. I was not going to get out of the car. Eventually, he would have to let me, a diplomat, go. It certainly broke up the day with some innocent excitement, so long as you were not in a hurry. It was one of the few times I met "regular" Russians.

Why was the Russian language so difficult for foreigners especially me to read? Cyrillic is unlike Arabic, Chinese, or Japanese all have alien letters you need to learn. In Russian take a word that looks like PECTOPAH that translates and sounds like Restaurant. Another example is the country CCCP, the Cyrillic abbreviation is SSSR for what we know as the USSR. It stood for the Union of Soviet Socialist Republics. The problem is the alphabet includes a letter your brain has always said is a C but in Russian, it's an S, or what looks like a P is an R. Plus, we had little practice speaking Russian in Moscow's foreign enclave.

What does this have to do with driving in the Soviet Union? Joann tried hard so she recognized the Russian alphabet. She could proudly sound out the words at about kindergarten reading speed. I never bothered because my little brain saw PECTOPAH, and it took forever to realize it was a restaurant. So, when driving along the highway, you see a Cyrillic sign showing you where you want to go. Joann would try gamely to sound it out. Meanwhile, we were past the exit and the next *raz* (U-turn place) could be some way down the road.

A bank colleague of mine in England was obsessed with Frank Sinatra. I am not much of a night owl. Sinatra's song "Strangers in the Night" would pop into my head as I drove home late at night from some function. The inner ring road had a special lane for the Zil (Russian luxury car) to transport Communist bigwigs or foreign dignitaries from A to B. When the party leaders were tucked in their beds, I sometimes met a Mig fighter trundling along the special lane. Why a fighter jet was towed along a public highway is just one of those Russian mysteries. The covered fighter jet was towed to some airfield. The wind sometimes gave everyone a brief glimpse of the fighter underneath the cover. These fighters would be followed very obviously by a gaggle of diplomatic ducklings. Various Western military types from different embassies followed the plane's slow progress in their cars. I can imagine the late-night spy rota, "Okay John, you have midnight driving duty around the ring road tonight". All embassies had different D numbers so you could tell they were diplomats and where they came from. My little green Zhiguli was D01, Americans had D04 on their number plates.

Most foreigners only get to meet Russians who are outsiders and dissidents in the communist system. The average Russian would avoid people like me. The social costs of consorting with foreigners could be very high. On a frigid night as you were driving home at two or three in the morning, you would come across Russians who would hitchhike because the danger of frostbite was possible. Maybe they didn't see your diplomatic number plate as you approached in the gloom. I would sometimes stop as I knew picking up someone was safe at the time.

These infrequent trips would take me to areas of Moscow where I would normally not venture. The few times I did it I got a brief taste of the friendliness of ordinary Russians. Many of my hitchhikers would show an interest in Westerners. They were friendly because they knew "Big Brother" was not watching. In exchange for a lift, I would be invited into their apartment. As I had to drive home from an area, I was not familiar with, I would politely refuse vodka and brandy. I opted for a tea sweetened with jam. We had a good time exchanging questions and answers despite my poor Russian. Two hours later I would be back on the road consulting my trusty CIA map to get home.

Russians often help stranded drivers. I never saw a Russian AAA or tow truck. For some reason, taxi drivers were the ones who might stop and help a stranded motorist. I once ended up in a huge pothole on a side street. The rear wheels have sunk into the small pond with soft sand and mud. As I struggled to get nowhere, a taxi driver stopped. He pulled his bigger Volga in front of my stranded car. He opens his trunk and produces a sturdy rope. In a few minutes, my car is free, and the taxi driver has a big grin. Most of us carried a few packs of cigarettes for such occasions and he was happy to receive them along with my thanks. My current AAA membership is much more expensive.

SEVEN

GEMP

COLLECTIONS, ATTACHÉS, AND CORRESPONDENTS

JOANN: I'VE ALWAYS BEEN A COLLECTOR, LONG before coming to Moscow. Most of my collections were either inert or dead. Rocks and minerals, fossil marine life, pressed plants and flowers, dead bugs and butterflies, and animal specimens in jars of formaldehyde. A miscarried human baby, the most disturbing and bizarre to behold, now makes me cringe. But I'm a scientist and biologist, so I had no qualms nor put any limits on what specimen I would collect. Some specimens were even alive.

In Moscow, I collected invitation cards, mostly for social functions. Sometimes a dinner party but mostly foreign embassy receptions, often with drinks and caviar. I could never get enough of those dark beluga eggs. I'd spread them thick on crackers or dark rye bread. Bad Joann. Today, I have cringe-worthy moments as I think of endangered species like the beluga sturgeon. The sturgeon and their eggs are illegal for U.S. import, but you can buy hybrid sturgeon caviar to get around the ban. Only in America do you circumvent the law with mutant strains and chimeric fish eggs for one hundred dollars a tin. But for seven thousand dollars, a small business will still sell you an 8-ounce tin of "purebred" beluga caviar. A mere snack for greedy guts Joann.

I'd make the rounds in the evenings to embassies from everywhere. My trusty three-by-four-foot CIA map helps me find my way. The embassies are marked with red triangles, the country names are in English. On my map, they aren't too difficult to find. They are clustered in the West and South-west areas of Moscow. But the actual roads and street signs are in cryptic Cyrillic while the street names on my CIA map are typed in phonetic English. There's no GPS navigation, no cell phone or friendly electronic voice to give me directions or tell me where to turn but I somehow find my way. My torn, dog-eared, creased and wrinkled map of Central Moscow survived all these years, as did I, a little worse for the wear.

Invitations kept arriving in my school mailbox from a collection of people. I didn't understand why these people would invite an American teacher until I saw a pattern. The invitations were mostly from parents of my middle school kids. They were diplomats, ambassadors, attaches, aides. I remember a reception with the Malaysian Minister Counselor, two of his kids were in my classes. Parents from embassies or foreign offices, mostly the US, UK, Canada, Australia, and New Zealand, mingled among the many partygoers. From the far north, I taught the son of Iceland's Ambassador. To the south, the daughters of Ugandan diplomats and Kenyan royalty. Among the party guests were journalists and correspondents on both sides of the Atlantic from CNN and NBC to the London Times and Daily Telegraph. Businesspeople, from entrepreneurs to Estée Lauder, were also a part of the mix. You've got to wonder how many spies might have lurked in the darkness or operated in broad daylight.

And then there were those attachés. Attaché, the word conjures up images of spies, espionage, and collectors of information. The hunter-gatherers, nomads that hunt, fish, and forage. Guys and a few gals with attaché cases filled with secrets, political, military, cultural, or agricultural. Anything relevant during the Cold War.

Attachés, attached to a mission, had certain areas of expertise such as the military or defense. The role of the cultural attachés would depend on the country, their purpose could be broad or specific. A cultural attaché once took me on what I thought was an information-gathering assignment. At his office desk in the embassy, I noticed a few opened Newsweek articles with people's names highlighted in yellow. By my estimation, not very top secret, but he quickly closed and shuffled them into a drawer. There was a closet full of books near his desk. Banned books that might interest Muscovites for one reason or another. He selected one for a dissident Russian writer. It was a gift, a treasured book in English, unavailable to anyone with ideas that might deviate beyond the accepted norm. Cultural attachés cultivated people. It was a seeding of Western ideas, a form of schmoozing, or maybe plain American propaganda. Later the attaché confided, or perhaps he was bragging. "I'm the second-best Russian speaker in the American Embassy. I'm a spy, you know." I nod yes. I'm thinking, then why are you telling this secret to the walls? Every foreigner must assume that all walls have ears.

Attaches, aides, and foreign service diplomats well-versed in the language, the culture, and the history have since become a dying breed. The old guard could blend in, a real asset, whether an attaché with a command of the Russian language or just an ordinary teacher. Expertise combined with the ability to mingle, lets you hide in plain sight, where you might pick up some nuggets or buried treasures.

Attachés are the flies on the walls. It's the job that sustains them. An addiction they cannot live without. Attaché. A "diplomat who collects, analyzes, and acts on information". But perhaps they imagine themselves as something more exotic. Who can resist the mystery? Working undercover as an infiltrator, a secret agent, poking around in other people's business. Enlisting others as collaborators. Ya gotta love the world of Ian Fleming and those imaginary characters we all aspire to be, especially 007.

I often wondered if the "teacher" who spoke Armenian and Russian was just a teacher. Or was she a covert version of the cultural attaché i.e. spook? At an American Embassy reception, my cultural attaché friend and this teacher greeted each other with a fleeting "Hello" and nothing more. I must have looked curious. He volunteered, "We knew each other at USAID". If you combine the words USAID and Spy in Google, nothing comes up that connects them. Nothing incidental or coincidental. But I wonder, was it a training ground?

On a few occasions, I dined at the popular Georgian restaurant, Aragvi. The same teacher and her friend, an American business lady, could be seen dancing a bit too wildly on the dancefloor with some middle-aged Moscow apparatchiks. Were those fat bald guys on the dance floor from the Caucasus or other Soviet states? Maybe business "entrepreneurs"? I couldn't imagine them as paramours. As I watched, she looked over, embarrassed at being flung about by those exuberant Georgians and Armenians. Could she and her friend be American sparrows? Or maybe just plain spies. When in doubt, I make things up.

Worth waking up for on Saturday mornings, the American Embassy cafeteria, aka the "Snack Bar", was where people met. My Canadian neighbor arrived early at my door because people from other countries needed an American friend for access. The snack bar meant strong coffee in the morning and "steak-cheese-onion" for lunch. The Russian head cook calls out your order and first name. Just about everyone was partial to this weekly treat, a small steak smothered in cheese and fried onions. With French fries, of course. Fresh vegetables, especially in winter, were a rare commodity, so not much of a selection for vegetarians. One morning, I overindulged in strong coffee. By noon I'd suffered from extreme caffeination, my right eye twitched, and my smile froze as if botoxed. Not a pleasant experience. I felt like a jittery wind-up toy, a jitter critter with chattering teeth.

On another Saturday, I ran into a French photographer I'd met through an NBC friend. I joined him and a French journalist for coffee. It wasn't French Roast, but what other choices were there? We talked for a while. The photographer translated for the journalist who spoke little English. The journalist's Russian might have been pretty good, otherwise, how could he find stories and infiltrate Russian society? The two Frenchmen wanted to show me something, but I was told I must never tell anyone. Ever! Ok, you got me, I'm intrigued and curious. What illicit secrets are in store for me? Hopefully, something illegal. Maybe contraband, something politically sensitive, or something very… French?

Saturday afternoon adventures could be anything, I was gregarious and always up for just about anything. If I didn't know what I was in for, then all the better. After all, my acquaintances were vetted by their embassies, or whoever else they were affiliated with. So, the Frenchmen seemed like a safe bet to me.

We drove to a foreign housing block. I don't remember exactly where it was other than somewhere in the north of Moscow. Before we enter the apartment, I'm warned, "Do not say anything once we enter." Both Frenchmen place their forefinger across their mouth, that universal gesture to seal your lips. The wide-eyed photographer whispers, "Be quiet, don't talk." But they continued to whisper loudly as we entered the sparsely furnished apartment.

The door to the bedroom is closed. The journalist, who speaks little English, waves his hand and whispers "Voilà!" He opens the bedroom door to show me something I have sworn I'll never reveal. I nearly gasped when my eyes spied on his top secret. It was the quintessential collection of all Russian contraband. On the walls hung hats, not ordinary fur *shapkas* but Russian military hats from all branches and ranks. Yes, I'm impressed.

Even more imposing were the "Heads". Most were busts… all of Vladimir Lenin, some small, many large, and some so huge I wondered how the journalist could fit them into the room. Let alone smuggle them into his apartment—it must have been under the cover of darkness. It could not have been easy with a Russian military guard, stationed in his sentry box at all foreign compounds.

I'd started my collection of Soviet *znachki*, metal pins, and badges. My Lenin head pins would grow over time. But those Lenin busts? How the hell did he ever get them out of the country? I still wonder.

But oh, the universal urge to collect! Not just things, but people too. People became part of my collection. I became part of theirs. We all become a piece of someone else's collection. Some pieces we toss, others we treasure. But only a precious few do we keep forever.

Bill, an American preacher, and I had random conversations. I don't remember what religion he preached, but he tried to convert me to his brand of God. Good luck with that. He lived in my apartment block, one floor below. On a Saturday morning at the snack bar, he intercepts me before I can find my friends. It was a cold autumn day. In my furry long-haired alpaca coat, I looked like a fluffy fawn-colored creature. I hadn't yet transitioned to my full-length winter sheepskin. Baah. He introduced me to a tall blue-eyed guy, younger than me, handsome enough, who was at his side. I'll call him Ryan. What Bill wanted was a friendly fur-ball companion to brighten somebody's day. "Oh no," I thought, "Another matchmaker!" If he couldn't convert me, he'd marry me off.

I wondered what I was in for. Another Saturday misadventure, perhaps this time delivering smuggled bibles? Or maybe a prayer meeting, speaking in tongues, babbling in a foreign language understood only by some higher being. I didn't know what to expect. As it turned out, Ryan, who lived in a Midwest state, came to Moscow as a patient. He would receive an experimental eye treatment not available in the U.S.

Despite Russia's repressive regime, Soviet medicine excelled during the 1970s, especially in developing new eye techniques. Professor Fyodorov (from the Institute of Eye Microsurgery) pioneered radial keratotomy, which improves short-sightedness (myopia). An expat I knew who played Platform tennis, underwent precise scalpel cuts on her corneas. As the fine lines healed, they would reshape her eyeballs. Her eyes were red and irritated at first, she complained of seeing fine lines and sensations of sand and grit. But over time her vision improved remarkably. And so did her paddle tennis game.

But Ryan had another eye condition, one that deteriorates over time and eventually leads to blindness. There was no treatment available in the U.S. Over the next few weeks, he would undergo injections of an experimental drug, not in his eyes but in his hip.

"So, Joann would you show Ryan around Moscow?" Of course, I would. I've never been short of compassion for someone with medical needs. Especially, handsome ones.

"Yes. Where would you like to go?"

"The Moscow Zoo." An interesting choice, I thought, but then again, I'm a biologist. I love animals of every kind, especially the big cats. When teaching in London two years earlier, I chaperoned a small group on a two-week safari to Tanzania. Most memorable was Lake Manyara where the tree-climbing lions hung suspended on fig trees and acacia branches, lounging and dozing to avoid the heat of the midday sun.

I would pick Ryan up the next day at an Intourist hotel. He had a girlfriend back home, but she couldn't afford the trip's expense, nor could any of his family members. So, he was on his own, in an unknown place, receiving experimental treatments in a country shrouded in mystery. Pretty scary stuff, in a scary place during scary times.

"Zoo" is on the back of my CIA map of Central Moscow in tiny light grey print (is it disappearing ink?). Using the "Index to Streets of Central Moscow" under the section "Public Buildings and Parks", the last entry is Zoo at N1 W3 on the grid. Map reading may be a dying art today but there are still people who know how to read printed paper maps (dinosaurs like me from the Jurassic).

I'd visited the San Diego Zoo and the well-kept wild animals in England's Chessington Zoo, so my expectations may have been high. But to compare them all would be unfair. The Moscow Zoo first opened in 1862. It had an ever-expanding population of animals and by 1979 the facility was run down, its equipment broken after years of neglect. There weren't many visitors. At times it seemed as though we were the only ones there.

It was a depressing cloudy day. Maybe it would have been more inviting if it had been a sunny day in June. The enclosures were in a sorry state, as were some of the occupants, animal and otherwise. But we were determined to see the big animals. The lions and tigers and bears, oh my! And then we found the cat house. A blast of pungent air overwhelmed our senses on opening the entry door. Wondering if we should venture onward, we persisted, nevertheless. Bravely we went where no other Westerners had likely gone before, well at least not on this chilly autumn day. A heady aroma of animal excrement overpowered us. Like a fine blended wine, there were overtones of uric acid, tinges of earthy straw, strong hints of fecal essence, and suggestions of a distinctive lack of care.

But I remember the distressed animals pacing. Back and forth, their repetitive pacing. Backwards and forwards, to-and-fro, those frustrated, ferocious, angry tigers were mad as hell, held captive in the tiniest of cages. And the scruffy lions lounged lazily, unable to sleep, having no place to hide. Ryan nearly gagged as we paced quickly, in one direction, towards the exit at the end of the corridor. We trotted full throttle towards the zoo entrance, eager to exit, we didn't stay long among the cages and confines of the zoo. We'd had enough of the floral bouquet of fetid feline feces. So must have those unfortunate big cat captives, breathing the stench as they gnawed putrid decomposing meat in their squalid quarters. What might those tigers be doing in the forests of India? Or a pride of lions in the African savannahs? Did they have memories of life in the wild?

The 1980s were not the best of times for the Moscow Zoo, the conditions only deteriorated further. In the 1990s, the city constructed a new complex with enclosures for those big felines, the Amur tigers, Asian lions, leopards, and other cats. Life improved for the now sleeping tigers and lounging lions. The hunt would only be a distant memory for these solitary tigers and lions.

Ryan would embark on his eye treatment on Monday. He wanted fresh fruit, he needed fortification. But fresh fruit is a rarity in Moscow during winter. We drove to the diplomatic *Gastronom* No. 1, a special Soviet grocery near the American embassy. Produce was scarce and supermarkets didn't exist in 1979 Moscow. The *Gastronom* sold basic foods but only to diplomats and accredited correspondents who had access to it. And you needed D-coupons bought with dollars or other foreign currency. So, as a mollycoddled American, I had my D-coupon stash for everything from food to gas to special souvenirs. Imported Moroccan oranges had arrived, but not much else. A treasured bag of a dozen would help Ryan get through the daily hip injections he'd start on Monday. I promised an outing next weekend, something with less of a stench. But the next Saturday at the snack bar Ryan was limping as he walked with Bill past my table. "I'll call you", he promised.

Sunday morning, he called. "It's just too painful. My hip hurts so much from the injections, I can't take any more. I'm flying home tomorrow." I didn't know what to say but managed a few groans and fewer words. I remember that young man and our day at the zoo. I remember his quest to hold on to his precious eyesight. And the disheartening disappointment he must have felt when his dream of a possible cure disappeared.

On Friday nights with our boss Gene, a half dozen or more of us teachers pile into his van and begin our rounds. Our rotation starts at 6 pm at the Australian Embassy for a beer with the Ambassador. Only in the great outback of Moscow does the Ambassador socialize with the hoi polloi. Around 8 pm at the Canadian Embassy, some play card games, some play snooker, while many of us focus on snacks and more drinks. Around 10 pm we head for the highlight of the evening, the Marine House Bar at the American Embassy. This is where everybody young, mostly single, and looking for a good time would come. It was not just the highlight of the evening but the biggest event of the week. It was way too much fun, and you'd never know who you might meet. I remember hanging out with students from Columbia University. The embassy opened the bar to people with Western and European passports from France, Italy, Germany, Turkey, and more. But who could keep track of who was who on evenings fueled by beer? Luckily, we had our designated driver.

It was easy to roam the Embassy confines. On my wanderings late one Friday evening I ended up in the embassy courtyard. A group of Russian staff, mostly drivers, invited me to join their card game. They were jovial but not drunk as they were likely on night duty. Embassy drivers were provided by Intourist, aka the KGB, which meant they had rules to follow. But rules were subject to interpretation. The Marines did stop serving booze at midnight. Not quite as loosey-goosey on the rules, or so I thought. But with the combination of youth, beer, dancing bodies, sexy gyrations, and the obvious pheromones that permeated the bar's ambiance, anything can happen. The Marine guards, their testosterone raging, could make them ripe for any *Kompromat* offered them. A Natasha, Tanya, or Katya, most likely a set-up, a honey pot, might lead to their downfall.

On a cold winter night at the Marine House Bar, I danced with Jim. Dancing led to snuggling as I sat on his lap and whispered sweet nothings in his ear. What I whispered, I would never repeat (at least not here) and I'd hoped that the next morning all would be forgotten. Bad Joann. Very very bad Joann.

Collections: Some people collect things, inanimate bits of memorabilia, from tiny pins to enormous busts of Lenin. Some collect paper images, tiny stamps, or massive posters. Other people collect words and numbers, those details and secrets that might tell a story. Then there's the ephemeral, the transient, those snapshots, photographs of people and places, frozen in time, during moments that can never be recovered. And we all collect each other. Some people are seasonal like deciduous trees, while others are everlasting evergreens like pines and firs.

ВОСЕМЬ EIGHT

DISSIDENTS, ARTISTS, AND REFUSENIKS

JOANN: MEETING ORDINARY RUSSIANS WOULD TAKE time. Introductions were key. A journalist's wife introduced me to a Moscow University (MGU) student interested in western literature. Novels in English were mostly banned in the Soviet Union and impossible to find. In college, I'd changed my major from English to Biology, and my literary interests devolved from Dostoyevsky to Durrell.

MGU was not far from my apartment. In the student's miniscule dorm room, he showed me a cupboard where he hid away his contraband of about ten books. Most were classic Western literature that in my opinion were nothing controversial. It didn't make sense to me.

If you could only have ten books, what would you choose?

During that time, ignoramus that I am, I sorely lacked any understanding or compassion for the plight of the Russian people. Repression, oppression, and authoritarianism were not part of my vocabulary. I'd arrived in a country I knew little about, neither its history nor its culture. Nor could I imagine the lives of ordinary people who didn't have the freedoms we have in the West. I had plenty to learn about how the Soviet State used all its power to suppress dissent.

I was born in a beach city, Santa Monica. This California wild child lolled about all summer on sandy beaches—El Porto, Hermosa, Manhattan, and Playa del Rey. The big waves at El Porto pier brought the boys of summer and the "Surfin" Beach Boys were among them. I wanted to be a "California Girl". The Beach Boys' refrain, "I wish they all could be California girls", echoed in my vacuous brain. I was out there having fun in that warm California sun. But I—unlike the tall blonde California beach beauties with their baby oil sheen—was a short curly-haired brunette with a dark natural tan.

What I knew about the U.S.S.R didn't go beyond the lyrics of the 1968 Beatles song, "I'm back in the U.S.S.R, You don't know how lucky you are, boy, Back in the U.S.S.R." The Beatles lyrics to "Back in the U.S.S.R." was a parody of the Beach Boys "California Girls." The Beatles were inspired by the Ray Charles song "Georgia on My Mind" when they wrote another chorus, "The Ukraine girls really knock me out, They leave the West behind, And Moscow girls make me sing and shout, That Georgia's always on My, my, my, my, my, my, my, my, my mind."

I had a lot to learn. Like, what exactly is a dissident?

A dissident is a person who expresses their dissent. They usually disagree with the majority. They may challenge beliefs, doctrines, or political and religious institutions. Anti-war sentiments challenge the aggressors, those who start or provoke wars. Anti-anything sentiments challenge the status quo.

Creative people whose cultural ideas and values do not conform to state directives are also considered dissidents. The authoritarian state dictates what is acceptable art. In the USSR, the only officially sanctioned art was Socialist Realism. Just imagine being told what you could or could not imagine.

In the 1930s, guidelines were drawn up under Soviet leader Josef Stalin that all paintings, sculptures, posters, photographs, and other visuals must depict optimism and promote Soviet ideals. The arts must portray the ideal life in the USSR. Literature and music must also subscribe to that message. The portrayal of the lives of everyday people must glorify the workers in factories, on farms, in construction, and all those good people who support the aims of the Communist Party. Glory to Work! Art is good if it serves the people.

During the Winter and Spring of 1980, Jim and I had become more than friends, we were always together, even if only by telephone. We dated traditionally and went to hockey games, like Red Army vs Traktor, soccer games in Lenin stadium, and even the Ballet, but Jim preferred athletic events. We both fell asleep during the Opera.

Our friend Marcia taught Russian at the Anglo-American School. An aspiring

Dissidents, Artists, and Refuseniks 63

Happy Communist Couple on the Collective Farm

Columbia PhD, she'd earlier met Russians who were not ordinary Russians. Ordinary Russians would have too much to lose if they befriended Westerners. But Marcia had friends—dissidents she'd come to understand and know very well. I could never fully grasp their plight, but Marcia's impeccable translations gave Jim and me a window into their world. We were thankful she shared her deep insight into these wonderful people.

In the Spring of 1980, Marcia introduced us to her artist friend Sasha (Alexander Kalugin) and his wife Tamara. I remember intimate evenings at the Kalugin's apartment where we'd crowd into their small apartment. Marcia, an incredible linguist, had another dimension—she could also swear in every Slavic language. With her irrepressible smile and humor, she would translate seamlessly. We spoke almost no Russian, and the Kalugins spoke no English. Tamara would lay out a generous array of whatever delicacies she could find, exotic sausages, breads, pickled things, and whatever she likely queued hours for. We'd cluster around a communal coffee table with cups of whatever to warm up the evening.

Sasha and Tamara lived in typical Russian housing. Poorly constructed, you would not want to stand out on the balcony. Balconies were known to crack, bend, and fall off. There was no miliman at the entrance. But, be assured, dissidents of any kind who brought foreigners into their homes were watched closely, often by their neighbors.

We met people like Sergei, a Soviet Jew, who did not have permission to emigrate. A long list of Refuseniks were denied their right to leave the Soviet Union. One afternoon Sergei visited me. He asked me for an unusual favor. My first thought, it was me he wanted as his American wife. But it seemed almost any American wife would do. Playing along, I made a few suggestions. But none were beautiful enough for him. He wanted to have his cake and eat it too.

At another Kalugin gathering, a party of dissidents, poets, writers, artists, and refuseniks crowded their small space. Marcia gave hints of what was going on and who was saying what. Poets read their lightly veiled satire and criticisms of the Soviet regime. But the irony, humor, sarcasm, and sense of the absurd came out mostly in jokes about repression, the regime, their lack of freedom, and the futility of their daily lives.

The CIA collected Soviet jokes. Just a few years ago the CIA finally declassified its collection of humor along with millions of deadly boring Cold War documents. The Russians' skill with jokes hasn't completely died. One is particularly apropos today for Putin's reign of terror: The ghost of Soviet dictator Josef Stalin appears before

Russian president Vladimir Putin and says, "I've got two pieces of advice for you; kill your political opponents and paint the Kremlin blue." Putin replies, "Why blue?" Why would he want to paint the Kremlin blue? He ponders. What's wrong with its existing Red? Changing the color of the Kremlin would require some thinking, but Putin will kill his political opponents without a second thought.

The secret police watchdogs spy on suspected dissidents and subversives of any persuasion. In the Soviet Union, Socialist Realism regulated emotional expressions. No negative thoughts, only uplifting messages were allowed. And the color "red" must predominate, not blue. Sasha's artwork was deemed "not official" for many reasons. He suffered a lot at the hands of the State. Kalugin believed that what is imagined can be real. And what is real can be imagined. His earlier themes were sometimes religious, often spiritual. He looked to Russian icon paintings and Russian 20th-century masters—Kandinsky, Chagall, the Spanish surrealists, and Hieronymus Bosch—during his earlier work. Sasha evolved and created his unique mythology, a multilayered mix. My favorite piece is neither political nor religious but an etching and watercolor painting of a colorful cockerel, the first in his series. It hangs in our kitchen.

Sasha's profound stutter made the simple act of communicating and talking a monumental effort. Was his stutter the reason he poured out everything in his art? Perhaps in some way, he was unable to keep up with his thoughts.

Sasha told Marcia his story about why he had a stutter. It goes like this: "What he told us (which may or may not be true) is that when he was a little boy, he and his brother were left at home alone one night when his parents went out to visit friends. He was really quite little, but babysitters apparently weren't a concept. I believe he and his family were living in Estonia at the time; his father had been sentenced to some sort of mild internal exile for some reason (I can't remember his "crime"). Anyway, the house they were living in caught fire. Sasha and his brother had an argument about what to do. They decided that the best thing to do was to hide, in the burning house! At the eleventh hour, his parents came running home and rescued them, but Sasha was terrified by his near brush with death and was left with a stutter ever after. (Assuming, of course, that all of this actually happened and that Sasha wasn't spinning a yarn).

In the Soviet Union, one of the big-time psychiatric diagnoses was "sluggish schizophrenia", something that, of course, doesn't really exist. One of the "symptoms" of sluggish schizophrenia was stuttering. So, Sasha was always conveniently arrestable.

Kalugin's Colorful Chicken "Petux krikin"

Back somewhere in the 1982-83 academic year, Sasha was picked up and dumped yet again in a psychiatric hospital. A grad school friend of Marcia, who had access to Stockman's (a department store in Finland), boldly marched into the hospital and asked the chief doctor what it would take to get Sasha out. Without even a blush, the doctor named a particular model of Nike running shoes. Her friend immediately ordered them from Helsinki, and Sasha was sprung. Nice, no?

For days and days Sasha would draw or paint, sometimes not even stopping to eat. Obsessive and detailed, complicated and astonishing, fantastic and realistic, but not in line with Soviet Realism's glorifying messages about the Soviet Union. He expressed the irony of how the Soviet people lived an absurd, red-bannered world. His work abounds with grotesque manifestations of tacky Soviet propaganda, the lack of everyday comfort, and the total loss of individuality. He combined nostalgia and surrealism with the past spiritual life of Holy Russia. Monasteries and fantastic Monsters interplay in a strange, unified existence. Sasha's early trauma in his childhood, his resultant stutter, and his detailed visual imagery might have added to his creative eccentricities. Those wildly colorful paintings and etchings with phantasmagoric images had to come from somewhere.

He was a gifted genius, but at times, Sasha's intense creativity spilled over in a drunken haze, his only other outlet. His fate brought him many trials. He was interrogated over his symbolism (religious, fantasy, or abstractions). People like Kalugin who did not agree with the guidelines of the Communist Party were put in jails or placed on "the list for psychiatric treatment". The Soviets questioned the sanity of these dissidents and might confine them to mental institutions, often interned for political reasons. Sasha suffered multiple visits to psychiatric hospitals (fourteen in all) where he was sometimes forcibly treated with mind-altering drugs. The 1970s and 1980s were a difficult period for Sasha with his many "treatments", despite his wife's continual support to prove he wasn't mentally ill. A dissident, Sasha was a man suffering from his convictions. The horrific practice of committing dissidents for crimes of imagination, mystical, or spiritual enlightenment, might horrify us in our too often indifferent world.

Like other unsanctioned artists, Sasha was not allowed in the Art Guild. To be a member you must conform to the dogma of Soviet Realism, the only government-approved art form. Consequently, he was unable to get art supplies. Only card-carrying members of the Art Guild could purchase the tools of their trade. But Jim found a way to get a few art supplies for Sasha on a trip to Finland. Sasha's paintings, graphic etchings, and drawings rolled up easily to fit in the diplomatic pouch. I smuggled some out for an exhibit in New York. Bad Joann.

One evening I went with friends to a Moscow exhibit of avant-garde art, most of which was deemed "unofficial". Outside the Soviet apartment block, Big Brother, an obvious goon, paced outside, back and forth, back and forth. Keeping his lists and checking them twice, he knew from the foreign license plates who was naughty, not nice. The D01, D04, D05 (diplomat), and K (correspondent) numbered plates of Westerners, the U.K., U.S., Canada, and more. Who was arriving and when did they leave? Other visitors, likely locals, made it on his "suspicious character" lists.

Some artists were "semi-official" with acceptable landscapes, while others were more Turneresque and therefore not Realism. Sasha helped other artists, he included just a few pieces of his own. I expected to see more of his work, but some dissident artists were more privileged than others. A pecking order existed among them.

In the fall of 1980, I agreed to host an exhibition of Sasha's art in my apartment. On one Saturday morning, someone I did not recognize, nor did he give his name, approached me. He pulled me aside on my way to the embassy Snack Bar. "You cannot use your apartment to exhibit art." I hardly remember whatever else he said. I was dumbstruck, I felt like I'd been given a hard slap on the wrist. "Ok, I understand," I think I said, not oblivious to his strong reprimand. Do not fraternize with the natives, especially dissidents. I'd been told in my briefing about the Rules of Nonengagement and that engaging with Soviet citizens is not encouraged. So, American Big Brother was watching me too. Bad, very bad Joann.

Dissident, the word itself conjures up images of incarcerated prisoners who commit the crime of speaking their minds. Those freethinkers in thought, philosophy, ideology, politics, and religion must all watch their tongues, or they may end up with monumental consequences. They can be discredited, arrested, hounded, persecuted, incarcerated, banished, forced into exile, or worse. Some things stay the same, and today's Russia is no different. We are in many ways still "back in the U.S.S.R."

In today's Russia, Aleksei Navalny, incarcerated dissident and unrelenting critic of Vladimir Putin, languished until he died in the "Polar Wolf" arctic penal colony. During the freezing dark of winter, he spent three hundred days in solitary confinement in an airless, cold, damp, 7-by-10-foot concrete "punishment" cell. Inmates were only allowed one book. His only complaint was, "I want to have ten books in my cell."

For those of us who still don't understand, we are all dissenters of varying degrees.

Dissidents, Artists, and Refuseniks

We all have opinions and sentiments, we may not always agree with others, but dissent often comes with consequences. As with any action, there is a reaction. Newton's third law of equal and opposite reaction holds true in the physical world. In the world of people, sometimes the smallest and seemingly trivial action can provoke consequences hugely skewed out of proportion. Bad things can happen anywhere in the world, but especially in totalitarian dictatorships and other repressive regimes. Sometimes, there are unintended consequences even in free societies and democratic countries.

During my California college days, when I wasn't in a science lecture, dissecting lab animals, or working to pay my tuition, I might get involved with student protests. During my little free time, I was more likely lounging on the lawn during hippy "love-ins". I did take part in the Vietnam War protests. It all seemed pretty harmless to me. There were few repercussions or risks for the students. That is, until 1970 when the National Guard opened fire and shot and killed students at Kent State University. Apparently, Newton's Third law didn't apply equally to anti-war student protests, where an action was met with an extreme and disproportionate reaction, a violent massacre. Was it state-sanctioned violence when the governor called the protesters "worse than Brown Shirts and communists."? Or when he labeled the students as "the worst type of people that we harbor in America." Some potent provocation in my estimation. Even in the best of democratic societies, things can go horribly wrong for dissidents. Today, student protests have returned in America but not at the scale of the 1960s-70s. Let's hope that history does not repeat itself.

There was a joke in the Soviet Union about holding a blank sheet of paper, because "everyone knows what the paper is supposed to say." In 2022, following the Russian invasion of Ukraine, the police in Moscow arrested people for holding a blank sheet of paper during anti-war protests. The Russian regime had mastered mind control. They could arrest you for what they *think* might be your thoughts. Even if you write nothing, your message is clear to the thought police.

George Orwell's "1984" modeled Big Brother on Josef Stalin. Things haven't changed much under Putin. After the invasion of Ukraine, the word "war" no longer exists. The banned word "war" had been replaced with "a special military operation." The "1984" slogan "War is Peace" could therefore be replaced with "A Special Military Operation is Peace." Putin's totalitarian absurdity at its finest.

Meanwhile, in America, a narcissist co-opts the stories of Russian dissidents. Feeling persecuted, he claims that everyone is out to get him. He portrays himself as a "proud political dissident" and repeatedly says "I am a dissident." His "torture" he compares with Navalny. He proclaimed "It's a form of Navalny. It's a form of communism or fascism". Not knowing that communism and fascism are incompatible terms, he combines the two inflammatory words to create fear and fury. But he misses the word "totalitarian" in his dream for his future America.

In America, free speech is protected by the First Amendment. With the Rule of Law and a justice system, freedom and democracy will hopefully prevail. But if you dare speak (or write) your mind in Russia today, it's off to the Gulag you will go. Whether in Siberia or in a remote penal colony in the Arctic Circle where Aleksei Navalny tragically died at 47, all for bravely speaking his mind. Sudden death, or whatever the euphemism is, he was murdered after many systematic, deliberate attempts to kill him. In the Soviet Union and Russia today, political thugs assassinate their opponents. Was our American narcissist, like Navalny, poisoned with a nerve agent? Novichok in his underwear? Was he tortured and beaten? Was he left in the "Polar Wolf" arctic prison to freeze to death?

Would the Western world sit back while their citizens, dual nationals, and Russian political dissidents suffer the same fate as Navalny? We in the West believe that it is our duty to protect our nationals and that solidarity between the USA and its allies is imperative. The moral dilemma of making deals with the devil, a Faustian bargain, requires difficult decisions. And a deal for freedom might not be possible without bitter concessions.

On August 1, 2024, the largest prisoner swap between Russia and the US since the Cold War. In a historic 24-prisoner exchange, the complex deal involved seven countries to secure the release of those unlawfully detained in Russia. It took months of negotiations to come together, especially under extreme secrecy. Before this prisoner swap, on December 8, 2022, NBA Brittney Griner, charged with smuggling cannabis vapes, was exchanged for a convicted Russian arms dealer, Viktor Bout, the "Merchant of Death". It's a high-priced swap when vape pens are traded for combat weapons.

Wall Street Journal reporter Evan Gershkovich was sentenced to 16 years in prison for espionage. We followed his plight closely during his four hundred and ninety-one days in Lefortovo prison. Former-marine Paul Whelan, convicted of espionage for twenty-five years, languished in a high-security prison for over five years. The bargaining chip for both Americans was an FSB assassin, Vadin Krasikov, who killed a Georgian-Chechen opponent of Russia in a Berlin park. He was sentenced to life for a "state-ordered murder". Vladimir Putin's pal Krasikov was the lynchpin for securing the release of Gershkovich and Whelan.

There is no free speech in Russia. Dissident writer, Alsu Kurmasheva, a joint US-Russian citizen who, for two decades, worked for Radio Free Europe. She'd been sentenced to six and a half years for spreading false information about the Russian army. Kurmasheva, Gershkovich, and Whelan were greeted on their arrival on US soil by President Joe Biden and Vice-president Kamala Harris. The prisoners released in the US were designated as "wrongfully detained."

Kremlin critic Vladimir Kara-Murza, a Russian-British citizen, denounced the war in Ukraine. He was convicted of treason in a show trial. He suffered the consequences of dissent in Putin's Russia—two attempts at poisoning him and twenty-five years in prison. In 2024, he won a Pulitzer Prize for the Washington Post columns he wrote from his prison cell. He was released in Bonn, Germany. Kara-Murza viewed what happened to him as an expulsion. He added that there are "hundreds of people in prison solely for their political views, and more and more are on the lists of political prisoners."

American Marc Fogel, a history teacher for nine years at the Anglo-American School (AAS), made the biggest mistake of his life and was sentenced to fourteen years in a hard labor camp. He brought in medical marijuana in his suitcase through Sheremetyevo airport. In 2021, the Anglo-American School in Moscow became a charter school. Teachers were no longer under the US Embassy umbrella, like us. They lost their protection with diplomatic immunity. Cannabis offenses like Marc Fogel's would barely raise an eyebrow in the U.S. In many Western countries, those products are legal. I do worry about the unfortunate plight of detained and incarcerated individuals. Using "prisoners" as pawns in a geopolitical struggle is a dangerous game that Putin is playing to get what he wants.

During the Cold War, marijuana brownies might have led to my demise. Gulp! Today, there are many people held in long-term detention for minuscule offenses. I will never step foot in Moscow again. In Moscow today, opposition politicians are in exile or assassinated while others are political prisoners. Russian oligarchs who displease Putin face tax fraud charges. The Kremlin allows no dissent. Putin feels even more emboldened, he believes he's untouchable. For so many years, he's kept an iron grip on Russia. That's the way dictators work. He does whatever he wants, whenever he wants. And today in Russia, people are arrested and detained for as little as laying flowers at impromptu memorials.

The message is clear, toe the line or otherwise bad things might happen to you. You can be assassinated by gunshot as you walk across a Moscow bridge, or they will find other ways to kill you. Putin has a long reach and has eliminated people overseas. Maybe a chemical nerve agent, like Novichok, or biological poisons like ricin-tipped umbrellas. Or physical means like window falls, torture, or repeated beatings that will eventually lead to your demise. And then there is Putin's personal favorite, "Vlad's tea" laced with radioactive polonium. It not only kills you, but it also makes you glow.

ДЕВЯТЬ / NINE

SOVIET LEADERSHIP AND BOOKS CHANGING HISTORY

JIM: WINSTON CHURCHILL ELOQUENTLY DESCRIBED the Soviet leadership. In a radio broadcast in October 1939, he described the Soviet Union: "I cannot forecast to you the action of Russia. It is a riddle wrapped in a mystery, inside an enigma. But perhaps there is a key. That key is Russian national interest." This quote is still a good description of Soviet and post-Soviet Russia in many ways. Soviet leadership, like many communist countries, could be a mystery to anyone in the West. The riddle for the capitalist West was and is how the communist system worked. When you think you have understood then something will come along to show how little we in the West understand this enormous country. The Soviet Union was always a puzzle, difficult to unravel, it stood as an enigma that defied our understanding. Putin has created a narrative that selects different parts of history and wraps it up as neo-Russian nationalism.

Russians in 1980 Moscow were proud of their sacrifices in the "Great Patriotic War" (World War Two). Forty-five years after the end of the war you often saw old men with their medals on their suits, and sometimes missing arms or legs. More Russian soldiers died in that war than any of the other allied countries. Joann and I were often struck by the number of old women you saw working on Moscow streets. Widows got a small pension which they needed to supplement with work.

In Soviet eyes, it was Russia that played the major role in defeating Germany and the Nazi threat.

I never had a calendar in Moscow, but I got to know certain days marked for their importance. Russians loved any excuse to have a fireworks display. The cityscape would light up with some pretty spectacular displays. The commemoration of the end of the Patriotic War was time for a big fireworks event. Russian television devoted significant time to veterans and running patriotic World War Two films. We found many Great Patriotic war memorials throughout Eastern Europe. In sharp contrast, Russia's role in World War One was rarely mentioned. No Nazis were available in 1914-17, and Russians fought for a czar. The Soviet system portrayed Nazis as the root of all evil in the world. According to Putin's current chosen narrative, Ukraine is the new Nazi haven that needs to be obliterated. Ironically Russia still took heavy casualties in World War I.

We could never ignore the billboards filled with the current propaganda line when we walked around Moscow. Whoever was the current Supreme Soviet leader had their photographs on numerous street billboards. We saw two leaders in our two short years, 1979-81. Why were pictures of leaders so prominently displayed everywhere? I suspect it was the quick leadership changes after Brezhnev died. Another part is that generally in communist countries I think the elite always worry that everybody would forget what they looked like. Leader security in Soviet times meant the chance of seeing the top leadership in person was a rare event for the average Russian.

Soviet newspapers quoted anything the Supreme Leader, or the rest of the Politburo had said on any particular day. There would be more "latest news" as I watched the national evening news broadcasts and English language Radio Moscow. You got a daily dose of some leader of the Marxist utopia, visiting manufacturing plants or earnestly listening to some farmer on a collective farm. As a confessed political cynic, I have difficulty believing a 0.5% increase in the harvest would make leaders jump for joy. How did the leaders feel having to stare at a tractor production line? I always wondered what was going through any politician's mind. Do car or tractor assembly lines thrill the communist functionary? Who knows how they felt? This is part of the Churchillian enigma, I suppose.

I should point out that many political leaders in the Western world tend to want their photo opportunities and quotes in the press. Propaganda is something only the bad guys do, right? Instead in the West, national and local news outlets, spin doctors and political flunkies tell us we get valuable information. Western videos often show the politician looking slightly uncomfortable in suitable protective overalls and a safety hat perched on their head. This performance is supposed to show how our politicians at worksites mingle with the working people. Again, you can wonder what is going through the politician's mind at these events. Does hi-vis yellow go with my complexion? This bloody safety helmet feels as though it might fall off my head. However uncomfortable for politicians, it is democracy in action to show the "little people" that they are working for them. It could also be seen as political theater as they wield those gold-plated shovels of earth at groundbreaking events.

I love the story of one of the several recent UK prime ministers, Boris Johnson, who hid in a fridge at a factory visit. He wanted to avoid answering some awkward questions from the press. It turned out to be a public relations disaster. I imagine some low-level PR person would get the blame. The Western press people have a very different take on any politician's "visits" compared to their communist reporters. The Western press can be fierce in their criticism. No negative reports would be seen on Soviet news.

Language and image are tools politicians use extensively. I am always impressed with the power of a good political image or clever language. The reverse is true if you hide in refrigerators, awkwardly wear a hard hat, or leave the script and speak off the cuff. Any politician prays to avoid a "hot" mike that captures their less glorious speaking moments. Vice-President Biden was caught saying "It's a big fucking deal," at Obama's signing of the Affordable Care Act. Soviet leadership used language and images to project their power and the country's progress. Putin's penchant for huge tables and vast rooms seems part of that power projection he learned under communism.

The communist leadership felt it important to write books about themselves. They want to describe their achievements or thoughts on how communist society was always progressing. There is a heavy emphasis on their important part in that progress. So, in Moscow, I bought the autobiography of Leonid Brezhnev: *Trilogy, Little Land, Rebirth, The Virgin Lands* in English. Part one "Little Land" is about Leonid's active fight in the Great Patriotic War from 1941 till the victory in 1945. He wrote about this because we are told "people from all over the world asked to recall his ordeal of fire." This quote jives with the need to show a Russian leader's contribution to the Second World War. We may recall that President Kennedy's WW2 exploits were written about in detail. Leaders show in their writing how personal events they document contributed to the political system and the leaders they are now.

Brezhnev on a Typical Soviet Cement Block

Leonid (or his ghostwriter) often waxes at great length in true Marxist style. The Virgin Lands is about his agricultural administrative work in Kazakhstan in the 1950s. I quote, "Yevdokia Andreyevna Zaichukova was nearly fifty when she came to the Virgin Lands (Kazakhstan). She kept her youthful zest, willpower, and strength of character, and above all she had the ardent heart of a Communist and patriot." Later this patriotic lady tells the local District Committee, "I want a post on a poorly performing collective farm. I want to leave my current management post on an efficient collective farm." One assumes this little anecdote shows the sacrifice good communists make to create a better world. I confess it is a great read if you have trouble sleeping. Booker or Pulitzer Prize contender, it is not.

Western countries are not immune from these memoirs, autobiographies, and personal political philosophy books. A jaundiced view sees this personal propaganda especially when the politician is about to run for higher office or reflect on their career. I recently tried to read a well-respected US congressman's book. The format follows a pattern throughout these types of books. You get the politician's personal history and edited events. It is always difficult to puzzle how big an impact the person had in the events they describe. They identify what they see as wrong or right at any given moment. Did this thinking happen during the moment described or is the writer giving you an afterthought? Books are sprinkled with the person's view of politics as they see it or how they would like things to be. The Brezhnev book is a good example of his less-than-stellar leadership posts before he was promoted to the Politburo and eventually took over the top position. His prior achievements after the war were less than you might expect in a "great" leader of a powerful country. His humble beginnings and early career are a puzzle to how Brezhnev rose to power for eighteen years. Political memoirs are good puzzles to untangle reality, fact, and fantasy. At the same time, the book—*History of the USSR* I purchased was far more interesting, although the prose is often as turgid as Leonid's opus. I read about Josef Stalin who led the Soviet Union from 1924 to his death in 1953. There are estimates that more than twenty million would die during Stalin's rule. The list of crimes against humanity is long. Stalin saw enemies domestic and foreign. There were the feared Secret Police who arrested anyone who they thought had wrong political thoughts. Mind reading must have been a required skill for an NKVD operative (forerunner of the KGB). The Stalin "courts" were often show trials with a predetermined outcome.

Ukraine's famine from 1930 to 1934 is known as the Holodomor. Holodomor is Ukrainian for hunger and extermination. Nearly four million Ukrainians died. Whole villages had their farm products taken, often leaving the people with nothing to last the winter. A widespread famine killed another million Russians at the same time as famine spread across the Soviet Union. Stalin's Ukraine policy was to make up for the shortfall in agricultural production and exterminate undesirable Ukrainians. It was also the time when several rebellions by small landowners (kulaks) were ruthlessly forced to join collective farms or eliminated. The Soviet Union's collective farm system couldn't provide enough food. Stalin's great solution was to steal Ukrainian food to prop up his failed farm policies.

Whole groups of Soviet and conquered people would end up dead under Stalin's rule. For example, there were Cossacks from the Caucasus, Stalin considered the group to be a threat, despite being a Georgian from the Caucasus himself. He organized their transportation *en masse* by train and dumped them in Kazakhstan. Not all survived the journey or stayed in this poor Soviet republic. Then there were the Siberian gulags, firing squads and prisons. Russians still referred to "The Terror" under Stalin's rule. One reason we did not socialize with ordinary Russians in 1980 Moscow is that the culture of neighbor informants was alive and well. Fraternizing with Western foreigners had serious consequences for Soviet citizens in post-Stalin times.

How did Russian history portray this totalitarian strongman? The book gives Uncle Joe two brief paragraphs that mention him as an administrator with a minor role. It is said that winners write history. Nikita Khrushchev denounced Stalin's thirty-year dictatorship as "The Terror" at the 20th Congress. My history book clearly shows some careful editing in this official Soviet history. Stalin transforms from a Second World War winner to a minor historical footnote. He was a mass murderer of epic proportions. It is a great example of a Russian enigma. We often hear in the West that Russians still want and have a "strong" leader. I can only speculate how Putin will appear in distant future history books. Will some future Russian leader erase Putin's leadership?

Over the years I have kept reading biographies or investigative journalist books on Russian leaders. I generally avoid most personal memoirs or autobiographies that I always suspect are far too close to the events they describe. In a biography, the writer is removed from the person they write about. You must judge the relationship of the author with his subject. Is it propaganda puffery or a balanced historical narrative? Investigative journalists who write books tend to pick people with "interesting" exploits. They have less interest in the excessive promotion of a leader. History is less "fact" and more one interpretation. The example of a "glorified" British colonial history has undergone a recent re-interpretation. Recent colonial history downplays the apparent civilizing effect on the "natives" and remembers the harm and thievery that enriched the British Empire.

Probably the strangest biography on a Soviet leader I read was a memoir of Nikita Khrushchev. He was the leader from 1953 following the death of Stalin until 1964. Who wrote it was in doubt for many years. The Politburo led by Khrushchev's successor Brezhnev in 1964 forced Nikita to say he never wrote the book. The official version of history at the time was that the publication was a fake. Years later Khrushchev's diaries appeared in the West to provide convincing evidence that the biography was authentic. We have another instance of the winner (Brezhnev) rewriting history. Khrushchev's denouncing of Stalin was repeated when Nikita's version of history was officially denounced. Khrushchev joins a long list of Russian leaders who magically disappear.

Khrushchev was a man who rose to leadership from great poverty. He was born to parents who were very poor in a small southern Russian village close to the Ukrainian border. People who met him found he was a true Soviet puzzle. He could be charming and funny or volatile and threatening. Given his background, he could be blunt and let everyone know exactly how and what he was thinking. The story of him banging the table with his shoe in the United Nations has taken on legendary status. Less known was when he visited America, he was impressed with American ice cream. So much so that he made sure ice cream was manufactured in the Soviet Union. Joann and I can say it was good if limited in flavors to vanilla, chocolate, and rarely strawberry. Odd though it seems, eating ice cream outside in the middle of winter remains one of our fond memories of the Soviet Union. Thanks, Nikita!

Few Soviet leaders acknowledged their wives had a part in their story. Stalin had two wives. His first wife was believed to have wanted to leave him in 1932. She ended up committing suicide, at least that was the official version. Often there are few pictures of Soviet wives. Yuri Andropov (a leader of the KGB) who came after Brezhnev was a shadowy character. There was little mention of his two wives. Marital bliss was not on his agenda because, under his KGB leadership, he was too busy suppressing dissent in Hungary, Czechoslovakia, and on the home front. He orchestrated the Russian invasion of Afghanistan for Brezhnev. His part makes sense because the Afghanistan invasion took place and certainly had an impact during our time in the Soviet Union. The 1980 Olympic boycott is one of our other stories.

Brezhnev had a severe heart attack in 1975. Andropov and others in the Politburo were probably running things for many years. I remember seeing Brezhnev on our rented color TV. It was obvious he was very ill, his complexion looked pretty odd. His speech was slow and sometimes he slurred as he spoke. It reminds me that there were plenty of stories where Churchill had difficulty giving a speech. In his case, the overindulgence of alcohol was blamed. There is a parallel in that Churchill and Brezhnev's wives remained in the background. Communist history gives very little detail about the leader's spouse(s).

The only wife before Raisa Gorbacheva who was mentioned as having an impact on the man would be Lenin's wife, Nadezhda Krupskaya. Vladimir and Nadezhda are framed in our bedroom above where we sleep. I will let you work out which one is above my head. A biography of Mikhail Gorbachev by William Taubman impressed me. In the biography, Raisa Maximovna Gorbacheva plays a prominent part in her husband's life. Mikhail and Raisa were seen as the last committed communists who tried unsuccessfully to change and save the Soviet system. Gorbachev would live to see the demise of communism with two little-known figures, Boris Yeltsin and Vladimir Putin, changing the country's course away from communism. Gorbachev became another of those disappearing Russian leaders. It is difficult not to feel sorry for the Gorbachevs as they tried to emulate the little Dutch boy sticking his finger in the dyke to prevent the flood. They failed.

Supreme leaders or autocrats certainly do not like books that show them in a bad light. *Putin's People: How the KGB Took Back Russia and Then Took On the West* is a book by Catherine Belton. She was a former Moscow correspondent for the Financial Times. Ms. Belton learned to her "cost" financially that writing an investigative book on Putin and his cronies comes at a heavy personal price. She ended up in court several times with her publisher defending herself against a gaggle of oligarchs who didn't like what she wrote. She had to admit there were a few errors to be edited but the overall themes remain. Yes, it is one author's interpretation of history but her narrative blends with other reports on Putin's crony state. The book showed why Putin has become a menace to the West. The bottom line is that many of the world's bad people now use the Western courts to silence their critics. Bad people still murder, torture, and imprison to keep power but they have discovered the legal systems in democracies are another useful tool. It is just an extension of the "legal" system in Soviet and post-Soviet justice. The goals are the same. Silence the critics or those who threaten them.

Putin's career in the KGB started in East Germany. Part of his job allegedly was to finance and provide weapons for the Bader Meinhof gang (a.k.a. Red Brigade). This murderous group was about creating chaos and very little else. Young Putin learned the ideals of communism were easy to set aside, all he had to do was find a group, left or right, in the political spectrum in Europe that showed themselves against Western democracy. The aim is to keep the political pot boiling and make people think Western democracy is a failure. Putin still has the personal dream that he can destroy Western democracy. It was the same aim he had in the1980s Soviet Union. With that lens, many of his current actions and decisions make scary sense according to his worldview. He grew up in an organization that had the goal to destroy Western democratic values. The Soviet propaganda he grew up with told him repeatedly that the Soviet Union was an ideal until it wasn't. Putin rules a mysterious country, in a system we struggle to understand. After two years of living in the Soviet Union, I can never claim to understand Russia completely. I am as mystified as Churchill.

ДЕСЯТЬ / TEN

SHOPPING FOR ANYTHING, EVERY-THING, AND ART

JIM: **THE FOREIGN AND DIPLOMATIC COMMUNITY LIVED** a life that was light years from the average Soviet citizen. Stories of Soviet corruption, inefficiency, and smug feelings of superiority were rife among Western diplomatic circles. The Soviet Union would cease to exist a few years after we left. The Communist society even in 1979-81 was under pressure. What follows are brief stories of us shopping and selling different things. Some represent anecdotes from our brief encounters with Marxist consumerism in Moscow.

Often Joann and I opted out of the diplomatic system where everything was shipped in for you. Some foreigners would even ship basic goods like milk from Finland. We on the other hand learned the Russian art of careful examination and sniffing milk cartons in domestic shops. Milk is milk after all. In Russia, it came in pyramid cardboard cartons. There was a two-step process I followed, which was to pick up the carton and see that the contents were not leaking. A gentle squeeze helps to see if any milk drips onto my hands. Next, bring the carton up to my nose and sniff. If it passed the 'squeeze and sniff test' I would take that milk carton and pay. The only problem with this test was if milk from another carton had spread across the shelf. The question then is to decide on the location of the leak. Is your carton the one leaking or did it just pick up sour milk on the shelf?

We did not refuse all the "comforts" of the British and American commissaries. For a fleeting moment when we were dating, I may have entertained an awkward question. Was our growing relationship cemented by American Betty Crocker upside-down cake mix or British Bird's custard? I shamelessly asked Joann to buy a whole case of Dr. Pepper from the American commissary. A purchase that several friends found amusing. My excuse is that I had never savored that soda until I was in Moscow. I still occasionally drink Dr. Pepper. On the other hand, I have never craved or eaten a Betty Crocker baked delight since we left Moscow.

Capitalist-style shopping trips to the Stockmann department store in Helsinki were an infrequent treat. They had to be infrequent as I could put things on our accounts. Yes, we enjoyed our purchases. But the bills to settle our accounts later could temper anyone's enthusiasm to purchase. We mostly bought winter stuff like coats and "moon" boots. Moon boots were something we would probably never wear anywhere else. It was obvious that Muscovites thought foreigners in moon boots were the height of some hideous and hilarious Western fashion statement. Thick insulated calf-length boots require some arm strength to get on when they are new and still stiff. Moon boots had a certain amount of grip so that you could walk on the icy Moscow pavements. Finns taught us by observation the art of walking on icy patches. Put each foot out at an angle and waddle like a giant penguin. You take smaller steps than you normally would and certainly avoid being in a hurry. I loved our shopping visits to Finland. The Finns, like many Scandinavians, were good English speakers. This contrasted with most Americans and Brits who rarely speak second languages.

As you waddled in moon boots penguin-style in Finland, you could hear the Finnish sound like the "Muppet Swedish chef". The Finn's lilting tones would always make me smile. In contrast, Russians always sound angry in tone although they are not. I made the mistake of walking in the Moscow winter without a hat. Wielding a broom, a small fierce-looking old lady, known in Russian as *babushka* shouted "*shapka*" along with a stream of friendly advice. It certainly startled me as she barked this out. In Russia, every old woman could be your long-lost grandmother. Their self-appointed task is to ensure you don't catch a cold and wear that hat.

"Okay Grandma, I will wear my hat in the future, I won't do it again, I promise."

Could not wearing a hat be genetic? My sister visited us twice in Moscow and those fearsome old ladies reprimanded her for not wearing her hat. I only ask because our father was punished several times for not wearing his hat in the British army. He told me once he had to paint all the stones white in the parade ground. Stupidly he told the sergeant he had finished. He ended up painting those stones twice in the oppressive heat of the Indian sun!

Back in Moscow, I went appliance shopping. I mentioned on a whim to a correspondent friend that I missed television. His voice drops to a conspiratorial whisper.

"Okay, do you have a lot of US dollars?"

"Yes, what do I need them for, don't I need rubles if I want to buy a Russian TV?" He just smiled.

He took me for a drive into a distant suburb of Moscow I had never seen before. We arrive at Aladdin's cave in the basement of a typical Russian high-rise apartment. The place has radios, black and white TVs, and some grand-looking color TVs in good wooden cabinets. The lady in charge of the cave and my friend rattle away quickly in Russian and come to some agreement.

"We need your dollars now." I cannot remember the amount, but I was curious because my purchase seemed cheap. We heave the color TV into the back of his car with a little effort. I discover more about my "purchase" as we drive.

"You have just rented a TV," I am told with a smile.

"Okay, great. So that is why it seemed so cheap?"

"No, it was cheap because you paid the rental in dollars."

Sometimes I am a little slow on the uptake, but I ask the question. "So how long was the rental and what happens when I leave Russia." I worry my credit rating will be affected. What happens if I fail to make further payments or do not return the TV at the end of my stay? Joann always teases me because I tend to obey rules. It's very much a British thing!

"Welcome Jim to the black market. Your US dollars will be useful to the "shop" lady. I guarantee that when you leave, your TV will disappear after you have left the country. I assure you some unknown Russian will benefit from your abandoned TV." I think my friend was referring to the people who came to foreign apartments after they were vacated. As well as checking the microphone bugs were in working order they could "recycle" my TV into their apartment. What an efficient system to combine espionage and television rental in one neat package.

I enjoyed my "rental" TV for the rest of our time in Moscow. There were a couple of channels to watch. As I understood little of the language I favored sports, so ice hockey or soccer was a usual choice. I tried to improve my Russian. I enjoyed *spokoynoy nochi*. A cute little bear or mouse with big ears appeared early in the evening to tell little kids it was time to go to bed. This creature be they he, she, or it, and with a five-year-old voice, included a simple bedtime story. Just about my level of Russian which otherwise included asking how much my beer would cost and simple greetings or goodbyes. I even found a few commercials; they consist of riveting and eye-catching scripts like "Buy soap". I could never work out if the goal is to improve sales at soap factory 57 in Omsk or Tomsk or a subtle message for Russians to make more use of the hygiene product.

Joann's upright piano was another whim we realized. Joann did play it a few times. I suspect it was to put right a childhood trauma. When her family moved to a new smaller house in Los Angeles, it meant her upright piano was sacrificed. She told me a sad tale. "My parents gave me a cardboard keyboard to practice for piano recitals. After a year, I gave up piano lessons with Sister Mary Elephant. I've never forgotten how I lost my piano."

Neither of us can remember where the piano came from but we both remember the sale and removal. Two gentlemen had been hired to remove the piano for the person who had purchased it. The two men were about 5 foot six or less, clearly from one of the Asian Soviet Republics, both appeared wider than they were tall. They slipped two long canvas belts underneath the front and back of the piano inside the wheels so the belts could not slip off. Then to our astonishment, the belts were put on their foreheads. I have seen heavy appliances carried with similar canvas belts in the US, but the weight is carried on their shoulders. Their neck muscles bulge as they take the weight and then in synchronized movement, they say one—two (*odin, dva*) as they take the piano out of the apartment and down the stairs from the second floor to the waiting truck. Joann gives them a six-pack of American beer. Her piano disappears off into the sunset. We look at each other in amazement. "That piano was heavy," Joann says. "Those two guys would not look out of place in an Olympic Weight-Lifting contest."

Shopping for what you need or want, took up enormous amounts of time for the average Russian in those days. Demand always outstripped supply. We learned about the attaché case that many Russian men carried. Inside was a string *avoska* (possible) bag in case you saw a possible desirable item to buy. Your string bag held any trophy you might purchase on your daily travels. The shopping rumor network in Moscow was world-class. The network told people Polish frozen peas were available in a certain location. Suddenly a line forms and passers-by would ask why they were in line. On finding out what was on sale they would join the line and abandon whatever else they were about to do. At one time toilet paper was in short supply when we were there. I remember seeing a happy man with a string of toilet rolls around his neck.

Another time there was a long line outside an appliance store. The store had East German washing machines. Right or wrong, Russians assumed that an appliance built outside of Russia would be more reliable and worth the extra money. Shopping and joining lengthy lines were just part of daily life. There were many reasons for a poor Soviet product. Employment in communist Russia was guaranteed for life. We saw people doing very little in a fine industrious-looking fashion. They reminded me of British road workers where three men need to watch someone dig a hole. The profit motive was replaced. The Soviet economy's answer was quotas produced from government planning. If your quota was to assemble fifty washing machines a day, it did not seem to matter if five were defective. The day's quota had been achieved. In many cases, the Soviet citizen was right to be suspicious of big Soviet-made purchases. Joann and I followed Russian consumers' customs. Where possible, we tested the product we were buying before leaving the shop.

It certainly was a surprise to us in the supposedly egalitarian society, shopping was not always equal. The average shop in the Soviet Union was open to all. In addition to our milk, Joann liked to buy the Russian bread. The "regular" stores could be depressing for customers. As we walked down the aisles in a "regular" grocery store many shelves were empty or had just a single product. Fresh produce was not something the Russians would find in these "regular" stores.

There were two other levels of shopping. There were stores exclusively for the elite of the Communist Party. We could only guess what was in those stores because there were guards to prevent ordinary Soviet citizens or foreigners from entering. The other level of shopping was strictly for foreigners, again the entrance was guarded. It never ceased to amaze me that every Soviet citizen could identify a foreigner by sight. It is like there was a sign on your forehead saying foreigner. There were always stories, maybe apocryphal, that you would be stopped in the street and asked if you would sell your jeans. I imagined finding a convenient alleyway, taking off my jeans, and receiving a pile of rubles. Besides the practical problem of what you wear home and the cold as you strip off your clothes, there was always the possibility of being accused as a black marketeer. Neither Joann nor I did any of these shady back-alley transactions.

The final level of shopping was the foreign currency stores (*Beriozka*). These stores were only for foreigners. They did have some interesting things to buy. The drawback was Soviet retail marketing techniques did not include "service with a smile." You could stand there at the counter for some time. There may be one or more sales assistants but you, the customer, are invisible. Patience was a virtue. It was a case of waiting it out and eventually and reluctantly someone would ask you what you wanted. We did find the wait worthwhile. Joann specialized in Olympic pins for the Moscow Olympic Games we would never see. She also has a scarf depicting two smiling Misha bears, the Olympic mascot. I took a liking to pins showing motorcycles and airplanes through the ages. The prize purchase was a pin of *spockoynoy nochi* that I had seen on my rental Russian television.

My first degree was in geography, so I liked maps. I still have my "Atlas of the USSR" bound in (you can guess) red leather. Maps in the Soviet Union interested me because there were often subtle omissions, transport routes added, or suspicious placement of certain places that did not jive with Western maps. Soviet paranoia went to great lengths to confound any enemy. The atlas was only the size of a regular paperback, so I had to smile at the idea of some invading commander squinting at a map this size. "Okay chaps the battalion will advance in this general direction and Baikal should be somewhere there and about that distance." Just a thought. Current Russian generals seem to not believe in the accuracy of their maps. It explains why they lob many random missiles in the vague direction of the target. Sadly, Ukraine is the brunt of this Soviet-style missile and drone strategy.

During Joann's initial security briefing at the American Embassy, she got a map of "Areas Closed to Foreigners in the USSR". This useful map prompted me to shop for picture books that showed us areas we could not visit. The photography in some of them was spectacular. My favorite was a book about Kamchatka, a 1,250-kilometer-long peninsula, in the Russian Far East, with wild natural beauty. There may be some less bucolic defense installations that are not photographed. Kamchatka is remote, but you can see it from the Alaskan Aleutian Islands. This was probably where the vice-presidential hopeful, Sarah Palin, must have stood when she claimed she had seen Russia. I also liked picture books of things I thought I should not photograph. The Moscow metro was truly breathtaking. Each station had different art and stonework decor and was always clean and tidy. The metro's cleanliness contrasted with the generally dingy London tube stations at the time.

Everyone used to buy what people sometimes referred to as *beriozka* junk. Machine-made Matryoshka dolls, *Khokhloma* spoons and bowls, black, red, and gold painted with flowers. Also, Easter is an important date even though officially the Soviet Union was atheist. "Religion is only for old people", was the usual Intourist guide's explanation when we visited churches. But painted wooden Easter eggs were available in shops. We also purchased small beautifully painted *Palekh* boxes or similar ones from other Russian villages. Recently we visited the Religious Icon Museum in Massachusetts, and I came up with a theory. "Look Joann at these icons with their tiny figures painted on many of them. They look like the paintings on those boxes we bought in the Soviet Union." As religion was supposedly dying in the Soviet Union, I suspect many icon painters turned to safe subjects to depict on these lacquered boxes. Russian fairy tales were often the subject of these boxes.

These lacquered boxes were not cheap. I suspect they formed a good source of foreign currency. They were only available in those foreigner-only shops. Forty years on our meager collection shows the passage of time. The lacquer is sticky, and the lids are difficult to open. A better purchase was a collection of hand-knotted rugs again only available in US dollars. These have stood the test of time and different climates. I have a small moral qualm based on Joann's school trip to the Caucasus. The schoolchildren were shocked to see children of their age working full-time in the carpet factories. The lighting was poor, and the girls often wore thick lenses in their glasses.

So where do you go for perishable and fresh items not found in regular stores? The answer is the open-air markets that were sprinkled around the city. A little basic free enterprise was allowed by the State in open-air markets. It was common to find people from the southern republics selling fruit and vegetables. The Moscow train stations that served Georgia or Armenia would have passengers laden with something that would be sold in the market. There were also locally picked mushrooms, and other vegetables, and some arts and crafts were also available. We bought two *matroshka*s painted by an enterprising local folk artist in the open-air market.

Our favorite market was euphemistically called the "pet" market. It was not somewhere we went to buy—instead, it was to look at what was on display. As you expect there would be pets for sale like multiple tanks of goldfish and other domestic animals. Of more interest would be the chickens and other birds that were clearly for eating or egg production.

I was always impressed with Joann's red fox hat she bought in a Moscow shop. I always wanted a "real" Russian hat (*shapk*a). I did buy one in a shop, but it was only rabbit fur. Both hats gradually molted in our wardrobe, and we threw them away.

Love and Vegetables at the Moscow rynok

Happy Couple in the Moscow rynok

Rynok Woman with chicken on strings

Like many foreigners, there is a market for illegal Soviet military cap insignia. When we packed to leave, I forgot to take my Red Army badge off my rabbit fur shapka. Sadly it "disappeared" before it left Soviet customs, but they left the hat. It tells you how thoroughly our outgoing shipment was looked at.

Why did I not buy my Russian hat in the pet market? Any hat purchase was very much alive when purchased. The deal was you got fresh meat along with it for the Sunday dinner. Then the skin could be made into a hat. I did not fancy bringing this living fur hat in a cardboard box to my apartment. I did not trust my hat-making skills. The thought of the process of killing, skinning, and eating did not appeal at all.

I did acquire one pet, a long-haired Siberian cat, from a family at the British Embassy. No doubt the cat originated from the pet market. The cat came with the purchase of their car. The saying "buyer beware" worked in the Soviet Union. A long-haired cat from Siberia would withstand the punishing winter, but this feline was more the cat from hell, a slightly warmer climate. His favorite trick was to lie in wait and ambush me. He would jump out on me unexpectedly and get a firm grip on my skin as he hung on me with splayed legs. As far as he was concerned, the litter box was merely optional. I spent hours cleaning the kitchen linoleum. I love animals and big soft me swallowed their sad tale. I suspect it was more they did not want to pay for the quarantine boarding of animals required in Britain. The moral of my sad pet story is "Don't look a gift cat (horse) in the mouth. Instead, keep your eye on those claws digging into your skin!"

Joann and I's budding romance nearly ended by the Siberian hell cat. I was off on ironically the Trans-Siberian train trip. Joann kindly offered to look after the cat. Joann used to comb her beautiful hair before going to bed. On my return, Joann looks threatening.

"You know what that damn cat did?"

Sheepish "No," I think I know the next words; she does not look ready to embrace me after my journey.

"I was combing my hair and suddenly your cat leaped with claws onto my back."

What can I say? I decided discretion was the better part of valor. "Did he hurt you? I am sooo very sorry. Maybe he was upset being away from his normal surroundings."

Joann in full flight is not to be trifled with.

"The worst thing is the cat chewed my Saint Basil!" This was a small wooden souvenir depicting the church we all know in Red Square. Joann had bought it from the foreign currency shop. Saint Basil is thrust in front of me. "Look he chewed the top spire and one below on the onion domes."

I think I saved the relationship with a suitable amount of groveling. I restrained myself from a laugh or smile about deconstructed St. Basil. When I see it today, I cannot resist a smile when I look at the remodeled Saint Basil if Joann is not in the room.

It is at this point that you find out as I did, several people at the British Embassy were very aware of this feline from hell. Several of them had suffered slight injuries and bore the scars from when they had dinner with the cat's owners. He would lay in ambush normally in the bathroom and spring out with claws ready. It is a clear choice of the puss or Joann. This was non-negotiable for my relationship with Joann, so the cat had to go. The British librarian at the school took the cat away one morning. She told me that she resisted the offers of people to take the cat from her in the vet's waiting room. Maybe they thought the cat might make a nice fur hat? I can only speculate that he went to Siberian heaven despite his misdeeds.

On a happier note, we were struck by the vibrant level of culture and art in the Soviet Union. We loved the ballet and could get cheap tickets through our embassies. We got to watch ballet in the beautiful Bolshoi Theater several times. It was a once-in-a-lifetime experience. My parents visited us twice and my mother asked if we could go to the opera. Please don't ask me what opera it was. My sister thinks it was Prince Igor. Joann, my sister, and I all felt the performance was far too long. All I recall was a gentleman on top of a medieval tower and various squawking ladies entering or exiting at different intervals. Joann and I are not opera fans, and I fell asleep. Mum told us afterward, "It was wonderful!" Dad bought the music. I guess I was a good son after all.

My musical tastes are broad except for opera and English folk music. I arrived with around a thousand albums from my DJ days and had a significant vinyl-buying habit. *Melodia*, the one Soviet recoding label allowed me to indulge my craving. I extended my classical music collection. The recordings were good. My best record-collecting coup was a multiple-disc set of the ballet Spartak (Sparticus). A part of that music was the theme song of a popular British sailing ship soap opera "The Onedin Line." The sad bit is that we never saw the ballet Spartak because tickets were always sold out. More vinyl to feed my bad habit was available at the Anglo-American school where we worked. These record sales were of CBS and affiliate label recordings. These sales happened a couple of times in our two years. I had to be careful that Joann was not supervising me when I studied all those wonderful records. "Is ten, okay?" I ask hopefully, to be met with a frown. One way to remove Joann's frown was to include

Bolshoi Theater in 1980

some Leonard Bernstein classic albums that I knew Joann liked. Vinyl junkies would do anything to get their fix!

Art shopping also led us to a friendship with a Russian artist, Sasha. We used to visit their apartment where he lived with his wife and young daughter. A Russian teacher, at our school translated and we spent many enjoyable evenings. I remember one evening Tamara, his wife, provided a special treat. She had spent three hours shopping and bought some "herring-like" fish. It was another example of how difficult and time-consuming Soviet shopping could be.

My parents gave everyone including Sasha a good laugh. I had brought them to meet the family when they visited us. My father posed a question. Dad had zero Russian and decided to use a mime to ask a question. He thought he would convey his question as though he was playing charades. In my mind, I can see him mimicking hitting something with a hammer and chisel. Sasha is puzzled for a moment. Suddenly, he is inspired by my Dad's pantomime. He can barely speak he is laughing so hard, "*Nyet, nyet*, I am not a sculptor." Everyone is now laughing hard including my father, a normally uptight, serious bank manager.

One evening Sasha talked about one of his paintings.

"Look this is a picture of me lying in the gutter. It was a cold night. Over there on the left is the large goat and a bear. They are coming to save me."

The painting tells a lot about Sasha. He like many Russian men might disappear for a few days on a drinking binge. Vodka consumption between "friends" could be measured in "two bottle nights." It took a long time for him to tell us the story as he had one of the worst stutters I have ever encountered. The goat and bear were with the van that cruised the streets and transported people to the drunk tank for their safety. A night outside in the middle of winter would be a possible death sentence. The next morning the drunks would emerge with no charges lodged.

Soviet society had a very different way of dealing with drunks, always men, on the street. In most Western countries drunks are studiously ignored. Western people suddenly become blind and deaf. Most people gaze anywhere but at the drunk who may be shouting or singing. I remember on one city street seeing a man who was bleeding heavily and very drunk. Two pedestrians spent time assisting him.

Sasha and his wife, Tamara, were wonderful people. They were generous, funny, and always interested in conversation in their apartment. Sasha was also a great artist. He and his wife were like many Russians generous to a fault. One time they came for dinner, and he gave us an abstract painting that sits on our wall today. When Joann was pregnant other gifts were exchanged including a baby dress and icons with mother and child. But I have given you three clues as to why he was not an official artist. Drinking was a lesser transgression but was a strike against him. His stutter was a second "problem" for the authorities. His worst crime was his artwork was not socialist realism. This style portrays uplifting patriotic scenes, like muscular factory workers or peasants in the fields. Sasha's work was varied, like his fantastic goat and bear. It depended on what materials he had at hand.

Sasha told us he had spent some time in psychiatric hospitals, not as a volunteer patient. Psychiatry in the West these days is portrayed as all Kumbaya and gentle therapy. The dark side of psychiatry history is easy to forget. Electro-shock "treatment", and removal of frontal lobes is not what we like to remind ourselves of in past Western medical practice. My great-grandmother was left-handed. She was beaten on her left hand at school until she learned to write with her right hand. In the Soviet Union portraying fantasies or religious subjects was a clear indication of "mental illness." He also felt his stutter was something the authorities thought they could "cure."

His artwork and other unofficial artists would be at very private showings. Many of these would take place discretely in foreign apartments. Russians who had showings in their apartments could be hauled off. Joann saw a Russian goon from the authorities taking careful notes of who was turning up. We went to several of these clandestine gatherings. At his home, we purchased two of Sasha's abstract paintings. We also have a folk tale in a very surrealistic style. I gave my parents one of Sasha's religious ink drawings of Saint Basil. Our favorite picture Joann bought was a multi-colored chicken standing in front of a tiny hen house. Our trips to Helsinki sometimes included a list of art materials Sasha would like. The department store, Stockmans, was not bulging with paints, pastels, art paper, or canvas. Luckily, we navigated to an art store. I wondered how Sasha would feel if he could have been with us and purchased his art supplies.

Simple tasks for Westerners, like shopping, owning a car, or obtaining good home appliances are easy. For Russians, shopping could make life monotonous and at the same time a real struggle. Soviet shopping involved dealing with long lines, empty shelves, and possible indulgence in the black market. Cars were given out from lists where the prospective driver may wait many years. There is a saying in a tiny New England state, "I know a guy" who could help you obtain something. Some Russians had the same guy, mostly connected to the Party. Everyone else did not have such a friend.

ОДИННАДЦАТЬ

ELEVEN

FUN AND GAMES IN MOSCOW

JIM: **IN A SMALL FOREIGN COMMUNITY, THERE WAS A** limited but world-class range of Soviet entertainment. The Soviet Union offered ballet, opera, and sports to us. I avoided the circus in Moscow. I am not a big fan of animal acts. Foreigners were isolated from regular Russians at many events. I always wondered if we were considered infectious by the average Soviet citizen. No ordinary Russian could afford the tickets to many events we got heavily discounted from our embassies. For example, a hockey ticket costs $3 to us from the embassy "concierge". These were not cheap seats "up in the gods" but premium viewing a few rows up and near the center line. I have no idea what a Russian paid. My Russian friends never spoke about visits to the ballet or opera.

In addition to Russian culture and sports, we occasionally ate out. Although it reads as a restaurant (in the Russian-Anglicized alphabet Restoran) I often referred to it jokingly we were going to the "*Pektopah*." For dinner. Someone else had the same sense of humor and called their cat *Pektopah*. A cute name for a cat. Restaurants were expensive, so you rarely saw many Russians in them. If they ate out, they would go to cafes or as it translates in Russian, canteen. The word canteen describes well what food and drink was on offer, it was like circa English school lunches. Not exactly Michelin star-worthy cuisine. I tried a greasy sausage and bread with a cup of coffee. Although the sausage was greasy it tasted nothing like an English "banger' (pork sausage). I have a socially embarrassing reaction to cabbage and root vegetables often found in Russian cooking. I was limited in my choices of Russian cuisine. Vegetarians and vegans would be horrified to see mostly meat on most Soviet menus. My sister remembers the oily mysterious meat the hotels offered, so vegetarians were not missing out on much.

Soviet era eating establishments were odd places. The menu was limited so at the Kiev restaurant you got, no prize for guessing, Chicken Kiev. Another place served steak in a cathedral setting where you heard echoes of other diners. Service was slow, the few Russians who were there would order lots of booze while they waited for the meal.

My parents and sister visited us twice and they learned to be punctual in their hotel restaurant. It is a must in Soviet dining. Their guide told them the hotel breakfast was served at 8 am. The Meads arrive at 8:25. Their cold, congealed fried eggs had sat there since 8 am for their expected arrival. They made sure they were on time in the future. Each tourist hotel had a woman stationed on each floor who called my family if she failed to see them return to their rooms. It makes a change to the mint on your pillow!

There is always an exception, and we visited the Aragvi Georgian Restaurant several times. The food was much to my limited palate with meat on sticks and rice. Even better was the Georgian wine. Soviet-era wine from Georgia and Moldova was pretty good, other Soviet wines not so much. Poor Russian wine reminded me of when I purchased Chianti in those nice straw-covered creations at an Italian gas station. I think the wine was delivered in the same tanker as the fuel. At the Aragvi, there was plenty of dancing and people having a good time. I learned that only certain Russians would be allowed in. So, the clientele included Soviet celebrities, the KGB, and foreigners, especially their spies. One we knew as a "teacher" at the school was a frequent visitor. I know one is supposed to take these things seriously, but the spooks I met seemed sadly comic. One told me about making pit stops in the countryside so they could estimate the grain harvest. I guess satellite imaging has put those spies out of a job.

Any Russian who did sit next to you at some event or restaurant would tell you they learned English in high school. Soviet language education of foreign languages was obviously of a very high standard. It was like the random phone calls I used to get some evenings. The women who called me, never men, demonstrated high school English, of shocking fluency. Some would suggest we could meet, an offer I declined. Exhausting vigilance against compromising encounters was part of the hardship of living and working in Moscow. International phone calls to your friends and relatives avoid embarrassing or difficult conversations. We assumed the KGB probably monitored any international call. I should add that wrong-number calls were not uncommon as I never saw a telephone directory for Moscow. People had to keep a personal list of friend's phone numbers.

Less on the fun side, but supposedly good for you, I signed up for a Russian fitness class. Our instructor was a tall well-muscled military type. He demonstrated and then expected us to try. There was no correction, he seemed to think of other things while we strained away. The exercises were tough. I thought I would be fit enough to join the Soviet elite Spetsnaz soldiers, where our instructor may have come from. The striking feature of the lessons was that we had piano music supposedly to help us as we sweat. Our little Tchaikovsky would hammer away while chain-smoking. Obviously in 1980s Russia, nobody was aware of secondhand smoke problems. He could even keep the music going while he lit the next cigarette. It was the strangest fitness class I have ever attended. But it was not as much fun as encounters with Intourist guides.

Your Intourist guide to any Russian tourist site could produce history you never knew existed. The communist interpretation of history and culture was breathtaking and puts current spin doctors to shame. I will summarize the fun and games I enjoyed because of our Intourist guides. I ended up on a three-hour-plus coach journey each way to Suzdal from Moscow. Suzdal is a twelfth-century town steeped in history and boasts a large community of monasteries and priests. It certainly is picturesque from the outside. So much so my parents gave us an English painter's landscape that includes Suzdal in the distance. The painting might be a metaphor for many things in Russia, a distant view that defies a close look.

Our guide would usher us into this or that church, most of which we are told are museums rather than religious buildings. Why so many museums? Your guide always has the answer.

"Religion is mostly for old people. Most forward-thinking Soviet citizens may admire the architecture but are not believers."

You can translate this as: In the 1920s and 1930s the Communist Party had a massive propaganda campaign against the church. The party sponsored atheism. Even attending a church in the 1980s could mean you were photographed, and names taken by the security people as you left. Religious observance could have severe consequences for your personal and career prospects. No wonder the average Soviet citizen would not go to church. So, it makes sense that some churches become museums. The weird circular Communist logic is at work. Stop people going to church and you can claim religion is dying. People do not go to church, so it follows religion is dying. The Intourist guide at Suzdal spent little time explaining the 700-plus years of history the town represents before 1917. I love irony so I often think that the average pre-revolutionary peasant was not worth a mention. The nobility, middle class, and land-owning peasants were erased from the memory of your Intourist guide.

My second historical rewriting example is when Jim asks the awkward question. We are traipsing around the Peter and Paul Fortress in Leningrad (now Saint Petersburg resurrected after the fall of communism). It is a pretty grim place, and it was a prison. Our Intourist guide gives us a description of who was imprisoned in the cells.

"After the revolution, the fort was used to imprison counterrevolutionaries, remaining nobles, and bourgeoisie who fought against the revolution."

I have read about this period of history with great interest. I decided to have a little fun with our guide plus my bullshit meter was overloaded.

"Excuse me, I thought the bulk of inmates, men, and women, in this prison were Mensheviks?" This group was Marxist and part of the 1917 revolution, but the key difference from the Bolshevik group was they did not recognize Lenin as the Russian leader. The prison also held some early Bolsheviks who after the revolution had become a danger to the ruling elite of the party. These naughty Bolsheviks were often promoters of the World Revolution, not just a revolution in Russia.

The most famous world revolution promoter was the Bolshevik, Leon Trotsky. He was a great rival to Joe Stalin, so he needed to be exiled. He got an ice ax headache, from which he conveniently died in Mexico. Our guide suddenly ushers us on, ignoring my question. I guess some of the people who helped the revolution became surplus to the requirements of the ruling elite. Consolidation after a revolution can often include a purge of some awkward comrades through prison or death.

Russia is not the only country where awkward and unpleasant history is ignored or changed. The United Kingdom is currently coming to terms with its colonial heritage. Some of those beautiful National Trust homes built by Lord and Lady Muck were financed by profits from slavery or colonial theft. Tourists were rarely told about this unpleasant historical background. As Harry Frankfurt, an American philosopher, wrote there is a difference between a lie and bullshit. Liars know the truth and what they say is meant to deceive the listener. The Intourist guide is engaged in bullshit. They may or may not know the truth, they don't care what the truth is. They did not care if you believed the story. Their stories are all about conforming to the approved history. National Trust and Intourist guides give visitors the acceptable bullshit version of history.

Moscow was considered a hardship post in Soviet times. It was not just because of state-sponsored oppression. There was always the chance of being a target for Kompromat. Kompromat was an attempt to obtain information or even better photographic evidence to blackmail foreigners. Those late-night calls I got from nice English-speaking ladies were part of the test. Your contact with home was limited at best. I also found my "bullshit" meter" in constant use during those two years and that can be very tiring.

It was difficult to be completely relaxed when you were at a Soviet event. This explains why much of the 'fun' in Moscow had to be contained within the foreign community. The younger school staff would follow the same routine most Fridays. We would start at the Australian Embassy for early drinks. Then on to the Canadian Embassy where we would play cards and drink. Finally, the group would end up at the Marine Bar in the American Embassy for dancing and drinks. I found you had to pace your alcohol content. Regardless, I would persuade an American friend to invite me to brunch at the American Embassy on Saturday morning. I can still taste steak-cheese-onion and fries with coffee.

The point of all this is to suggest the routine could be monotonous. I am dangerous when I feel ennui setting in. So why not do something different? I felt sympathy for the kids at the school. Many diplomatic parents have heavy social and work schedules, so their children are left to their own devices or looked after by Finnish nannies. The school is small and limited, in the pool of friends they could have. There were limits to the children's social activities.

In the first year in Moscow, we are approaching Christmas. In Britain, no Christmas holiday period can be without a pantomime. This piece of "dramatic" art is unique to the UK. Some think it has something to do with French farce, but I think that is wrong. Here for the uninitiated is a brief explanation of the pantomime spectacle.

First, pick any children's fairy story, let's say Snow White and the Many Dwarfs or Cinderella. I chose these examples because they were two of my "brilliant" forays into plays 'as what I wrote.' I also had to organize, act, and direct these thespian extravaganzas. Two elements of casting are essential. The "principal boy" is a woman, and the script calls for a dame (old woman) played by a man. In Cinderella, the prince who marries Cinderella is played by a woman. We have been cross-dressing in the UK for many years before fashion caught on in the rest of the world.

The ingredients of a good pantomime are double-entendre jokes. There is a fine line here as the audience consists of adults and children, so subtlety is essential. You want the double entendre to be understood by the adults, not the kiddies. They should be topical jokes, material snatched from the recent headlines of the day. Finally, we wrote "groan" jokes. These are jokes that elicit groans in the audience.

For example: "My trash can (dustbin in England) is full of toadstools."

"How do you know they are toadstools?" asks the stooge.

"Because there is not mushroom."

Or

"How do you tell a stoat from a weasel?"

"Well, how do you tell a stoat from a weasel? The stooge echoes.

"It's easy. A weasel is weasily distinguishable, and a stoat is stoately different."

I guarantee the audience will groan.

Pantomime has people running around aimlessly, with people not understanding the obvious, and lots of audience participation. Children will be told to yell or boo when the bad guy creeps up behind the innocent person.

"Kids can you tell me if the bad guy is behind me."

Of course, any child delights in taking part in the drama. Bad people like the Ugly Sisters or the wicked Queen in Snow White disguised as an old woman, encourage the audience to boo when they appear. It may not be Shakespeare, but people enjoy playing the fool.

This brief outline is consistent with what I tell my unsuspecting principal. I tie it up as part of those essential soft skills for management. I cannot believe he bought it!

"It'll be fun, Gene, and it will bring the faculty together. The kids will see us teachers in a different role. Parents will have good feelings about how we, the faculty, are prepared to cross boundaries." He gives me his blessing.

One afternoon I demonstrated how to use a film strip projector for the faculty, and I mentioned the idea of doing Cinderella. The British and Commonwealth (Australia etc.) teachers know what is involved in pantomime. My North American colleagues need some information. As I did with the principal, I summarized what pantomime is.

"Would you like to try it?'

There is a generally positive reaction.

One American teacher asks tentatively, "Will there be tryouts?"

I suspect in her high school past her unsuccessful try-out made her 'gun shy' about thespian arts and her competence in them.

"There is only one consideration. You must under no circumstances be able to act."

I deliver this rule with a straight face. It takes a moment, but the faculty then starts to laugh.

Writing a script is essential, using it in the performance is optional. I found three bottles of wine, some beer, and a few snacks made for Tolstoy-like prose. At least that is how it sounds to the well-oiled participants at the time of writing. People compete to make the jokes funnier. I seem to remember we did a couple of rehearsals. The cast could easily tell who could remember their lines and who ad-libbed well.

Cinderella was one performance only. The audience in the school's assembly room had a good time, and the actors were "brilliant". We had piano accompaniment by the music teacher. The ugly sisters were ugly, and Cinderella got her prince. One of the "highlights" was the dance of the Sugar Plum fairies. This happened as Cinders was getting ready off-stage to go to the ball. I persuaded the principal and myself to wear winter long johns, tutus, and heavy boots for our big dance. I even had a sight gag as my wand was distinctly droopy.

In my mind, teaching is a strange occupation. You spend a lot of time alone with a group of children. The whole process can feel very isolated. I have a veteran teaching friend who complained to me.

"One year I would like to be promoted from fourth grade I have taught for many years. The kids progress. But, after many years in that age group you, the teacher, can regress. I think my speech and mannerisms reflect the fourth graders I taught."

A social event like a pantomime reminds people they can have fun as a group. It shows another teacher's facet to the students and parents, which is generally well-received despite some teacher's initial reservations.

Life in the foreign community in Moscow for those two years was rarely dull despite the vigilance in some situations. Our life was a sharp contrast to how the average Muscovite lived. They did not enjoy the freedoms we had. I am not only thinking about politics and repression.

ДВЕНАДЦАТЬ / TWELVE

LADIES PLAY BROOMBALL AND BOB HOPE

JOANN: FOR EXERCISE DURING THE MOSCOW winter, Jim and I signed up for the Soviet-run "Keep Fit" evening classes. A Russian drill sergeant, athletic and buff, puts us foreign ladies through the paces. She bellows instructions for jogging and running, round and round like a swirling herd of cyclone reindeer, our hooves hammering on the worn linoleum floor.

To set the pace, a Soviet piano man tinkles the keys with stimulating Red Army marches. Some tunes I remember from the Red Square military parade. What I recognize most is Tchaikovsky's rousing 1812 Overture, without the cannons. Driving music, starting slow, accelerating as we warm up, to push us along, inspire us to strive to do our best, a test of Soviet discipline infused with the psychology of self-perfection. Piano-man plays and plays, nonstop, while he smokes and smokes, nonstop, lighting one cigarette after another, chain-smoking so much I wonder who will pass out first from lack of oxygen, him or us.

And then there was Broomball. You might think you know this game, but I doubt it. Our women were not quite the gentile types who played broomball in Canada back in the early 1900s. Those women looked like proper Edwardian ladies in white dresses with dark trimmings and sashes. Their caps looked like today's baseball helmets but couldn't have afforded much protection. Their brooms were common, long-handled

Anglo-American School Ladies Broomball Team

straw ones, their balls may have been small soccer balls. By the 1960s, broomball in Moscow had become a wild and wacky sport played among the foreign embassies. In 1979 I bravely joined the Anglo-American School women's team with other teachers and staff.

From the photo you can see our attire had evolved, as had the sport. We were not the proper "ladies" of yesteryear. Propriety and decorum were a thing of the past. Our Anglo-American School red-hooded sweatshirts gave a formidable impression as did our helmets in patriotic colors, red, white, and blue.

My broomball buddy Anne supplied the Anglo-American School team photo. She's in the bottom row, second from left. I'm to her left, the one with the goofy-looking grin proudly displaying my broom. Our broomsticks were unlike the long-handled straw broom the Canadian ladies used in the early 1900s. The short Russian handmade birch broom is called a *venik*. We had an excuse for a do-it-yourself stick-wrapping event, not as in gift wrapping, but the intricate tape winding at our team "hen party". More of a cockerel, I find the experience very intense and was determined to create, not just a thing of beauty, but a frightening weapon of mass destruction. I mold and shape the damp straw, then bind it tight with tape and string. My broom's tiny birch branches, most often used to sweep the floor, have been magically transformed into a threatening rock-hard hooked instrument of evil. I call mine the "red devil" and adorn it with diabolic red cryptic symbols to unnerve the opposition. I freeze my broomball stick solid before each game, an "illegal" trick. Shame on you, you might say. But, vertically challenged at barely five feet, and a miserably pathetic athlete, I needed some advantage to help level the playing field. Bad Joann.

Not for the faint of heart, broomball is a game where you slide across the ice on your knees at the speed of light. Plastic knee guards are essential as we chase a children's hollow rubber ball, all while wearing slippery tennis shoes. A determined few had special-order rubber shoes, but traction on the hard ice of a flooded court created perilous conditions for even the best of us, which I was not. The trick is not to panic. Yeah sure. Just throw yourself into the game. Just go with the flow. And use your stick! Nothing is more important than your broomball stick, sweeping wildly as you try to whack the ball, or mostly missing the ball and smashing your opponents.

In the Moscow 1980s, embassy broomball parties and the games themselves were notably the rowdiest. Broomball is, after all, a contact sport. We women were tough, but the men were a whole different story, absolutely brutish according to the aggressive British brute, Jim, in what he calls, "Diplomacy, Right?"

Our women's broomball league teams were mostly embassy-sponsored. The U.S. Embassy had their women's team with a big USA emblazoned on their white sweatshirts. The most formidable challengers came from Scandinavia, and less so other Europeans. But the great down-under Australia ruled the day and the night when the Australian women chanted their victory song, "C'mon Aussie C'mon". The Broomball championships culminated in the legendary Broomball Ball held in the ballroom of Spaso House, the residence of the U.S. Ambassador to the Soviet Union. What a stroke of luck since the legendary Broomball Ball was later held in Moscow's hotel ballrooms. Ambassador Watson in his infinite wisdom let us celebrate in his private residence.

Spaso House was a two-storied stone mansion built in 1913. It became the residence of the first U.S. Ambassador, William C. Bullitt, in 1934., He held the first of his legendary events, a Christmas Party, in the Chandelier Room. Seals from the Moscow Zoo were brought into the ballroom to perform a balancing act with a Christmas tree, a tray of glasses, and a bottle of champagne. When the seal's trainer passed out from drinking, the seals galivanted wildly about the house. But this was only the first of Ambassador Bullitt's extravagant galas.

In 1935 a new ballroom was constructed to entertain large groups of people. The U.S. Ambassador held the outrageous Spring Festival at Spaso House where the Soviets and Americans partied together in the ornate ballroom. Prominent guests, the author Mikhail Bulgakov, Soviet military officers, politicians, and Communist party VIPs intermingled among the four hundred guests. Stalin did not show but a host of other beasts were brought in. The Moscow Zoo supplied a baby bear, mountain goats, and white roosters. A fishnet full of zebra finches, pheasants, and parakeets hanging from the ceiling escaped when the bear, fed with champagne, got drunk in the early morning hours. The bear then peed on the red uniform of a Communist Revolutionary leader.

Ambassador Bullit's Spring Festival was mild compared to the pandemonium and drunken debauchery that Bulgakov envisioned in his Master and Margarita's Spring Ball of the Full Moon. Parties at Spaso House became few and unmemorable when relations between the Soviets and Americans turned increasingly chilly. The Soviets began courting the American Communist Party.

Fast-forward to 1980 when uninhibited, unguarded drunkenness might or might not have gone on at the Spaso House Broomball Ball. But neither Jim nor I would have witnessed anything as we were hidden behind a wall, in a nook filled with audio equipment. Yes, Jim and I went to the Broomball Ball but instead of enjoying the party, we might as well have been locked up in a safe room. Disc jockey Jim arrived in Moscow with his incredible LP record collection. His DJ past meant he'd amassed an enviable collection of rock, reggae, and heavy metal bands. All those "illegal" songs, sounds, and lyrics banned in the USSR, the music of Western decadence that glorified sex, drugs, and rock and roll. Jim's music did not measure up to the mandated messages of Soviet Realism. But the Soviet music he collected followed him to faraway places. His treasured record collection, he kept even longer than me!

In March of 1980, U.S. Ambassador Watson invited Bob Hope and his wife Dolores to Moscow. I don't think I need to say much about this iconic entertainer, comedian, and movie actor. Prolific, he brought his humor into homes and to troops worldwide during his 100-year life on this planet. Born in England, his immigrant family passed through Ellis Island as did mine. A natural, he would sing, dance, and perform comedy for pocket money at the age of twelve on the streets of Philadelphia. If he were a child today, he'd be considered a beggar or banned under child labor laws.

At one time, I learned calligraphy and brought my pen tips and special inks to Moscow. My middle school kids brought in a scroll to sign inviting Mr. Hope to visit the school. They only knew him as the legendary comedian from their parents' generation. The paper quality wasn't the best, but I scribbled my bird-scratch, and the kids circulated the scroll for signatures.

On his arrival, Ken admits he held Bob's hand for way too long in a handshake as he waited for a photo op. The Anglo-American School auditorium filled with about 250 kids sitting on the floor. Most kids were too young or from far-away countries and were clueless about Bob Hope's notoriety and celebrity.

Jim shares how his little kindergartner kids stole the show. He remembers "The school gym had no tiered seating so the little tykes from the two kindergartens are right up front." Mr. Hope was a skilled performer, he probably thought to keep his remarks short. 'Okay, anyone got any questions for me?' The hands shoot up from several of Jim's little charges. Bob picks a young one who stands and asks his question. 'How big is your garage?' You can guarantee of all the possible topics to ask a world-famous entertainer he had not expected that one. 'It's pretty big.' By now the room is laughing and Bob only asks the older students questions before it is time for him to leave.

The British Embassy held a cocktail party for their native son, Leslie Townes "Bob" Hope. Jim was invited, he had the right passport but, as usual for him, he was underwhelmed. Jim saw this as a stuffy class-ridden cocktail hour. He never got anywhere close to Bob.

Ambassador Watson opened his home to Bob and his wife, Dolores. They graciously agreed to entertain "the troops". Pleading hardship for his embassy staff, Tom Watson thought we all needed cheering up. Just months before, the Soviets invaded Afghanistan and the Americans and British pulled out their teams in the largest boycott in Olympic history. It was not quite a USO show, but, oh what a night it was. Bob and Dolores Hope entertained a few hundred of us Americans lined up in chairs in the Spaso House ballroom. Bob's ad-libs, traditional jokes, and Dolores singing and dancing, more than delivered. And yes, they did boost everyone's morale.

In the Spring, Jim and I start lifting weights in the evening. I'm out of my comfort zone and Jim pushes me beyond my pathetic athletic inability. Eventually, little camel humps develop on my skinny stick-like arms. I'm at the peak of my physical fitness, feeling like a bodybuilder, a fine muscular specimen. We practice arm wrestling and Jim shows me how placing your body just so can give you an advantage. He would feel my muscles and measure the girth of my upper right arm. I'm feeling so confident that I challenge my eighth graders to an arm-wrestling contest. The strongest young lady succumbs, but not without a struggle. Most of my students towered over me. Three young men volunteer, vying for male domination over the weaker sex. My first challenger, an American, fought hard, we clenched our teeth hard, which is not good for the TMJ joint. A few grunts later, he caves in. The next boy drops out, afraid of humiliation. But a big Swede, notorious for his Nordic strength, thought he would teach his science teacher a lesson. The grunting noises of the young man and his teacher might have been misinterpreted by anyone loitering in the hallway. But even the Swedish Viking Dog couldn't beat the American Bulldog I'd become.

I'd played a lot of badminton in my past—I was even quite good at it. But Platform tennis was new to me. Not to be confused with the pickleball or paddle tennis game played with rackets. The racket is solid, the ball is squishy rubber. Platform tennis is played on an elevated tennis court shrunk to one-quarter its size. It was surrounded by chicken wire that contained the play. Your tennis shoes get traction from grit on the deck. Holes on the surface and heat under the platform meant we could play, even in harsh Moscow winter. The court on the grounds of Spaso House had a cozy warming hut.

I played mixed doubles with yet another U.S. Ambassador's Aide, not the "Apocalypse Now" Aide from last summer. This guy could really play the game and I'm excellent at the net, so we were a formidable challenge. We went all the way to the final round but after fifteen grueling sets, I ran out of steam. It was all my fault we lost. But we decided to partner again next year.

ТРИНАДЦАТЬ / THIRTEEN

DIPLOMACY, RIGHT?

JIM: LIKE ALL KIDS, JOANN AND I DREAMED OF MANY possible careers in different fields. In my case, veterinary and dental careers appealed. Not in our wildest dreams had we thought a diplomatic career was for us. Two years in Moscow's diplomatic community confirm our negative thinking about our diplomatic employment. Diplomacy for us as Olivia Rodrigo sings, was a "Bad Idea, Right". Joann and I had no foreign service training to see when our actions may not have been diplomatic.

Diplomacy is a theme when it comes to playing broomball. I will briefly summarize this sports spectacle and let me set the scene. Broomball in Moscow is played on a frozen tennis court. This version of broomball was unique to Moscow. It is not to be confused with the Canadian broomball played on a large ice hockey rink. Snowbanks surround the ice surface on the tennis court. Hockey goals are at either end of the court. A small child's plastic ball is used, no hockey puck. The ice is kept super-slippery using water sprayed on the ice. I thought the watering of the ice was like a handheld Zamboni. The difference with a hockey Zamboni is that watering the ice decreases the chances of quick movement. The opposite effect for ice skaters and hockey players in skates, they go faster because of the Zamboni's ice preparation. This slick Moscow ice surface and our footwear did not help much with our speed.

Georgian woman with Birch Broom Venik

Broomball players wore either trainers or imported special broomball shoes that gave us only a slightly better chance of moving. The only protection I and other players have is a hockey helmet, elbow, and knee pads.

We bought short Russian brooms (*veniks* made of thin birch bundles) wrapped with tape and given a curve to help hit the ball. I wonder what the old Russian ladies who wield these brooms sweeping streets outside their apartments thought of our use. Pint-sized hockey sticks are great for five-year-olds, but not for full-grown adults. In brief, this is a pretty stupid idea thought up by bored foreigners to while away the Moscow winter. I remember someone saying a crushed beer can was used before the plastic ball. After a few beers, broomball with a beer can would look like a great idea, right?

There was an expatriate folklore surrounding broomball wrapping as a team-building event. Joann played for the Anglo-American ladies' team, who met to make their sticks at a wrapping party. I was on the men's school team, but we needed correspondents and others to make up the numbers. We also had a wrapping party like the ladies. That is the diplomatic way of saying it was an excuse to drink with your teammates. Maybe the alcohol explains the varied bends in our broomball sticks. Some teams used the freezer to stiffen their sticks before games. Joann put hers in the freezer. I frankly saw little advantage in this. Moscow winters are cold when we play so why waste time artificially freezing your stick?

Nothing could help me move smoothly and gracefully across the ice without skates. The fun for the crowd was watching adults struggle to move toward the ball. Think of the cartoons you saw as a kid, where people on ice run desperately in place going nowhere. Sometimes we fall flat on our chests or become upturned turtles on our backs. I always think of the Disney segment where Bambi and Thumper were on the ice. There was only one way to build up speed, run a few steps along the snowbank. Then use the knee pads to drop into an extended slide across the ice. You are a hero if you judge the angles of attack right and can hit the ball towards the opponent's goal. Alternatively, I often looked like a fool as I slid several feet across the ice flailing away desperately but nowhere near the ball. I will let you guess which movement caused more audience laughter.

There were several teams from the diplomatic and foreign communities. Just like many sports, the spirit to win during the game was very high. One of our team supplied special broomball shoes from Canada that our team hoped would give us an edge. Our school team hockey shirts were adorned with an American Express logo.

An enthusiastic member was a big, tall, Norwegian Olympic cross-country skier. He took the game and the opposing team seriously. Any prudent opposing team would watch out for the Norwegian when he used the snowbank's run-and-slide tactic. One unfortunate SAS (the Scandinavian airline) team member did not see my Norwegian friend sliding at speed towards him. Our Norwegian laid him out and the game had a short injury break. Ever the diplomat our Norwegian told us in the huddle, "It was okay, he's only a Swede. He will be fine." Historical note required. Norway used to be part of the Swedish empire and sometimes history plays a part in national attitudes. It is not unknown for Norwegian TV to make fun of Swedes and Sweden in their shows. Our Norwegian friend did what Norwegians do with Swedes in a game situation.

I was a defensive center back in soccer. Others tell me I have an aggressive streak that comes out when I play or coach games. Maybe it is true, I once shocked the opposing soccer coach of a five-year-old soccer team. I quote, "My ants will beat your ants." Next time you get a chance to watch five-year-olds play soccer. You will see them all moving like ants crowding around the sugar, in this case, the soccer ball. All my coaching sessions explaining their different positions on the pitch, fly out of the youngsters' heads. Why not? They only want to kick the ball!

I played defense with Ken, my Canadian colleague. Ken was a two-way player in Canadian football and was built that way. Ken and I extensively used the snowbank to build some speed. We slide and push opposing forwards away from our goal and maybe into the snowbank.

One American TV correspondent asked me to do a short interview about broomball. As usual, my diplomacy skills, or lack came to the fore. Fired up from a win, I described in detail the joys of taking out the opposition as a defender. It was no surprise that my interview ended up on the editing floor. The TV correspondent thought aggressive remarks by his child's kindergarten teacher were probably not a good segment on major American network news. I guess he was looking for that cuddly feel-good end segment that network news loves to finish with. In sports, I am not cuddly during games.

I brought my record collection to the Soviet Union including music I collected as a DJ for over twenty years. At the end of the season comes the "Broomball Ball" at the US Ambassador's residence, Spaso House. Jim and faithful assistant Joann are to supply the music for the event. Spin a few records and get everyone dancing. What could be wrong with that? I used to do a lot of mobile discos. I often played in odd venues with certain "challenges." Only Americans have challenges, in England we have problems. The problems include hauling heavy speakers up many flights of stairs

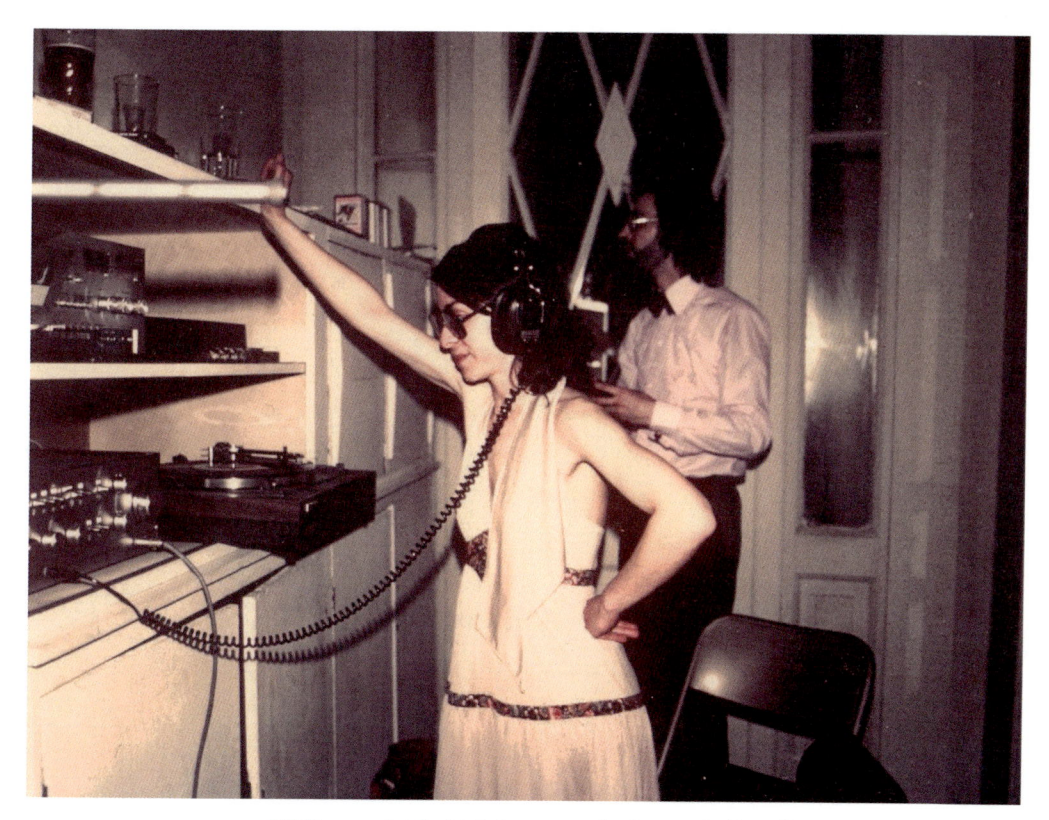

DJ Jim and side-kick Joann at the Broomball Ball

and using matchsticks to jam bare wires into odd-looking electric sockets. These are just some of the challenges I encountered running a mobile disco. Spaso House had the right equipment, including double turntables and a microphone so no heavy hauling was required. But when we arrived that evening, I was shown a little alcove with a wall between us and the dance floor.

Joann and I look at each other and shrug. I must be the Wizard of Oz behind the brick curtain. DJs feed off the audience and gauge pacing and music choices. My telepathic powers are limited, and my Superman X-ray vision is non-existent.

"Joann, maybe you can see how things are going as I play."

Joann is a willing soul, I am hoping. "Sure" was her positive response. Over the years I have learned when Joann says sure she means maybe or never.

Through the wall, we hear presentations and various speeches in the ballroom. Then a head pops round the corner and says, "It is your time for the music." I plan to start with a bang playing a new Russian record purchase. I play about 30 seconds of the Soviet anthem (a stirring little tune) and then switch to Anita Ward's 12-inch

"Ring My Bell". I certainly made an impression with the Russian staff in the room. They later launched a small diplomatic protest that somebody would play the Soviet Anthem at a disco. I forgot they had never heard Jimmy Hendrix's guitar version of the "Star Spangled Banner". It is easy to cross diplomatic lines.

Diplomacy is always something to keep in mind when you are a DJ. I should have remembered my disco past and why I used to charge extra to do weddings. A seemingly happy event that includes a lot of alcohol consumption by the time you are expected to perform. Tough crowd, you are always going to tread a fine diplomatic line. Play a little of this and a little of that with constant twiddling of the volume control. The senior members of your audience "Turn the volume down." When are you going to play a waltz or foxtrot?" "I love Frank Sinatra, can you play one of his tunes?"

The Sinatra or waltz was a great way to clear the dance floor. Usually, a single couple would venture out to "trip the light fantastic" to a foxtrot. The one couple who requested the foxtrot is dancing lightly to the music, they are having a great time. Meanwhile, most wedding guests stand impatiently at the edge of the dance floor. They are not happy. The young in the crowd are fixing your humble DJ with an icy stare. At which point I became fascinated to queue up for the next record, headphones muffle whatever is being said and I avoid eye contact at all costs. The younger crowd sends requests for the latest hits. "Turn up the volume we can't hear it". What is the volume level at a wedding that will please the youngsters and not antagonize the older audience? I was tempted to suggest the seniors remove their hearing aids, but diplomacy says no, bad idea, right? It shows any happy matrimonial event could teeter on the brink of disaster for the humble record spinner. When I could see the dance floor, I still had to walk a fine diplomatic line.

Back at the Broomball Ball gig, I hope all is going well. The only advantage of our wall at Spaso House was that ignorance is bliss. The broomball crowd, teams from Australia, the Anglo-American School men and women plus teams from Europe said they had a good time. I played all the hits from the late 79s and early 80s I had that evening. Edwin Starr's H. A. P. P. Y Radio even made the Russian staff smile. The ambassador's Russian staff are lined around the room. They watch everything going on. Maybe they thought this English DJ might have another diplomatic problem. Or perhaps they hoped I would play a popular Russian pop hit? Your guess is as good as mine. However, my preference is to see people have a good time. In my defense how could I be a smooth diplomat when I cannot see the audience without popping my head frequently around that damn wall?

Joann and I saw "diplomacy" in an ice hockey game between the Soviet Union and Finland. It was supposed to be one of those "friendly" games. If you think about the NHL All-Star hockey game, there are lots of goals and very little physical stuff. In this friendly between Finland and the Soviet Union scoring was the secondary aim for both teams. The prime goal was fighting and checking each other very hard and often into the boards. The small crowd of Finnish spectators were enthusiastic. They cheered whenever a Russian player went sprawling on the ice accompanied by the Russian crowd's boos. The Finns were whipped into a frenzy when the Finnish team won the game. A diplomatic and historical note is required. Finns took great exception to an abortive invasion in 1939-40 by the Soviet Union. History and sport are a potent mix. At the Winter Olympics of 1960 at Lake Placid the US hockey team's "Miracle on Ice" defeated the heavily favored Soviet team. It could have been named the Cold War played out on ice!

For me, sports and diplomacy are always a personal problem to understand. Terry and I were invited to play mixed doubles tennis in the late Spring of 1980. We are to play on those former frozen broomball/tennis courts. We turned up at the British Embassy to play an English married couple. I have always had difficulty recognizing when the game is more social than a game you try to win. My favorite US football team the Las Vegas Raiders say, "Just Win Baby." My Scottish soccer coach gave us a basic strategy talk. "Just stick the ball in the net more than the opposition. Stop them scoring, however, you can." See, even professional soccer can be simple!

As our English opponents saw it, we were to gently loft the ball around the court in social tennis mixed doubles. It is sooo nice that we all get a turn to hit a few shots. This gentle exercise was a good way to spend a few pleasant hours. I ask my partner, "Maybe we will get Pimms or strawberries and cream after the match?" Terry looks puzzled. "You know, like they sell at Wimbledon." Terry cracks a big smile. She has been to the Championships at Wimbledon with her husband.

Male players should not hit balls hard at the opposing woman when she stands at the net. I was a good little diplomat for a few games. Then a slow serve came across the net and the ball sat up, inviting a crushing forehand return. Diplomacy flies out of my head, and I hit the ball hard over the net landing on the lady's hip. Oops! Our opponents retired and I was never asked to play at the British Embassy again. I think it is why I tend not to play mixed doubles. My American partner smiled. The score Jim 15 Diplomacy 0. Love or Jim's lack of it.

You will notice in this chapter that history and culture play a big role, especially in sports. Norwegians and Finns have a certain outlook in these stories on Sweden and Russia respectively. A brief read of history shows you why. Many people erroneously believe that British people like to play the game irrespective of the result. I sometimes wonder if it is because we only have a small sporting talent pool, we celebrate our few winners. The UK gets a gold medal in the Olympics, and we must watch the replay many times. The British also watch a likable UK loser like Eddy the Eagle who had no chance of Olympic glory. He just wanted to try ski jumping, he was hopeless, but he gave the nation a good laugh. I think sometimes social class in Britain plays a part. The upper classes often pretend not to care about winning. "We just love to play, winning is so unimportant." Working-class people in the UK enjoy sports where we win. Whenever I watch a professional soccer game with thirty thousand people, we jump up and down, delivering a mighty roar or singing in unison as our team scores. Screw diplomacy, we are number one!

ЧЕТЫРНАДЦАТЬ

FOURTEEN

TRAINS, PLANES, AND TRUCKS?

JIM: MY LOVE OF TRAINS STARTED AT A VERY EARLY age. My father bought a model railway set as a present for me. It was supposedly my toy. However, for a long time, I could only watch my father control the two trains around a track he built. Further evidence of the ownership of the train set was when he brought it to America supposedly again for me. One afternoon I found my father setting up the track in the lounge and showing my young daughter how it worked.

What should I do in the Christmas Break of 1979? Joann is off to ski with another teacher. I do not participate in downhill skiing. I have watched winter sports on TV. I have seen skiers crash and break things. I like all my bits in one piece. Ken suggested that while he and others went skiing, I could try the Cresta Run toboggan track. I am half-tempted as it does not involve great heights, but it does involve speed. I miss my motorcycle with the wind rushing past me as I travel. However, my daredevil enthusiasm was curbed by a motorcycle experience just before I came to Moscow. I took part in a motorcycle racing course at the famous Brands Hatch track in England. I learned two things. First, eighteen and nineteen-year-olds are fearless and laugh at death. My twenty-nine-year-old me is convinced death is a real possibility on a motorcycle driven to its limits. Second, as we approached the first corner the youngsters threw their bikes at an alarming angle and flew way ahead of me. I am left puttering around for the five laps we have. I would rather not say how many of the riders lap me. The thought of careering down the toboggan track with little control seems reminiscent of recent motorcycle racing memories. In my mind's eye, I see those young daredevils fly into that first corner at Brands Hatch and me in the dust. So, the Cresta Run idea is a definite no.

 Snow has been falling in Moscow since late September. The ground will be snow-covered until April. Before and after the snow blankets the ground, Moscow endures the muddy months normally in September and May. This is a time when many Canadians curse. Snow can be brushed off, but the fine clinging Moscow mud is a real challenge. The mud is on your car, your clothes, and your shoes. If you leave on your outside shoes, it will coat your apartment floor.

 It's December so no mud just snow. Four of us from the school think a trip on the Trans-Siberian Express to Lake Baikal would be memorable. What a great idea! More snow stretches endlessly, with millions of trees. The Siberian average temperatures make the Moscow winter feel balmy when just below freezing. Siberia in December is often 20 degrees below freezing if not more. The Trans-Siberian railway goes from Moscow to Vladivostok. But Vladivostok is the home of the Russian Pacific fleet and is a no-go destination for foreigners.

 There are four of us, so we take up a four-person sleeping cabin. Anne and Laney are teachers like me, and Terry is the American wife of the school principal. The idea of "express" in the name of a Soviet train needs a little modification. Our trip is 2,702 miles and will take about three and a half days to Irkutsk across five time zones. By comparison, a trip across the USA is only across the three major time zones. You travel across seven time zones to go from Moscow to the Far East coast. Irkutsk is a city on the southern end of Lake Baikal. I cannot give you the exact speed of our train, but it certainly was not a Western European or Far East high-speed train. There were frequent stops of fifteen to thirty minutes. We could get out and stretch our legs but listened carefully to the instructions for getting back to our cabin.

 At the end of each carriage is a person with a hot water urn. Tea is available and I took full advantage of it. Day one on the train we look out enthusiastically. By the third day, the monotony and flat snow-covered landscape is beginning to get to us. I cannot resist, "Look," I cry out, "there's a tree." This particular tree is probably the latest of the

Train to Siberia: Moscow to Vladivostok

hundreds of thousands that have passed by the train window. My companions don't seem to enjoy the joke after a couple of repeated cries. To paraphrase Ronald Reagan, "Once you have seen one tree you have seen them all." A biologist will tell you Siberia has different spruces, firs, and pines but as our "express" trundles outside our window there is an evergreen blur. The scenery overwhelms you and the snow never ends.

One highlight for us was a horse trotting along the road by our slow-moving train. The Siberian sledge (*kibitka*) has one horse pulling the sledge along. The horse had a "necklace-like" arrangement with a few bells. I could imagine the bells tinkling along in rhythm with the hooves. It would have made a great Christmas card picture. As usual, my camera was buried somewhere in my luggage. This horse and man move along a seemingly endless road with no visible destination. The scene emphasized how beyond the urban environment in Moscow, there is a very different world. Cities, like hotel rooms, look the same. The villager riding his sledge represented a very different lifestyle. The man and his horse are not part of the uniform modern world. Here in the open Steppe people live a completely different life in small villages across Siberia. I doubt that Marxist-Leninist principles are in their daily thoughts. The harsh climate, getting around, limited shops, food, and friends were the mainstays of their lives.

We eventually arrived at Irkutsk station after more than three days on the train. A short taxi ride and we are at our Baikal hotel. Three days in close quarters with limited washing facilities means our personal freshness left much to be desired. So, a hot shower was first on our agenda. The view from our rooms is spectacular. The lake stretches for miles and is covered with snow and ice. I cannot resist. My geography teachers would scold me if I didn't mention Lake Baikal covers 12,248 square miles and represents 20% of the World's total fresh water. It's big, or as my Scottish friend Anne could quote Billy Connolly, it's fucking huge!

We can see how thick the ice is when we walk out onto the ice. It gives you an idea of how deep Baikal is. All four of us become children sliding across the clear ice patches. Trucks are crossing Baikal in the distance. During the freezing winter, there is a seasonal road across the ice. Another fun Geography fact, Baikal has depths that range from 2,442 to 5,387 feet (one mile deep). Staring into the depths impresses me with the dark clear water. I have driven up Pikes Peak in Colorado and that mountain is as high as Lake Baikal is deep. A lot of times you got told how this or that in the Soviet Union is the biggest when frankly it is propaganda puffery. Baikal is the real thing, a natural wonder of the world. I class it the same as my visit to Victoria Falls in Africa with the Zambezi River thundering endlessly. The present-day climate changes have transformed Victoria Falls into a slow trickle during long droughts. Sadly, the pristine environment in part of the Soviet Union, including Baikal, was threatened by mineral and other resource extraction. We are our own worst enemies when we think the world only exists to supply our wishes.

Two things that caught my interest in Baikal. The first was a tour of the Natural History Museum. There are animals that you can only find in Baikal. There is a native species of sturgeon and a couple of fish. What I found most intriguing is the Baikal freshwater seal (*nerpa*). We have all seen pictures of seals flopping around on land. This is not an animal made for long treks on land. The map shows the lake is far from the sea in any direction. I have no idea how the *nerpa* got there. The river system that feeds Baikal comes from underground springs. The only visible large river meanders east, west, and finally north across northern Russia. The river stops in a mountain range a long distance from the Arctic Ocean. I throw a metaphorical herring in salute to those migrating Baikal *nerpa* forefathers and mothers.

Something else captures my attention. There was a hill close to the hotel. "Wouldn't it be great to walk up and see the view?" Terry is game to accompany me, my two other companions not so much. If you have never walked in two or three feet of soft snow you cannot imagine how tiring it is. The hill is big, and we had no proper snowshoes, and we sank with every step. It required taking an all-fours posture when we scrambled up the steeper slopes. We must have been mad. As we struggled, we could imagine our friends sitting relaxed with drinks warm and toasty in the hotel bar. A considerable time later we collapsed at the top of the hill. I took a picture of Terry lying horizontally on the snow. She is too exhausted to make a snow angel and so am I. The view was spectacular. However, thinking of the trip back down the hill is not something we are looking forward to. Sliding like a turtle on its back helped the descent in the steeper places. I keep thinking back to those Baikal seals struggling, like us, in the snow to get to the lake.

Our stay in Baikal was brief. We have plane tickets to return to Moscow. The direct flight is supposed to be about six and a half hours. Did you notice the word "supposed" in the last sentence? We take off from Irkutsk with the usual sharp ascent we have come to know and love on Russian domestic flights. Every trip reminds you these guys at the controls are either training to be or retired Yak military bomber pilots. I think they are avoiding imaginary anti-aircraft fire from unseen ack-ack guns.

Terry is not a great flier. As the plane rears up in the sky she grabs the hands of two of us, but once we reach cruising height she calms down. After three hours the plane starts a rapid descent in true bomber pilot fashion. Terry is grabbing hands again. We all think it is far too soon, we cannot be in Moscow. This is not a regular occurrence on a so-called direct flight. We land and we sit on the tarmac for what seems an age. Eventually, we are told we are in Tomsk. You could have told us we were in Father Frost's Grotto as we could see little from the plane. Cultural note, Father Frost is the Russian equivalent of what we call Santa Claus.

A quick refresher of my "forbidden areas" map showing where foreigners cannot be, Tomsk is one of them. The Russian passengers make the four of us very uncomfortable as they pointedly stare at us. We did not ask for this attention. However, in true Soviet style, there is no way foreigners can be allowed into the Tomsk terminal. Therefore, all the passengers must sit patiently on the plane. Our Russian comrades are grumpy about these foreigners. Whatever is wrong with the plane must be remedied with everybody on board. Time passes and the dark is closing in. Suddenly without any explanation the plane taxis out and gets ready for departure. You can imagine how "great" our nervous flier is feeling. All of us are less confident," Let's hope the wings stay attached." Anne remarked as a joke. Terry looks extremely pale, and she is crushing supporting hands. Delayed in our scheduled arrival we are finally back in Moscow.

There was another occasion when Joann and I experienced the g-forces of rapid upward acceleration in a plane. Returning to Moscow on a British Airways flight from our Christmas break, we are on final descent. I am in a window seat. "Look Joann we are about to land I can see the runway over there." Let's do a quick review. Runway over there, plane over here. I am not a pilot, but I think we should be over there where the runway is. Suddenly the plane lurches skyward and we experience full power ascent. The flight attendant is sitting just behind me. I see naked fear in her eyes. This is not good. I grab Joann's hand. We later learned that a snowplow was on the runway where we were supposed to land. The unexpected racing of the engines to keep the plane in the air cost British Airways thousands of pounds to repair the damage. A quick circuit around the airport and we landed safely. Passengers, as often happens, applaud and breathe a sigh of relief. Statistics say planes are the safest form of transport, but I prefer trains. I cannot say much about truck safety records, but automobiles seem to provide plenty of slaughter on the roads worldwide.

Those nice ground-bound trains took a group of teachers on a lightening tour of two small Baltic countries, Estonia and Latvia. Did you ever wonder why Estonia, Latvia, Lithuania, and Poland are vehemently opposed to the old Soviet Union and the Putin-version of Russia? You could add Ukraine to that list of people hostile to Russia, millions died in a famine engineered by Uncle Joe Stalin. As the saying goes 'Who needs that sort of friend'. A quick check of the history shows many of the citizens in the five countries have been killed, jailed, or exiled in the colonial-style Russian Empire. In Ukraine's case, they are currently dying at the hands of the Russian invasion. Here is a true piece of Putinesque logic. Why does Putin invade a country he claims does not exist? Nothing like recreating the good old days of Empire, Vladimir?

We start with Tallinn, Estonia. On our arrival, Joann befriends an English-speaking Estonian on the platform. She tells Joann, "Look I can see Finland, but I will never be allowed to go there." As they speak, Joann sees a "gentleman" who seems very interested in their conversation. It was obvious this member of the Soviet goon squad was on the platform to "greet" our arrival. All travel is booked through the embassies and Moscow authorities. They like to know where foreigners go at all times. So, it is no surprise a watcher is waiting for our train from Moscow to arrive. Where possible foreigners get stuck with an Intourist "guide". Think of it as an unwanted and unfriendly chaperone who feeds you with authorized Soviet history and takes notes of any infractions on your part. We had no Intourist guide for this particular trip. Joann and the Estonian woman would be enough to get our "greeter" interested in their conversation. Joann's new Estonian friend didn't care what she said. Joann and I hope that after the fall of communism, she had a chance to travel on the frequent ferries to Finland.

Those Baltic ferries were used extensively by Finns. In our hotel, we saw Finns drinking to a point of alcoholic oblivion that I had never seen before. Russians are good at downing a couple of bottles of vodka, but these Finns were possibly drinking world champions. One Finn explained, "Booze is cheap here, compared to Finland, so it is worth paying for the ferry and spending the day here." The drunken Finns were friendly and generally peaceful inebriates.

My friend Ken and I thought a sauna in the hotel would get the kinks out from the night train ride. We suddenly made friends with many more Finns and Russians in the sauna. In a male-only environment all that manly-man stuff came to the surface. The steam was scalding. I have sympathy for lobsters. The Russians were intent on bashing everyone with leafy birch branches. The Finns had an even better idea. They pour vodka on the sauna heating stones, instead of water. The sauna has a fine mist of vodka. Inhaling booze our new Finnish friends assured us meant we got the required effect but no hangover. Maybe it is true. But beaten with red welts on our bodies and feeling distinctly woozy, we staggered out of the sauna. We gave our new-found friends best wishes as we exited. I have enjoyed saunas with and without steam. However, this Estonian experience was not the pleasant, relaxed state I usually associated with a trip to the sauna.

Breakfast, the next morning at the hotel was fairly peaceful, a late-night ferry had taken our drunken Finnish friends back home. The next batch would arrive later in the day. We decided a walk would be in order. Joann and I went to the beach to see where the Olympic sailing would take place in the Summer of 1980. The memory reminds us that we never see a single Olympic event because of the British and American boycott of the games.

As usual with Soviet train travel, we arrived at the Tallinn station late afternoon to board our overnight trip to Riga, Latvia. Our group was told we must visit the cathedral in Riga that boasts a world-famous pipe organ. I hate to be pedantic but where is the biggest organ? If you try to find out, it is a frustrating piece of musical trivia. My research said Riga boasts a pipe organ that has a beautiful sound. We stood in the church and admired the organ. We cannot tell if it has that beautiful sound

I researched because it was not playing. As usual, the next recital would take place after we left.

Overall, I remember being a bad church tourist in Soviet times. The outside domes and paintings are spectacular. Russian churches had a dingy unused look in most cases. On the bright side, the Riga churches looked like more went on inside them than their empty Russian counterparts. In Russia itself, many churches are only museums according to your friendly Intourist guide. Apparently in the 1920s and 30s Soviet propaganda was decidedly anti-religion. The new Soviet citizen was expected to be a good atheist. The few remaining churches were kept going for the deluded old folks who followed the old religious superstition. To reinforce the idea church attendance was a poor lifestyle choice for young Russians. The authorities took photos and lists outside any working church of people attending the services. Good communists would take careful note and avoid such places. The two Baltic countries we visited provided a sharp contrast. The many working churches were mostly Lutheran rather than Russian Orthodox. A small sign that the citizens of Estonia and Latvia had a very different view of religion from their Soviet counterparts.

After dragging ourselves around the sites the group is hungry.

"This looks like a good restaurant," and we crowd into the foyer. Our best Russian speaker approaches the desk and asks for tables in Russian.

"No, we are closed." The tone is hostile.

There is no 'sorry' in the refusal. Maybe this is just the usual Soviet level of customer service we had come to know and love. Our translator turns around to give us the bad news in English. We are tired and hungry so several of us express disappointment, all our muttering is in English. None of us want to get on the night train back to Moscow hungry. The woman behind the desk stops us as we are about to shuffle out dejectedly.

"Are you Americans?"

"Yes, mostly Americans and British with a few other English-speaking countries."

"Please come upstairs we have tables for you." No explanation for the turn of events is ever given.

The upstairs room has no other diners. We ate a wonderful fondue meal, one of the best I have ever tasted. The service is excellent, and the beer keeps coming.

I am at the window and can look down at the street below. Suddenly, I see a three-man squad of Russian troops. They are marching down the street on patrol with bayonets fixed to their shiny modern AKs (automatic machine guns). It seems to me that the Soviet authorities had little confidence in the Baltic populace and so a military presence was required. This is why speaking Russian in the Baltic countries is not a guarantee of a warm Latvian or Estonian welcome.

    I have always preferred train travel. Even as a seven-year-old, my Mum would pack me on a train to my grandparents' house. Grandma would meet me at the station, and we walked to her house. My only task on the train was to count the number of stops. My counting stops made sure I got out at Ashtead station. How our lives have changed. Sixty years ago, my parents had no qualms about putting me on a train. Joann and I have traveled countless miles in many countries by train. I always enjoyed my Soviet train trips even though many took place in the dark. Look, I see another tree and there's snow!

ПЯТНАДЦАТЬ

FIFTEEN

KIEV (NOW KYIV) AND KOMPROMAT

JIM: **THE MOSCOW FOREIGN COMMUNITY WAS ALWAYS** changing. The school year may run from September to June. This was not always in synch with diplomats and commercial people. The school faculty had a mix of internationally contracted teachers but there were not enough to cover all classes. So, the rest of the teachers and ancillary staff were employed as "local hires".

One of the local hires, a diplomat's spouse, taught 2nd grade. She had to leave at the beginning of 1980.

What effect does all this have on my kindergarten? My wonderful Australian aide had a full teaching certificate. In this teacher emergency, she was asked to take the primary Grade 2 class of the departing local hire teacher. So, Jerry, the wife of an American businessman, is taken as a local hire teacher's assistant. She had no teaching experience. A willing soul, she stepped into my classroom and helped me for the rest of the year.

Jerry, her husband, Joann, and I decided to take a weekend trip to Kiev Ukraine. The travel was arranged through the American Embassy. As it was a short trip, we were to fly to Kiev and return in time for school the next week. I said things in Moscow could change at short notice. Just before we were to go on the trip Jerry's husband had to leave the country and re-enter. Something had happened with his business visa.

It was a common experience, for people who were not diplomats to deal with Soviet bureaucracy. The result was three of us decided to take the Kiev trip. Meanwhile, her husband fulfilled the Soviet bureaucratic dance to retain his commercial visa.

Let's talk about Aeroflot during the Soviet era. Flights were very cheap on internal flights. Imagine you are sitting in your seat on the plane before takeoff. No, the flight attendant does not show you how to adjust and lock on your safety belt with visual aids. Your belt may be twisted and stuffed down the cracks between the seats. Sometimes the belt does not have that satisfying click to show it is locked. Your safety is very much a do-it-yourself activity. The atmosphere in the cabin may evoke an eau-de-livestock of past passengers. The air conditioning on internal flights seemed to be optional.

We have flown on many airlines, and Aeroflot stood out for its take-off and landing style. The plane taxis down the runway then as the plane takes off you are thrust violently back into your seat as the plane makes a steep ascent. Landing is the opposite. The same steep descent may leave you dangling forward in your seat. You pray the belt did lock when you last checked. Flying in the Soviet Union was not for a nervous flyer.

On this Aeroflot plane from Moscow to Kiev, we attained cruising altitude. The tradition of peanuts and drink trolley passengers might expect on any airline never appears. The flight attendants bring around small plastic cups half filled with water instead. A rather stale bread roll is your in-flight snack. You may inspect your plastic cup. I did so, as there were no peanuts, and have little else to do. I found scratches as well as those fingerprints to indicate heavy extended use. Don't ask if before each flight they were cleaned, I have no idea. In the Soviet Union, you are told that there is no unemployment. All able-bodied Soviets have a job. I swear, one flight attendant's job description is to put multiple fingerprints on the cups. Their job skill includes having good greasy fingers!

One unsuspecting foreigner on the flight makes a polite request for more water. The attendant looked surprised, even shocked, and studiously tried to ignore him. Eventually, with a shrug, she takes the cup and returns with it again only half filled. The unfortunate passenger can only grab hold of the bottom of the cup and discover it is hot boiling water. Customer service could have a different meaning in the Soviet Union. The moral of the story is do not ask for extra water!

Love in Kiev (Kyiv) Ukraine

On Saturday we wandered around the center of Kiev with no particular destination in mind. To say Ukraine's history is complicated is an understatement. Only Putin seems to think that Ukrainian history is simple. Putin believes Ukraine should be part of the reconstituted Russian Empire. It was ironic we spent time in the Maidan (also called Independence) Square. Maiden means town square. This would be the site of the Ukraine Maiden uprising (2013-14) against the Russian puppet who ran the country. Over a hundred Ukrainians died with many casualties as the people protested in February 2014. The earlier Orange (2004) and Maiden Revolutions would sow the seeds for Putin's meddling in Crimea and Donetsk followed by a so-far unsuccessful country-wide invasion.

As we stood in the now famous square the largest building had an oversized poster of Brezhnev. This reinforced the domination the Soviet Union had at the time in Ukraine. I saw government buildings with the crest of the Ukrainian Soviet Socialist Republic, a country that was seen as an integral part of the United Soviet Socialist Republics (CCCP in Russian Cyrillic alphabet stands for USSR in the Western alphabet). The USSR is not to be confused with the current country of Russia today. Putin's claim that Ukrainian society does not exist is based on its Soviet-inspired history and cheerfully ignores Ukraine's separate history, culture, and language. It is right to think that Ukraine has had several periods of domination by foreigners. The Ottoman Empire, Poland, and Russia have all played a part in Ukraine's past. Now it is the new Russian Federation that has colonial designs on Ukraine. I should have bought a tee shirt saying I had been to the Maiden in Kiev. Instead, we have photos to prove we were there.

I am less enthusiastic about our Saturday evening entertainment. Joann had been to the Moscow Circus. I avoided that dubious delight. My personal preference is to see animals in their natural surroundings. I am not happy to see animals dressed up in silly costumes. I think it is degrading and possibly cruel to make them perform what I consider "tricks" for human consumption. I always have an evil thought that I would like to see the lion or tiger have a nice snack out of their "trainer". My concern for animal welfare rests on the odd horror stories we hear about how the animals are trained and 'cared' for at the circus.

The Kiev Circus is not to be confused with the American, Ringling Bros. and Barnum & Bailey Circus. Eastern bloc circuses had jugglers, contortionists, acrobats, clowns, and animal acts. The performance followed a very Eastern European storyline. Scripts involve fairy tales or proverbs. The human acts were more like Cirque de Soliel, not the Western traveling circus. Circus in Soviet times was a state-run enterprise with the usual propaganda goals. We in Russia are better than the degenerate West. Communist countries, and even Russia today, see sports achievements as ways to showcase their superiority. To do that no drug or harsh training regimen is bad. Just like those elephants, bears, and big cats in the circus, communist athletes are ruthlessly trained and shown to the world.

Competition for places in the circus under communism was fierce. The lure of possible travel outside Russia was part of the allure for Soviet citizens. Athletes, circus performers, ballet dancers, and other artists had certain privileges within the Soviet system. Relentless government propaganda lionized these groups. They were held in high regard by the average citizens. An international tour would also provide an escape as happened to several prominent Eastern bloc performers. That was how Mikhail Baryshnikov ended up in America via a Canadian defection in 1974. Mikhail was born in the Latvian Soviet Socialist Republic and held Soviet citizenship while he danced in Leningrad's Kirov Ballet (now known as Saint Petersburg). Mikhail has a link to Ukraine. In 2022 he formed a group known as True Russia with other prominent exiled Russians. They raised substantial money to support Ukraine as it fights the Russian invasion. He is no friend or supporter of Vladimir Putin's neo-colonial expansion.

The Kiev animal acts included bears being made to juggle balls with their feet and dance with ballet-like tutus and other pieces of human clothing. It reminded me of my father's story about dancing bears in India. As a nineteen-year-old, he saw a moth-eaten bear forced to dance for the English soldiers. The owner used a sharp prod to get the bear to dance. My Dad remembers the sad spectacle. Fifty years later he went to the same spot and was disappointed to find the dancing bears were still there in modern-day India.

The evening wears on and I worry about the camel act. To me, they are too close to where we sat. One camel looked very grumpy as he tramped around the ring. I am concerned that he might aim a ball of sticky spit at us, as grumpy camels sometimes do. The rank smell of the animals is powerful. All my expectations for the evening's entertainment are confirmed. There was a long interval in the proceedings. I persuaded Jerry that we should go and get ice cream. I wanted a little fresh air and to take a break from our uncomfortable seats. We left Joann sitting alone and joined the usual Soviet-style lines to purchase our ice cream. I wonder how long the second half will last.

JOANN: OH, THE JOY OF THE SOVIET CIRCUS. I REC-

ognized the contortionists from the Moscow Circus. Bending and folding like flexible gumby toys, the two Asian women intertwined as if one. The horses circle round and round, mesmerizing, but at times stultifying. I felt like I'd seen this all before, probably because I had.

In the 1970s and 80s, the Moscow Circus symbolized communist thought. Communism, its ideology, its totality, its overarching, overwhelming, unified oneness! All-encompassing, it depicted communist egalitarian values and amusement for the masses. Glory to the Soviet Circus! There's nothing like a feel-good moment steeped in heroism, nationalism, and a dose of anxiety.

Kiev in 1980 was not the same place it is today. But the Circus was ubiquitous. It was meant to entertain the people, never expensive, it was the art form of the proletariat, the working-class plebs. The dance routines would tell folk stories and legends to elicit feelings of national pride. Fairy tales and folklore were reimagined as patriotic stories. Those Circus renditions of folklore were embedded with morals and values as part of the communist regime propaganda campaign. Soviet folk stories are unlike Hallmark's heartfelt, family feel-good movies where everyone looks for the true meaning of love, usually at Christmas. Christianity was not promoted in the Soviet Union. Atheism had become the new religion.

When the lights lit up during intermission, Jim and his teaching assistant, Jerry, search for ice cream. Soviet ice cream had to be the best in the world. Really! But they didn't have the 31 Flavors or Ben and Jerry's. Ice cream was almost always vanilla. On rare occasions, you might find what they called "chocolate", slightly brown, still great but not much different than what was sold as vanilla. I patiently awaited my rich and creamy circus treat and happily sat while they would inevitably be standing in long lines.

To my left sat a young man I hadn't noticed yet. When we'd arrived and found our seats, I filed into the row. Jim followed on my right and Jerry to his right. There was a vacant seat to Jerry's right, likely the extra one booked for her husband who had to cancel.

I felt an arm brush up against me and was surprised when the guy sitting next to me struck up a conversation. "Are you here visiting Kiev? The young man said in almost perfect English. He was smartly dressed and attractive. "I heard you speaking in English." He looks directly into my eyes.

"Yes, we're visiting Kiev." I didn't offer much more than that. But I did notice him lean in slightly, and thought, hmmmm...now this might be interesting. Educated, he was engaging and skilled in the art of pleasantries. He asks questions like, where do you live and what do you do. At that time, I had no instinctive distrust and took people at face value. I said I was a teacher at the embassy school in Moscow. He told me he lived in Kiev.

"Are you enjoying the circus?" He asks. "Yes, so many unusual animal acts." I'm thinking about how pungent the animal smells are and how the camels came within spitting distance. I'd come across camels before, they can be nasty. But I comment, "… the last act, the two Chinese contortionists were fascinating."

My new friend says, "Yes, the contortionists are so…flexible. How they twist and lock their bodies together." He looked closely at my face to see how I'd react to his descriptions.

I don't think I had a reply for that one. But when he gently tapped my knee with his hand, I suspected he was not a random person. He was definitely in the early stages of hitting on me. He next tapped my thigh. Were his mannerisms suggestive? Most definitely, yes. Perhaps he thought I was the odd woman out. He probably presumed the couple who left for intermission were in a relationship.

"Kiev has so much to see, beyond what most tourists would find. Perhaps you'd like to see more of Kiev?" He taps me again mid-thigh as if punctuating his words. But as the young man talks Jim and Jerry arrive with cups of ice cream, and I eagerly find my excuse to end the conversation.

"Oh, thank you, Jim." I scoop up a bite that is just as delicious and creamy as the ice cream in Moscow, but this time I can taste the chocolate. I ignore my newfound friend.

The Circus acts continue. The second half of this long show culminates with what everyone waited for. Like Dorothy in The Wizard of Oz tells Tin Man without a heart and Scare Crow without a brain, "The lions and tigers and bears, oh my!". The lion act features a lone trainer and his whip. In this classic circus routine, no whip can deter an aggressive lion. But this lion looks drowsy.

I think about just who this seductive young man might be. His shoulder held firm against mine, his slight movements most likely intentional but at least he's kept his roaming hands to himself. And I reflect on what I was told at my U.S. Embassy security briefing—about being compromised and about the Soviet process of Kompromat.

I assumed that Kompromat was entrapment of men by a seductive woman. She acts as the lure, to entice a man to the boudoir. I don't remember off hand where this happened in the reverse situation. But I wondered if maybe I just experienced an attempt at exactly that. A "raven", a male seducer, trained by Soviet intelligence, either the KGB or the military. But I was not his intended target. He was after the wife of the missing businessman who left the Soviet Union to have his visa renewed. And was it not just too unusual for me to be seated at the Kiev Circus next to a handsome young fellow who speaks nearly perfect English? We were always seated in sections reserved for foreigners. When the Intourist ladies at the American Embassy procured our seats for any event or venue, we were never placed alongside ordinary Soviets. Never.

In the usual "honey pot" situation, and there have been many, the list of KGB entrapments is long. Foreign men are the typical target, they might be lonely, bored, or just looking for love or lust, whatever the case may be. But it will often be a chance meeting, someone who miraculously happens to be where you are. A curvaceous blonde, a lovely Katya, Natasha, or Tanya, seems smitten with you. She plays to your ego—makes you feel sexy and desirable. Or she might be very vulnerable and young. Maybe she's in trouble, looking for a knight in shining armor. And you are her hero, her savior and she is willing to do anything for you. You get the picture.

The women are trained or at least well-versed in knowing what they are paid for. These KGB "red sparrows" are professional, in more ways than one. They'll have objectives, you'll be set up. Set up to get you in a compromising situation, you may be photographed doing naughty things and now you are the vulnerable one. Sometimes called "sexpionage", you may have something, information, or documents, or you have contacts valuable to the KGB. Eventually, your lover or their handlers will try to extract something from you or enlist you in some way to do their bidding. The most likely targets over the years have been diplomats or foreign service officers from Western embassies. From attaches to senior aides, all the way up to ambassadors, all were desirable prospects. U.S. Marines, correspondents and journalists, academics and scientists, businesspeople, and politicians, have all fallen victim to bedroom set-ups. It doesn't matter what your inclination or orientation is, there will be a sparrow or raven you might succumb to.

The spies who seduce, the activities of "sparrows" and "ravens" in the KGB and other intelligence services, those Soviet secret agents. Right out of the tales of espionage, right out of the spy novels and James Bond movies. And don't we all love the intrigue? I would later find out just how much of this entrapment went on. Whether you were a foreigner or an internal dissident, you could be a valuable source of information.

I read about the marines in the U.S. embassy who, after I left in 1981, had fallen victim to their charms. Too many were enticed by "red sparrows", fell prey to romantic encounters, and breached and compromised embassy security. One was convicted of espionage, sharing secret documents, and revealing undercover agents in the embassy. Despite the rules and prohibitions against relationships with Soviet citizens, three Western ambassadors and at least one military attaché should have known better. People, both straight and homosexual, fell for the sex trap and destroyed their careers. One later committed suicide. The stories of Kompromat go on and on.

But there are plenty of unsuccessful attempts, nine out of ten attempts fail. So, Goodbye Gennady or Farwell Fyodor or *Do svidaniya*, Vladimir, or whatever your name was, you couldn't fool me.

ШЕСТНАДЦАТЬ SIXTEEN

PROPAGANDA

JIM: LIVING IN MOSCOW IN 1979-81 YOU COULD NOT avoid posters and billboards that extoll the glories of Soviet life. The irony is that this is seen as a period of stagnation in the Russian economy. The collapse of communism was not far away. The billboards in a physical sense attempted to hide from the Soviet public how bad things were. Who would want the country portrayed as failing? Posters can inform as they did during the World Wars. Posters can give a sense of the country moving forward and dynamism. They say, look at how great life is. Posters can also warn people about the "enemies". Posters also stop foreign travelers from seeing the closed city. In the far east port town of Nakhodka, the billboards we saw going through the town on a bus completely hid the people and buildings. Who knows if people lived there and what their everyday life was like? Joann and I are interested in the colors, the artwork, and the simple messages.

There is a misconception that propaganda is about promoting the big lie. "If you tell a lie big enough and keep repeating it, people will eventually come to believe it." This is wrongly attributed to Joseph Goebbels, the Nazi propagandist. As sometimes happens with catchy definitions and quotes, Goebbels never said it. He said an important principle of propaganda is that it must be based in part on "truth." Here is the tricky part. We know that political truth can vary depending on how that truth promotes a specific state-sponsored goal. Remember Trump's spokesperson, Kellyanne Conway who gave us "alternative facts." She defended the view that Trump's Inauguration was attended by a crowd bigger than the independent count. There is a clear message with just a hint of truth. Yes, many people were there but the numbers were adjusted so the new president could continue to boast of the "huge" gathering.

It is probably best to say propaganda is to promote state-sponsored aspirations in simple effective ways. We bought a lot of Soviet posters from the late 1970s up to 1981. They sat rolled up in cardboard tubes for forty years. After we visited a couple of exhibitions of Soviet posters, we decided to bite the bullet by backing them with linen cloth and framing all of them. They are now displayed on walls in our house.

Two of our anti-West posters are good examples of "truth" used in propaganda. One portrays a bomb with cross-sections cut to display that the bomb is full of American dollars and coins. It certainly was true that the United States outspent every other country on defense. Historians attribute in part the end of the Soviet system to economic pressure to keep up with American defense spending. Ronald Reagan's famed Star Wars initiative encouraged Soviet armament production they could not afford. In other words, there is some truth in the Soviet propaganda's message. Another poster shows a meat grinder where US dollars are ground up to produce anti-communist messages. Again, there is a kernel of truth in the message. There was a broadcast system in the West that aimed Western propaganda to a communist audience, Voice of America was a prime example. A poster of "Construction Man" depicts the Soviet's expanding construction under communism. My point is that propaganda is not an outright lie. It needs some truth, otherwise it is too easily dismissed.

It would be wrong to think that propaganda would not be used to cause some national self-reflection. We have a couple of *Krokodil* illustrations showing the weeds of Russian society. This long-running satire magazine (1922-2008) walked a fine line with the censors. They portrayed Russian drunkenness, laziness, poor departmental administration, and black-market salespeople. *Krokodil* was a magazine with a smile that wrapped a more serious point of communist society's failings. As the song goes, "Never smile at a crocodile … Don't be taken in by his big wide grin!" I always find it strange that Russians love to tell me jokes often with a political bite.

I liked the topical jokes when Russians talked about their life and leadership. Take these beauties from Wikipedia quoting jokes under Soviet Communist rule.

Dollars for Bombs

Joann and Jim Mead

Dollar Meat Grinder for Anti-Communism

Q: Will there be KGB in communism?
A: As you know, under communism, the state will be abolished, together with its means of suppression. People will know how to self-arrest themselves.

This joke is about communist theory that claims the state will wither away in the ultimate stages of communism. The KGB and many communist variants of the secret police were to be feared. A joke blunts that fear. There are many jokes about how the march to a communist utopia is always a long way off. Remember how Mao told the people about the "Long March", a real event from the Chinese Civil War. It is also a metaphor used as propaganda for the development of communism under Mao's leadership.

Or this one about Marxist rodent control.

Q: How do you deal with mice in the Kremlin?
A: Put up a sign saying, "Collective farm". Then half the mice will starve, and the rest will run away.

Collectivism of agriculture had disastrous consequences with frequent famines or shortages.

Or this simple one-liner about Leonid Brezhnev who loved symbols of his glory.

"Leonid is having chest expansion surgery to make more space for medals".

It is a feature of many countries to have the leadership sporting a lot of gongs (medals). I often wonder how reinforced their jacket is to support all that metal. In my opinion, Russians are masters of great political jokes, I suspect many North Koreans and Chinese have a growing storehouse of ironic commentary. This might explain why there is plenty of employment in censorship departments in communist and autocratic regimes.

All countries make use of propaganda for their purposes. In the Communist Soviet Union, there were no uncontrolled media outlets. The state, owned or regulated the airwaves and the press. What images did the average Russian have about Western democracies under Soviet rule? It is worth reflecting on. The Russian people were fed a steady diet that gave only the state-approved line. There was no counter information for the average person to compare with what they were told. Putin's Russia has continued the tradition of media control. In current surveys, Russians get most of their "news" from television. All suspect or critical TV stations disappeared a long time ago. Propaganda is very much alive and prospering in most countries worldwide.

The Soviet Union made heavy use of posters that had easy-to-understand information. Socialist Realism art can be found elsewhere in the world. But in the Soviet Union, it was the only government-approved art form. Other art forms, like abstract painting, were banned. The Socialist Realism style portrayed a happy or strong working-class utopian society. Men are muscle-bound with working bib overalls and often wearing hard hats. Women are neatly dressed sometimes with peasant-looking scarves on their heads. Russia, depicted in the posters, is full of massive buildings, futuristic trains, and feats of engineering. There is no garbage pictured in Soviet streets. Even the factory floor only has modern-looking machines. Your happy factory workers wear no tie as they talk to a supervisor wearing a shirt and tie plus a white coat. In a supposed egalitarian society, there was certainly a difference between managers and shop floor workers. Slogans are short and punchy. "Let's storm the production target" or "The USSR is the shock battalion of the world proletariat."

Here is an easy question. What was the favorite color of a communist poster? Only one point in this short quiz, the answer, of course, is red. I read that in the Soviet Union, there was a shortage of red ink for posters. So, most of our posters use only four colors. We have a complete set of "us and them" posters. Lots of red in "us" (Soviet Union), contrasted with The West (them) depicted with a dingy shade of brown below those utopian Soviet scenes. The wording is kept to a minimum and only used for approved slogans. Around the world, you will find committees dreaming up the approved slogan for this year. Our posters show Soviet pensioners getting their pensions from an attractive government employee. Smiles are all around as Grandpa holds the government pension check. There is a TV in the background and a landscape on the wall. Meanwhile, in the brown (them) section, a man begs for money as a fat capitalist and his wife walks by ignoring him. The Soviet Union has total employment. Of course, the dismal brown picture of the West shows a dole line of the unemployed. The man has a placard around his neck asking for work. A happy woman and child are ushered into their new apartment. Below the family is being evicted by a capitalist landlord all in that attractive shade of brown.

Another poster, "Glory to the Soviet People" has a crowd representing the many ethnic groups in the old USSR in front of a stylized red Kremlin area. This ethnic group harmony was not how things looked in Moscow. There was a defined "pecking

Glory to Work or No Work in the West

154   Joann and Jim Mead

У нас обогрета заботою старость.
У них обездоленной старость осталась.

Grandpa's Pension or Begging

New Home versus Poverty and Eviction

order" that Russians made with "white" Russians at the top of the list. In the West, a dingy scene shows a big money bag pulling the strings of Nazis, Colonial overlords, spies, and soldiers.

I was always interested in the use of Nazi characters in Soviet posters. This mindset comes from propaganda and the Great Patriotic War. That is the war everyone else calls the Second World War. Why was it labeled 'patriotic' in the Soviet Union? It is estimated that the death toll was around twenty million Russians. This means they had more casualties than any other country. I suspect many Russians continue to believe that their country is in a continual struggle against Nazism. The current invasion of Ukraine (2014-2024) is based, according to Putin, in part on the need to destroy Ukrainian Nazis. The Russian foreign minister identified for us the Ukrainian president, Zelenskyy, as a Jewish Nazi. I have no idea what that grotesque mental picture means. But to ordinary Russians, it neatly identifies an eternal enemy they recognize from propaganda.

Before the Great Patriotic War, the target of poster propaganda was to eradicate religion. Religion was always seen as a threat to Marxist principles. This anti-religion stance came from Marx who wrote that "religion was the opium of the people". The 1920s and 30s published many anti-religious posters. When Joann and I recently visited a Massachusetts icon museum I bought a book titled "Godless Utopia" by Roland Elliott Brown. There are depictions of a pope-like character holding burning copies of Marxism. Another shows a priest milking the udders of a church. As people enter the church another priest is filling his bucket with money. Propaganda showed the people as the enemies of communism. For example, nice old ladies fill bottles of regular tap water and sell it as holy water. Fraud and speculation were crimes.

During that time printing large numbers of posters was a problem in a country short of many resources. As I said, most posters only used four colors to cut ink costs. Popular posters, whatever that means, would also be available on small postcards. Wouldn't you like your friend to send you a postcard with the worker in a hard hat saying, "Work, build, and no complaining." or "Let's mechanize the Donbas." Certainly, it beats a picture of the Eiffel Tower or the Grand Canyon saying, "Having a lovely time wish you were here."

As the only approved art style, many talented artists produced stunning images. One of the most famous ones was M. Abramov. He was ironically a Ukrainian who worked in Moscow. I think it is wrong to discount propaganda posters. They quickly convey a message that is not easily forgotten. Take Rosie the Riveter and many British war posters telling people that loose lips sink ships. Modern political speeches often use snappy phrases that emphasize the point of the speech. "Stop the Boats" during the British Prime Minister's speech on illegal immigration. Or an American politician's podium has "Control our Southern border". Immigration is a problem in many places. Politicians have a staff to create the right slogan they hope will mobilize the people. The Soviet Union extensively used those snappy one-liners in posters and general propaganda. In the modern Russian Federation, they carry on the proud propaganda tradition.

СЕМНАДЦАТЬ SEVENTEEN

KIDS IN THE CAUCASUS

JOANN: MY YEARS OF TEACHING IN SOUTHERN CALifornia and London England brought many opportunities to travel on "field trips" with teenagers and adolescents. "Opportunity" might not be the right word, maybe misfortune or mayhem might more aptly describe a few, but none went off without a hitch. Mayhem comes first to my mind. On one trip to Spain with the American Community School, we ended up in Madrid on the day before Franco died, we crossed our fingers hoping a revolution wouldn't follow. Our first mishap was that the music teacher who organized the trip had abruptly left the school leaving three of us teachers to take the reins. At a dinner with Flamenco dancing (nothing we would have chosen), we three teachers drank wine with our meal, not knowing that some middle school kids were doing the same. The choirmaster teacher had told them they could drink in Spain, and he was right, they were served! Of course, some overindulged. Just imagine the uproar when the American parents found out and the headmaster's interrogation of us teachers when we returned.

Then there were the mishaps. A train trip to the French Alps for a skiing vacation with those same middle school kids was highlighted with broken bones and a train journey through France on our sleeper-train carriages "mistakenly" labeled "American Communist School". I couldn't help thinking that some farcical French train scribe created the sign to parody our American "Community" as "Communists". Did that sign portend my next journey in life? All aboard. Next stop, Moscow.

In April of 1980 about thirty of our AAS middle school kids and a half dozen teachers would embark on a journey to the Caucasus—the southern countries of Georgia, Armenia, and Azerbaijan. So, here we are during Communist times heading off to three old-world countries where our cultures would clash like a head-on train collision.

The kids are bright, savvy, and worldly in a good sense. But they are typical adolescents. Mostly brought up in Western countries, many come from the U.S., U.K., Canada, Europe, Australia, and New Zealand. Others hail from Africa and Asia. Some kids are bilingual, others are multilingual, and a few speak Russian. One American boy speaks six languages, his younger sister speaks four. Most of the kids had lived in democratic countries with relative freedoms of expression. But now they are living insular lives in Moscow and will be traveling in the Caucasus, countries with different values, cultures, ideologies, religions, and ethnicities. These countries are subject to Soviet rules and daily bombardment with Communist propaganda. Now don't get confused with the word "Caucasian". In the U.S. that term refers to "white people", but here the Caucasians refer to more than fifty ethnic groups who reside in the Caucasus.

So where is the southern Caucasus? Herein lies my basic geography lesson. Although I'm a biologist, I can read maps well. So, pull up your e-maps or ancient paper maps, if you too are ancient, to help you find this wonderful part of the world. Sandwiched between the Black Sea and the Caspian Sea you'll see the Greater and Lesser Caucasus Mountains. Our incredible journey takes us to the capital cities and surroundings of Tbilisi in Georgia, Yerevan in Armenia, and Baku in Azerbaijan. But do not expect to be taken on some typical tourist excursion, as many unforeseeable things happen during this trip. Our Russian Intourist guide will try to ensure we keep to her plan.

Four of us teachers are American, Marcia is the school's Russian teacher, Kate and Tommy teach math and history, and I teach science. Ken is Canadian, he is both a teacher and assistant principal. Our "teacher-mom" is the wife of a New Zealand diplomat.

Lucky for me, I'm just a chaperone, I shirk responsibility whenever I can. But my friend Marcia, a Russian teacher and scholar, reluctantly took over the role of leader. The teacher who organized the trip bailed out at the last minute and returned to

America. Marcia confides she was scared stiff when asked by our school principal to take over the project. "Ugh! I'm nobody's idea of an organizer," she says. But what a fortunate twist of fate for us. Marcia speaks the lingo! While most of us remain oblivious, she understands everything and knows exactly what's happening around us. Being fluent in Russian would open windows where most are sealed shut.

Before boarding our flight from the Moscow airport, Domodedovo, to Tbilisi, Georgia, we were in the departure lounge when a young seventh grader slinks towards the draped windows. Unsure of what he's up to, I watch him with his camera in hand as he slips behind the "Iron Curtain" of secrecy. My antennae go up and I wonder if I should join him. I'd love to get photos of the Soviet jet planes on those runways. Domodedovo had a mix of military and commercial planes. Maybe there'll be military jets to add to my collection? But before I could do anything rash and get us all into trouble, an imposing figure of a woman, an airport security guard, rushes over and pulls back the curtain. The iron lady gruffly grabs the seventh grader's camera, prying it from his grubby little hands. She opens the back of the camera and pulls out the film roll, exposing the film to the light of day and his mortal sin to passengers awaiting their flights.

Marcia wonders if she should call his parents to pick him up and expel him from the trip. But then they called our flight, Marcia reflected, "I had no choice but to let him board the plane. Yes, he was a little rogue, but, no, you don't leave a twelve-year-old alone in a Soviet airport." Having caused a fracas, he later proved to be one of the naughtiest. And the son of a defense attaché to boot.

I'd spent way too many years with middle school kids and understood their excitement, lack of control, and propensity for risky behavior. Some of us get stuck in that mode and never really grow up. Me for one. Still stuck in perpetual adolescence with a passion for breaking the rules, I'm certainly not much of a role model. Remembering my exuberant teenage years, I would certainly have been among the naughtiest of them. Bad Joann.

Without my photographs, my memories would be a blur of fuzzy impressions of people and places. Those images help me fill in the mental voids, those gaping holes and bits of debris in my mental mess. Photos capture things before they decay or disappear completely.

We fly from Moscow to the capital of Georgia, Tbilisi, and stay in a hotel near Rustaveli Square. The next day we explored the square, the local sites, and other ancient treasures of Tbilisi. In the center of the square, a huge statue of Vladimir

Stalin Statue and Museum in Gori, Georgia

Lenin watched over us during our stay. After the collapse of the Soviet Union, Lenin was torn down as a symbol of communism's fall. Later, it was replaced with a monument of St George slaying the dragon that had terrorized the people.

Our adventures begin on a bus trip to the town of Gori. Joseph Stalin's hometown seemed an unusual choice for our school kids, but the trip had been planned by the teacher who'd absconded. The Georgian word *gora* means hill or mountain. Gori is about 50 miles north-west of the capital Tbilisi and nearly 2000 feet above sea level. Just imagine a bus ride through rugged hills and dales on an early 1970s bus, sans seatbelts, driven by an exuberant Georgian.

In Gori's central square stood a nine-foot pedestal with a gigantic twenty-foot bronze statue of Stalin towering over us. We visited the Stalin Museum and a school library where our museum guide showed us little Joe's report card with his barely passing grades. What never came up was how Stalin, a poor student, somehow managed to build a life based on his ruthless behavior and callous disregard for humanity. Our tour guide never mentioned the Great Terror when in 1936 through 1938, in his quest for power, Stalin eliminated a million of his rivals. The statue was erected in 1952, a year before Stalin's death. In 2010, after much debate, Stalin's statue was removed, unannounced, in the dead of night. The purge of his statue was an attempt to demolish the past. The Soviets constructed huge statues of leaders they would later tear down, obliterating their history as they rewrote their past.

Our gregarious, boisterous bus driver sang Georgian folksongs as he drove us back to the hotel. It was a frenetic, wild bounce-out-of-your-seat ride. The terrain was hilly, the road very bumpy and, in the dark of the night, it seemed like Mr. Toad's wild ride. Today there's a smooth modern motorway.

Marcia and I both remember a bizarre, unwelcome episode while looking at some local wonder. A group of Georgians in some rural village gathered around, they had never seen a black person before. Two of our girls were 7th and 8th graders from East African countries. I recalled that one girl was a Kenyan princess. Marcia remembers a young girl from Uganda and reminds me that those were bad times for Ugandans, "What with Idi Amin summarily executing people like her father, a diplomat. She was as nervous as a cat."

These girls did not need any unwanted attention, but in the outback of Georgia, a person with black skin was a rarity. The Georgian students kept wanting to touch the girls. They were curious and wanted to see if their skin color would rub off. It would have been horrifically rude if they hadn't been so naively wondering. But

Unwanted attention

it was horrific for the young ladies, nonetheless. And it only got worse when two young guys grabbed hold of the girls, arm-in-arm, and insisted they line up with the other students for a photo op. Now, even more nervous, the girls were surrounded by about three dozen spirited youth. Their photographer fired away. Incredulous, I couldn't believe how quickly things were escalating. But I was intent on capturing the moment, preserving it for posterity, and I put my Rollei into my twitchy finger fire mode. Thinking that if the young men tried to steal away our girls onto their bus, I would at least have photographic evidence of the culprits. The fascination with our girl's black skin might not be unusual in this part of the world where the white race evolved. Did it all boil down to guileless human curiosity? Or was it ignorance? Or racism? Would our African girls have been accosted if they were boys? Sexism was likely part of the mix of motives.

That evening back in our Tbilisi hotel, "teacher-mom" and I found the hotel bar and decided to sample the Georgian wines. Grape growing in its fertile soils and winemaking goes back 8000 years! We couldn't leave Georgia without sampling a few. The Georgian Sapervi, a dry red, was our first choice, but we may have finished with a velvety, ruby red semi-sweet as a nightcap. Meanwhile, Marcia, Ken, Kate, and Tommy did bed checks. I wasn't surprised to hear that a boy was found hiding in the bathtub of a girls' hotel room. And he was the same troublemaker, a defense attachés kid, who had already caused that fracas at the Moscow airport by taking illegal photos of the runway. Bad kids. Bad Joann.

The country of Georgia and the U.S. state of Georgia are 6000 miles apart and as ethnically and culturally different as you can imagine. You don't need to imagine—just remember the cultural and ethnic dilemmas for our young ladies. The next day, we embarked on a train trip. Not the "Midnight Train to Georgia" as sung by Gladys Knight & the Pips. But we're leaving on the Midnight train from Georgia, on our journey from Tbilisi to Yerevan, Armenia. It was not quite midnight when the train departed at 10:20 pm. It is only 172 miles between the two capitals, but our overnight train journey in 'Sleeper Cars' takes about nine hours with so many stops along the way.

Once onboard, we would have the entire train car to ourselves, but there wasn't enough space for everyone. So, our Intourist guide and a couple of the other chaperones, me included, were sent to another car. Our quiet carriage was two cars up. A heavy-set, low-keyed conductor was as mellow as the tea he brewed in his steaming hot samovar. The air was humid and warm, those hot cups of tea made me drowsy. The rocking of the train sent me to sleep like a baby. Lost in sweet dreams, little did I know what went on in the other train carriage.

As Marcia tells it, the real nightmare happened in her carriage. "The conductor was as bent as a paperclip. He had taken a bribe from a couple of ruffians to turf some of our kids out of their compartment and hand it over to them (to the ruffians, that is)." Marcia's never-ending nightmare continued. "I had some very unpleasant words with the conductor, who seemed to have the inside scoop on my female ancestors, all of whom, according to him, were whores. But he eventually backed down." I would love to hear Marcia's more literal translation of what was said. There's so much more to this story that only she can divulge. Like, just who were her female ancestors? She tells me, "We made all the kids lock their compartments, though, and told them that they couldn't open the doors even to go pee." Groan.

I was oblivious most of the time, as usual. Marcia, on the other hand, was hyper-aware of the unfolding crises. Once in Yerevan, she reports, "We had rest time the first day, on the principle that the train ride, even in the absence of ruffians, would be wearing. Why did I take a nap?" I don't remember what I did that day, having slept so soundly during the night, I might have roamed around and about, but who knows what I was up to.

At dinner, we went down to the hotel restaurant to discover that one of the 8th-grade boys, the son of another US defense attaché, had dressed in drag. "Why did we ever allow defense attaches' kids to come on the trip? Bad decision." says Marcia. "The kid had on a skirt, make-up, the whole nine yards. But that sort of thing was illegal in the USSR. It made for a bit of a stink."

I can't help but wonder if fun was illegal in the Soviet Union. One must never, ever have fun. Memories of my adolescent and teenage "dress up" antics come flooding back. Growing up in Los Angeles, my brother Russell wrote scripts and filmed videos—when he wasn't creating art or growing weed. I starred in some of his "movies". My Drama Queen singing sister starred in stage musicals. Everything for us siblings revolved around Hollywood, the movies, role-play, and costumes. Not just playing but becoming someone other than yourself. We enjoyed our freedom of expression. I would transform, for whatever reason, into amusing characters. My alter-ego was a mysterious, crystal ball fortune-telling, palm-reading gypsy with a black mascara mustache. My brother preferred Drag Queens, a sacrilegious Virgin Mary, and Hitleresque themes. The latter got him in trouble. A fine specimen of California wild child, my brother was hard to compete with.

Worse still, those occasions didn't end in my teens, they only got more outrageous well into my twenties. Most often self-inspired, sometimes provoked by others, the goal was theatrics and spectacle. I remember what the British would call a "fancy dress" party in an Italian Alps ski resort. Four of us, American teachers from London, heard a rumor at our hotel that a bar in the village was having a costume party. We lady skiers improvised silly get-ups for ourselves. Two young English guys at the hotel were also keen on the "fancy dress" party. They found a blue floral dress, a dirndl skirt, and wigs. We applied their make-up, lipstick, and eyeliner. They were almost pretty and in the dim light of the bar, they looked convincing. On the dance floor, I hear yelping voices. And soon I let out a yelp too. An Italian groper, roaming the dance floor, was grabbing quick feels of us American ladies. But he made a fatal mistake when he manhandled the bottom of the young lady in the blue floral dress. A bigger surprise came to the roving groper. His mouth gaped like a grouper in shock and horror, as the lady-like Englishman revealed his true self. He pulls off his wig and then throws a right hook. So, our evening out ended in a bar room brawl and everyone fleeing. It could have been worse. Oh, the trials and travails of misguided youth. Bad Joann.

Was it in Armenia when our Cold War kids climbed up on a Soviet tank? Kids being kids, they were just having fun playing with toys and weapons of war. I thought

Cold War Kids

California Kid tries out Soviet Artillery

they were pretty creative. Some are on top of the tank, others hang on to the barrel or pretend to prop the tank from below. I pretended to shoot old Soviet artillery somewhere in the Caucasus. Relics from past wars. Can you find the Katyusha multiple rocket launcher and MiG-15 fighter jet?

The next day we went to Etchmiadzin, the ancient center of the Armenian Church. Beyond that, my memory fails. Maybe it was Garni Temple, a first-century Hellenic temple, but when you've seen one old temple you've seen them all. We also visited an archeological site where the kids got to do some digging. Ken tells a story about one of the boys who was infamous for the airport photo fiasco and hiding in the girls' hotel room bathtub. Our bad boy might not have been guilty this time, but he somehow provoked a scuffle with a scorpion. The rogue son of a diplomat got bitten.

"Our guide said that because the scorpion was a baby, its venom would not be developed so the bite was probably harmless. Not wanting to take any chances, we took him to a medical clinic in town. We were escorted into a room that had a workbench, two chairs, a refrigerator, and a wardrobe against one wall. When the doctor went to the wardrobe and took out a syringe wrapped in butcher paper, wiped it 'clean' with a cloth, and went to the fridge we left. Bobbie lived."

In Armenia, we visit a small rug factory where young girls, the same age as our middle school girls, are hand-knotting colorful wool rugs. They sit on wooden benches in rows at their looms tying and cutting the dyed threads. They pause to look up when they become aware of our group. What was going on in all these teenage minds? I wondered how our kids would react to these poor young girls working a tedious job, day in and day out. We're on a school field trip. They don't go to school. We watch their toil from a distance. We are the rich spectators of the young girls' enslavement. Some people are born into poverty, others are born into privilege. Our trajectories are immutably set in stone and unlikely to change.

The factory supervisor tells his girls they can pause their work to welcome the visitors. He apologizes in English for their plight. He sympathetically tells us these young girls are from poor homes, working to help support their families, or maybe they have no family.

Reluctant at first, but all the kids are equally fascinated and interested in each other. Our older girls lead the way and approach the looms, they begin to talk. Others are hesitant but connect with smiles, gestures, and nods. I heard the young loom ladies tell our girls, "You are all so beautiful." And they say in return, "You are beautiful too." They tell our girls they look like movie stars. In awe, they admired the daughters of diplomats and kings.

We teachers wander, observing their work and the kid's interactions. It's obvious the toll that the close work took on their eyes. One small girl wore very thick glasses. I can't help but think how it's all a matter of luck, the lives we are born into, and where we emerge in the world. Perhaps our kids gained some compassion for those without their privilege, the poor girls so early in life exploited as cheap labor. Denied access to school beyond the age of twelve, child labor was their lot. They would provide for their family or themselves. Our families had access to world-class education, travel, and opportunities beyond these children's dreams. The girls connected, drawn to each other, curious, but it was obvious that these girls would be cutting and tying at their looms long after we boarded our bus, onward to the next tourist destination.

On April 25, 1980, on an excursion not far from the Iranian border, our bus driver stopped to pick up a group of Iranian tourists whose tour bus had broken down. About twenty Iranians boarded our bus, well-dressed and modern, likely remnants of the more affluent elite. Just three weeks earlier, Iran was declared an Islamist State, and less than five months earlier on November 4, 1979, over fifty Americans were captured and held hostage in the U.S. Embassy in Tehran.

Many of our boys and girls offered their seats and some rose to their feet, but the Iranian ladies declined their offer, saying they would not be on the bus long. Conversations were warm, and mutual interest exuded. I was sitting with other teachers and our tour guide in the back of the bus. We watched and listened as friendly, curious Iranians spoke English with our kids, asking them where they were from and how they happened to be in this part of the world. Even in tumultuous times, our humanity inspires and connects us. About fifteen minutes later, the tourists left our bus and boarded another.

So, think about this. We're traveling in a bus near the Iranian border with kids from high-profile families, their parents are foreign embassy diplomats, attaches, ambassadors, and even royalty. So, how dangerous could it possibly be? If abducted and kidnapped, what ransom demands might this precious cargo command as potential hostages? How high might the price be on their heads? The new Iranian Republic already had fifty American hostages. Just imagine trying to negotiate the diplomatic mess to release thirty children.

Later that day, returning from some precious site, I heard our Russian Intourist guide chuckle. She must have heard something on the Soviet radio that she'd found humorous. I see Marcia sitting across the aisle looking aghast. She seemed stunned with a look of shock or horror on her face. She translates in English that there was a fiasco in a failed attempt by the U.S. Armed Forces to free the 52 U.S. embassy staff held hostage in Tehran.

"Operation Eagle Claw" depended on everything going to plan, there was little room for error. On a complex maneuver with a 118-man assault team, U.S. helicopters confronted sandstorms in the Iranian desert. A helicopter caught fire after colliding with a fuel-laden transport plane and eight team members died. The helicopters were left behind after everyone boarded the EC-130 transport aircraft and evacuated. One day had passed before the wreckage at Desert One was broadcast to the world by the Iranian government.

Our Russian Intourist guide didn't even try to suppress her laughter. Was it glee at the misfortune of Americans? Schadenfreude? A combination of the German nouns Schaden, meaning "damage" or "harm," and Freude, meaning "joy." Was it joy over the harm suffered by the "enemy"? Or the misadventure, the mishaps, and the ironic bungling of the US rescue mission? A sad day for one country. A source of mirth for another. The headlines in America read "Mission to Rescue Iran Hostages Fails".

With one more country to explore, Azerbaijan culminated in a fair share of excitement. In the land of fire, methane gas escapes from a butt crack in the ground, its ever-burning fire is considered sacred. Marcia reminds me we visited the ruin of a temple of fire worshipers near Baku, perhaps Surakhani, a Zoroastrian temple. The Zoroastrians would usually pray near a source of fire. How fortunate we had Marcia in this never-ending series of unfortunate events. She tells me that we were at the Fire Temple of Baku when one of the girls freaked out, convinced that there were snakes everywhere. It turned out that she was seriously unstable, which her grandparents (her guardians) had failed to tell us.

We also toured a caravanserai, a roadside inn where travelers could rest and recover from the day's journey. But that was where a little local kid ran up and grabbed one of the girls' breasts. Groan. There would be little rest for us during the final leg of our journey.

Marcia remembers more horror stories. "The hotel was yet another fine kettle of fish. A delegation of Libyan military officers was staying on the same floor as us. One of them climbed over the low wall separating the rooms' balconies and tried to assault the girls in the adjacent room." We were in a panic when one young lady had momentarily disappeared. I remember helping out with night patrol in the hallway, but Kate and Tommy stayed up much of the night outside of the kid's rooms. I still wonder if the young Libyans were "terrorists in training". I'm often guilty of an overactive imagination.

Today, Baku is known as a "city in the sea" called Oil Rock. There are over two hundred and fifty offshore oil wells. The oil drilling wells are connected, but in 1980 there were not quite so many. A guide from the oil company walked with us to the end of a very long wooden walkway. When we neared the oil derrick, he told us "If there is a fire, there is no escape. We would all die." Gulp! I'm now thinking it's time to go home to the safety of Moscow.

When we got back to Moscow, Marcia told Sasha a few harrowing stories. "Sasha asked what I had expected, given that we had gone to Zveristan." Stan, she says, needs no explanation. But for those of us who don't know, Stan means a settlement, where one stands, or a land. And "*zveri*" in Russian means wild animals. In the Caucasus there may be leopards, hyenas, and bears, oh my! But don't forget the other wild beasts, the kids, the natives, and a rogue teacher. We visited the land where the wild things are.

ВОСЕМНАДЦАТЬ EIGHTEEN

KOMSOMOL KIDS

JOANN: IN YEREVAN, ARMENIA, LENIN'S HUGE statue, 23 feet tall on a 36-foot pedestal, dwarfed everything and everyone standing below. The monument to Lenin was erected in 1940, but after the fall of the Soviet Union, Big Lenin was dismembered (decapitated), taken down, and demolished in 1991. This is sad considering it was one of the best during Soviet times. Lenin's influence on communist Russia outsized any statue of him ever created, until after the fall of the Soviet Union.

At Lenin Square (now Republic Square) we were welcomed by red flag-carrying, soon to become red card-carrying, troops of Young Pioneers. The red flags they hold and the red scarves around their necks signify everything young communists represent and their aspirations for the future. Did they know we were coming to visit? In April 1980, we were the only Anglo-American School group of international kids that visited Yerevan. I wondered if our welcome was a planned event.

Are the Young Pioneers like the Scouts of the United States or Great Britain? Jim and I will share our Scouting experience and compare the US and UK Scouts with the Soviet movement.

Growing up in California my older sister was a Girl Scout, so I joined the Brownies when I was seven. I wore a Brownie uniform, that same drab brown color our

Young Pioneers in Yerevan under Lenin's statue

Intourist Guide wore. My Brownie wool beanie always itched my scalp. Mom sewed a couple of boring badges on my ugly brown sash. I was not very accomplished. Today, the long list of scout badges includes STEM categories like cybersecurity. Now, those might have interested me. I never "flew up" to the Girl Scouts nor did I wear the glamorous green Girl Scout uniform with colorful badges adorning the sash. But at least I still have my gold-colored 1950s brownie pin with its little elf centered in a clover leaf. That pin was the first one in my pin collection. Today my collection is mostly the mascot Misha Bear and Moscow Olympic Sports events along with a few tiny Lenin heads.

If I'd grown up in the Soviet Union, I would have been a Little Oktobrist. Ages seven to nine, they were called 'the little stars'. At seven I would have been in a little star group. A portrait of Vladimir Lenin, when he was young, is centered on a ruby-red five-point star. It is the pin that young Soviet children proudly wore. I would love to add that pin to my collection today.

Each little star group of Little Oktobrists was assigned to a Young Pioneer leader. With an emphasis on preparedness, sports, and outdoor skills, the Pioneers (ages 9 to 15) were modeled to some degree on the Scout movement. They even wore

Little Oktobrists in Armenia

neckerchiefs, red of course. But the Young Pioneer girls and boys didn't "fly up" like the Brownies or Cub Scouts. They had no choice. The Communist government controlled the Young Pioneers. The Scouts are independent of their governments. The Young Pioneers' motto "Always Prepared", came from the Scouts "Be Prepared". The Young Pioneers pin has a grown-up Lenin head, centered in a star with a red flame. On the bottom is a banner in Russian that says, "Always Prepared".

Like the Scouts of the US and Britain, the Young Pioneers promoted a sense of identity and a sense of belonging. And they were taught Communist and Marxist principles. It wasn't anything like the national pride I was taught in my high school Civic classes. Proud to be American, I still pledge allegiance to the flag. I'm still crazy for the blue white and red, and yellow fringe. The soundtrack lyrics from the musical, Hair, became my brand of patriotism.

Vladimir Lenin's Young Communist League, ages 14 through 28, started after the 1917 revolution. There were 40 million in the 1970s and early '80s. Just like Lenin's statue, the Young Communist League was dismantled and demolished in 1991, after the collapse of the Soviet Union.

JIM: BOY SCOUTS IN BRITAIN: I STARTED AS A CUB

when we lived in Wimbledon. I loved collecting the badges and being part of the Cub Wolf pack. The wolf pack was led by Kipling's wolf, Akela. I read "Just So Stories" by Kipling, my favorite was Rikki Tikki Tavi, the snake-killing mongoose. Like the mongoose, I was very small. At school, I was sometimes called Weedy Meady. But I would take on anyone, just like Rikki.

When I was a Cub, one night stands out in my memory. Let's start with my terrible acting. I was all dressed up as Little Bo Peep. The curtain is raised, and I'm in a white, old-fashioned dress, flowery bonnet, and holding a Shepard's crook. I had a line about how I had lost my sheep. Coincidently, I had lost my lines. The light is on me, the audience is waiting. I look desperately across at the prompter in the wings. She repeats my line several times until this stage-struck eight-year-old proclaims, "I cannot hear you!" The audience laughs and I want to crawl into a hole. My sheep chorus sings about finding their way home. My theatrical disaster thankfully finishes.

I just want to get out of this stupid outfit. I climbed some stairs to the changing room. A boy stops me and says, "Girls can't go in the boy's dressing room!" My humiliation is complete, I say, "I am NOT a girl", and push by him. At least I didn't use my Shepard's crook on this boy, although that did cross my mind. My mother, who made up my face, just laughed, "You do make a pretty girl." Oh, thanks Mum, I now feel great. The whole evening was not complete. When I dressed in my Cub uniform and sat in the audience, I was called to the front by the Chief Scout. I am thinking, will people realize I was silent Bo Peep? Instead of more laughter, I got an award as District Cub of the Year with a trophy. Life can take strange turns in moments.

Unlike Joann, I did go from Cub to Scout until I was fourteen, even after we moved to Ringwood. I continued to collect all the badges and ended up with a Scout Cord, one rung below Queen's Scout top award. My father got a bank promotion, so we moved again. This was a feature throughout my school life. I found other activities; some good, others not so good in my new town. I guess you could say I became an English *Stilyagi*, a stylish young Russian. I do feel that Scouting gave me leadership and life skills. The big difference with the Soviet youth system is I never felt forced to do anything. I just had a good time.

Soviet children had an educational path that could lead to full adult communist

Glory to Lenin's Komsomol

membership. The Communist Party fostered a cult of childhood, idealizing Soviet youth. The Komsomol, Young Pioneers, and Little Octobrists played a role in shaping young minds and promoting socialist values.

These movements reflect the complex interplay between ideology, rebellion, and social change during the Soviet era. The Young Pioneers (Vladimir Lenin All-Union Pioneer Organization) was a "compulsory" youth organization for children aged nine to fourteen. Founded in 1922, Pioneers instilled communist values, hard work, and cooperation. The Young Pioneers replaced the Boy Scouts and Girl Guides (which were banned). The new groups emphasized loyalty to the Soviet state. The Nazi Party in Germany had a similar Hitler Youth group. Pioneers wore red scarves and participated in various activities, including community service and ideological training.

We photographed many of these young people as they laid tributes on World War Two memorials. As a side note, Joann and I saw no memorials for the First World War in Russia. The people who died in that conflict were part of the Czar's army. When 1917 rolled around, Russia was embroiled in what would be the creation of the Soviet Union.

The Komsomol (All-Union Leninist Young Communist League) was a political youth organization for older teenagers in the Soviet Union. Although often considered the youth division of the Communist Party, it officially operated independently. Its purpose was to promote communist ideals, discipline, and cooperation among young people. Established in 1918, Komsomol members graduated from the Young Pioneers and Little Octobrists. Radio Moscow sometimes told you the youth system was to develop the "New Soviet Man". The Komsomol played a crucial role in political education and social development, but its success varied during different periods of Soviet history. Russians who want to progress in their careers would belong to these state-run youth movements.

Not every youngster took part. *Stilyagi* (The Stylish Ones) was the Russian equivalent of the Western 'beat generation' from the 50s and later hippies and flower power in the 60s. The *stilyagi* were the first youth counterculture movement in the Soviet Union. These stylish rebels embraced Western music, fashion, and culture. They stood in contrast to the official Soviet norms and were known for their distinctive style and love for jazz and rock 'n' roll. Not a group to be identified with if you wanted that prized communist party card. This group was where many of our Moscow friends came from, they were outsiders in the Soviet system.

ДЕВЯТНАДЦАТЬ NINETEEN

DINNER WITH U.S. AMBASSADOR WATSON

Spaso House: Residence of the US Ambassador

JIM: During our brief two years in Moscow, we met people who would never be part of our usual circle of acquaintances. Diplomats, commercial people who work internationally, and correspondents from major newspapers. We even met spies from many countries including Russian ones. Many were less James Bond and more like "Get Smart", the American television spoof in the 1960s.

It was a fact of life that Moscow was just a moment in the lives of many in the foreign community. At the end of our first year, in the summer of 1980, a 'Goodbye Dinner' for the Principal, Gene, took place. This was held at Spaso House, the residence of U.S. ambassador Thomas J. Watson Jr. Son of the founder of IBM, he had retired as board chairman. President Jimmy Carter appointed him as U.S. Ambassador to the USSR. Tom Watson Senior may have founded IBM, but his son, Tom Junior, built the company into a global corporation based on expensive mainframe computers they sold and leased.

I purchased some special occasion clothes from a Saville Row tailor before my travel to Moscow. I had no idea what I would need in any formal diplomatic gathering, so I took his advice. Unfortunately, the advice the tailor gave me was based on his diplomatic clients and, as I clearly showed in many ways, I was not diplomatic. Joann and I have a dinner invitation to the American ambassador's residence. The question is, what should I wear in June? My infamous sheepskin coat with beaver collar is quickly removed from my mental list. I know I wore it in 90-degree Moscow heat, but I have no intention of a repeat performance. Over the two years in Moscow, I suffered enough jokes from my overheated arrival. The invitation gives no clue about the appropriate dress, but I think the three-piece pinstripe suit does not feel right. My choice comes down to the burgundy evening jacket, pink formal shirt with eye-catching cufflinks, and bow tie. Joann looks elegant in a dress she had her mother send for special occasions. In short, she looks great, I look and feel like a gaudy penguin. I am not sure either of us knew how the evening would play out as we parked the car and entered the residence.

During the cocktail hour, the men talk with the ambassador. Tom was interested in everyone; Watson exuded warmth and the social talk was relaxed. He told us a funny story about flying his helicopter to some private island he owned. The ambassador has private wealth I cannot imagine yet he had us laughing with his story. I was not the only one who felt anxious that evening. Anyone who like me watched Jeopardy knows that Watson, the early AI, competed against human contestants who vainly tried to beat the machine. I swear that Watson the machine is named for Tom Jr., because the father Tom Sr., was not a big fan of digital computers. Tom Sr. founded IBM on mechanical accounting machines. Tom Watson Jr. was one of those individuals who saw an opportunity and took it with both hands.

JOANN: MEANWHILE, THE LADIES, INCLUDING ME,

are with Olive, Watson's gracious wife. Olive, once a model on the cover of Vogue magazine, strolls along a Spaso House runway to show us her art collection. The centerpiece is a work by James Whistler, the famous son who painted his mother. Mom's portrait, Whistler's Mother, is housed in the Musée d'Orsay, Paris. We cozy up with drinks on formal couches, and then the banter begins. Donna, my Canadian friend, and I entertain with our recent visit to a Russian *banya*. Our story seemed to amuse Olive. She didn't get many stories like ours in polite conversation, nor would her security detail allow her that liberty. The *banya*, a public bathhouse, was in an old palace building that echoed its past magnificence. My first impression was its complete nudity. It is something that strikes us more socially conservative North Americans, we're not used to stark naked strangers in public settings.

The *banya* attendant gives us a wash bowl to begin our preliminary body cleaning. You might "bring your own bottle" to a party but in the Soviet Union, it is "bring your own soap" to the public bath party. First, you scrub down with your soap and soft sponges. Then we go through many rounds of showers that squirt water at us from top to bottom and side jets that get into every crack and crevice. It feels like being in an American carwash, but the Russian version is for people. After the Russian water hosing, we move on to small pools, some hot, some cold. We alternate between dipping in pools, steam room sessions, and endless birch twig beatings to stimulate our skin.

I'd opted for the extra add-on, a two-ruble foot treatment. First, the elderly babushka soaks my feet in a bubbly mystery liquid. Then, she pulls out a long razor blade. Yikes! Or as Russians say when surprised, *Ona*! I wonder if the babushka has turned into Baba Yaga, the mythical character who eats children in a fairy tale designed to frighten Russian children. The babushka brandishing her razor-sharp weapon made me wonder, "What does she think I've asked for? There's an anti-climax as she skillfully removes the calluses from my feet.

The British Dacha

Olive, Donna, Teri, and I bonded over those cocktails at Spaso House. Whistler's Mother and Baba Yaga, what an odd mix that made. And we were also an odd mix from the start.

JIM: THERE ARE ONLY TWO TABLES IN THE DINING room, each for six people. This is a big deal for both of us. Ambassador Watson is seated at one round table and his wife hosts the second. Joann and I are at Ambassador Watson's table with Gene and his wife Teri. We have no idea how the seating was arranged. Neither of us can remember what we ate. We were too busy listening attentively to the conversations and showed our best dinner table manners.

The goodbye to Gene and his wife took part in many stages, as they were both popular in Moscow's foreign community. Anglo-American School teachers and staff organized a party at the British dacha. The Russian word dacha is a country house. Dachas can be something as humble looking as a garden shed to some elaborate mansion and anything in between. The key point is that it is a seasonal place, often a second home, located away from their city apartments. The British dacha is old, welcoming, and cozy, it is a perfect place for a party.

I volunteer to DJ the party. Unlike my Broomball Ball gig, I do not create a small diplomatic uproar by playing the Soviet anthem. I stick exclusively with disco. People dance and drink, and all goes well. As the party ends, I play Ian Drury and the Blockheads', "Sweet Gene Vincent". Not exactly disco material but it emphasizes the point of the evening.

ДВАДЦАТЬ TWENTY

OLYMPIC DREAMS AND NAKHODKA NIGHTMARES

JIM: BEFORE THE MOSCOW GAMES, JOANN AND I WITH other Anglo-American School teachers dreamt of good money as we ferried around NBC television staff to different Olympic venues. We knew Moscow (sort of) and had our cars, and we were free because of the school holiday. NBC planned a group of several hundred personnel they would bring to cover the Olympics. We knew the roads (kind of) and we would be cheap guides to the city. The Soviet invasion of Afghanistan meant many Russian soldiers would have a long vacation with some never going to return. An American and British boycott meant our wonderful jobs and Olympic dreams evaporated. The British and American Embassies advised us not to go to Olympic events. Moscow would not be a place for us to stay, as many Russians were displeased with the Western boycott.

Joann and I made a quick decision. "Why not travel?" We heard about Pan Am issuing round-the-world tickets. Initially, this meant we fly across the Soviet Union and then take a boat to Japan from Nakhodka. From Japan, we would fly Pan Am to America. I would leave Joann in Los Angeles after I met her family. Then I planned several stops across America before I flew back to England. She would join me in England and meet my family. Finally, we would fly back to Moscow for the new school year. Simple in theory. In practice, it was a little different.

I went to the British Embassy and talked to my Russian hire "travel agent". "*Nyet problem*" (No problem), she tells me. She should have said "*nevazhno.*" It is not important, do not worry, roughly translated. As our story unfolds it will be clear that we should worry and there is an important missing detail in our travel arrangements. Our Pan Am tickets covered flights on other carriers. Flights in the Soviet Union were by Aeroflot. In America, I had internal flights on United Airlines. Our flight back to Moscow from London was by British Airways. All this meant that we only flew on actual Pan-Am planes trans-Pacific and trans-Atlantic.

The school has closed for the summer, and we boarded our Aeroflot flight to Khabarovsk. This is as far east as you could fly. Once there you board a train to take you to Nakhodka. This is a major commercial port with the Far East Steamship service to Yokohama Bay, Japan. The American map of the Soviet Union has lots of pink areas titled in its key as "Areas Closed to Foreigners". In other words where you, an American, could not go. Why this cartographic detail is necessary becomes obvious later, so hold that thought.

Our Moscow to Khabarovsk flight was not the typical domestic Aeroflot flight. It was classed as a continental flight of about 8 hours long, at more than 8000 kilometers distance, and flying through 8 time zones. You arrive having lost 8 hours, but according to your watch, you have lost no time. Joann says that 888 is a magical angel number. It means there are positive changes on your horizon, an abundance of something new. Maybe it's love?

Since Aeroflot was part of Pan Am's around-the-world service, the meals had to conform to international standards. So instead of scratched plastic cups and stale bread rolls, we are served delicious Chicken Kiev on china plates. Other international passengers, including a Czechoslovakian girls' choir, were onboard the flight and the choir would accompany us on the Far East Steamship boat to Yokohama.

In Khabarovsk, we boarded a night train to take us the rest of the way to the Pacific coast. I again recall Joann's embassy map with all those pink bits where foreigners cannot go. That map of Russia's Far East has lots of pink. To prevent commercial planes flying over sensitive areas Soviet night trains are the answer. A night train prohibits curious foreign passengers from seeing the countryside in daylight. There was a long list of things we were not allowed to photograph. Joann missed or ignored that particular memo, a dedicated collector with photos of military men, missiles, and tanks. In the Soviet's view, Westerners could not be trusted. In some cases (Joann), they were right. All foreigners are treated with suspicion and sometimes as possible spies. Add the fun fact that Vladivostok is a few miles from Nakhodka, the Russian Navy's Pacific base. Vladivostok is a port not on the Western tourist's list of attractions.

The rail journey between Khabarovsk and Nakhodka is close to the Chinese border. Soviet night trains I traveled on were usually slow, they chug along at whatever speed guarantees we arrive at our destination the following early morning. Joann is asleep rocked by the gentle travel motion. I am awake and I cannot get back to sleep. I decided to stand in the corridor with the early pre-dawn light. I can see the Chinese border. China and the Soviet Union may be comrades, but the border suggests there are limits to Marxist brotherhood. There are lots of watch towers with searchlights on and substantial barbed wire.

Early in the morning, the train stops at Nakhodka station. We have an escort who takes us out of the station straight onto a couple of Intourist coaches. Nakhodka is a closed city. This means there is no hotel for us to stay in. The coach trip to the port is surreal. We looked out of the bus windows and saw nothing but propaganda billboards. Do people live here? What do they look like? We have absolutely no idea. We get off our coach and are escorted into the customs and passport control building. Our ferry is tied to the quay. Now the fun is about to begin...

I pass through passport control with no problem. Joann approaches the control desk and hands over her passport. "No problem" in Moscow turns into a "big problem" in Nakhodka. Joann may be small in stature, but she is always feisty. She loudly demands to know what is happening. A man appears with a video camera recording the scene. I am sure we will not get offered a copy of this videotape as a souvenir of our trip. Videotaping is standard Soviet procedure to provide evidence of foreigners being "naughty." I can tell Joann is scared and angry by the look on her face. I try to return through passport control. I am stopped with a brisk *Nyet* (No). The officials point to the ship, they "suggest" I go aboard. Meanwhile, two armed guards take hold of Joann's arms. They frog-march her away with her feet barely touching the ground. I am thinking what am I to do?

I look around and see an old sofa. I created a plan. In a loud best British voice I announce, "I am going nowhere. I shall sit on the sofa until my friend meets me so we can get on the boat together. I have '*nyet problem and nevazhno*,'" I announce to anyone who cares to listen, "I have cigarettes in my bag so I will sit right here and wait until Joann, my friend, appears." Smoking does calm my nerves as I dream up three unpleasant scenarios. Scenario one, I will not see Joann again, they will drag me onto the ferry. Japan could be a solo journey for Jim. Scenario two, neither of us will board the ferry and we will somehow be sent back to Moscow. Scenario three, we will end up in some Siberian jail and our embassies will have to get us out, at least I hope they will. Other passengers have witnessed this scene. They look sympathetically at me as I muster that stiff British upper lip. I adopt an air of nonchalance I certainly did not possess.

What happened to Joann?

JOANN: "WHAT? I CAN'T GET ON? BUT I'M WITH HIM."
I point to Jim. "We're together."

Jim turns around and stares back at me, first in confusion, then in disbelief. "She's with me."

"You must come with me." The Soviet official spoke English.

"No! I'm not coming with you. I'm with him." I gesture again towards Jim.

I'm very agitated now. At first, I was angry and annoyed at what I conclude is just some bureaucratic screw-up. The man insists more and more, and I become even more and more belligerent. I wave my hands, flail my arms and expressively show my Italian ancestry. I insist I must get on the ship with my boyfriend. My voice gets louder (as if that would help). "What are you doing? Why? Why?" I yelp and squeal like a puppy.

Other officious people begin to gather. A cameraman appears with a large video camera on his shoulder. He walks towards me, much too close. It's obvious to me (and everyone else) that I'm the center of attention. People are watching, solemn but amused. None are willing to join in on the fun.

"You must come with us." Another man chimes in. Then two gun-toting guards flank me. Each one takes hold of an arm, and they frog-march me quickly to another part of the port terminal. One opens a door, and the other escorts me into a small holding room with just one wooden chair in the center.

"Wait here!"

"But, but …why am I here? What did I do? Please, tell me!" The door closes behind me. Click!

My anger has faded but I'm more nervous than ever. I am beginning to think I may be doomed to some unforeseen future. Fear sets in and I wonder why I'm sitting alone in this room. Am I under arrest? Did I do something wrong? My mind is racing, and I'm thinking. Have I been flagged for something I've done? Something illegal? And then my guilty conscience churns up the memories of all my delinquent misbehaviors. Naughty me. In Red Square, I took illegal photos of the missiles and tanks. Or could it be something about my Russian friends, the dissidents, artists, and refuseniks? But how would they know about these things? I manage a chuckle at my ridiculous thoughts.

And then I start to feel sorry for myself. And worry about what they will do to me. Maybe they'll put me in prison. Or set me up for something I haven't done. Have they mistaken me for an American spy? Hi ho, it's off to the gulag I will go. Or maybe some other notorious prison in Outer Siberia? It's all beginning to unnerve me. I'm crying and whimpering, again like that lost puppy. Get hold of yourself, you silly puppy. I must no longer squeal. But no, they can't arrest me, or could they? PNG, persona non grata, at best or worst … What is the worst thing that can happen to me?

I look at my watch, only ten minutes have gone by. In less than two hours our ship sets sail. But it's a Soviet-owned Far East Steamship boat so I hope the authorities hold the departure. I stare at my Misha Bear wristwatch, the mascot of the 1980 Olympics, the games that never were, at least not for us Americans and Brits. Jim and I had hoped to see the Games up close and personal. I am sitting in this room with nothing to do, so I visualize driving around NBC film crews. I am driving in my beige Zhiguli getting lost with a crew trying to navigate the Moscow Maze. But instead of the 700 people scheduled to cover the spectacle, only 7 showed up. Russian regrets? Certainly, the Russian ego took a big blow. But maybe they should have thought first before invading Afghanistan. Hey, but don't take it out on me! I didn't do anything! It's not my fault!

I keep checking my watch. Misha Bear looks up at me with his cute face, huge welcoming smile, and Olympic Belt with five rings. He reminded me of Mickey Mouse—big ears, big smile—and here I am, a kid from Los Angeles, remembering our annual trips to Disneyland. Will I ever get home again? The next stop after Japan would have been California. "Oh, East is East, and West is West, and never the twain shall meet." Rudyard Kipling had it right.

After nearly two hours I'm now in the depths of despair with only thirteen unlucky minutes until the ship departs. Nothing can slow the passage of time. But then the door opens.

"Come with me, you must hurry." The official hustled me to the boarding area. Jim is waiting, he has our backpack with my little Rollei inside. Together, we scramble aboard and look down at the terminal, relieved but still not knowing why. I take a photo from the boat as we say *"Do svidaniya"*.

Port or Nakhodka from the Far East Steamship

JIM: WE MAY HAVE ESCAPED FROM RUSSIAN SOIL, BUT

this ship is Russian-owned. On the first night, that enthusiastic teenage singing group from Czechoslovakia from the plane serenaded the passengers during dinner. It makes up for the cuisine. Unfortunately, the food is up to regular Soviet culinary standards.

During the night we wake up in our cabin. "Do you think we are going into a storm? The boat is starting to pitch and roll. Joann, did you see where the lifeboats or floatation devices were? I wonder if we missed the abandon ship drill by our late arrival onboard?" We stay planted in our bunks until dawn. Then I try climbing off the top bunk which presents a real challenge. The boat's motion makes descent down the ladder difficult. Neither of us are poor sailors who suffer from sea sickness, yet our balance is off.

"Breakfast?" I ask, "Why not." Joann replies.

The food hall is notably sparse. Our fellow passengers seem to have decided against breakfast. The Dutch couple we met at dinner last night are at our shared table. The garlic-laced sausage does not appeal as the boat heaves in the swells. We opt for bread, cheese, and coffee. I always wondered why cruise ships ply everyone with booze and games to occupy passenger time. I now know, boats and sea voyages are in one word—boring. Still, the Far East Steamship Company has provided further special entertainment.

We decided to take a turn on the deck. There are plenty of those angelic Czech voices. Sadly, the sound now is a nightmarish heave as the teenagers hang over the rail and vomit. After the interesting sights of people in distress, the white-capped swell, and the chilly bracing sea air we retreat to our cabin till lunchtime. "I cannot decide how I feel, how about you?" Eventually, we stagger to the fine dining hall like drunken sailors.

"The swell is not too bad I was told," our Dutch friend informs us. "It may get choppier when we go through the Sea of Japan." Oh good, I think, maybe I should have bought some sea sickness pills. Lunch arrives with more entertainment courtesy of the ship's kitchen. We get steaming soup bowls with lots of "tasty" squid. Joann is fine she regales us all with a tale of eating squid and octopus in Greece. "The only thing that resembles Greece Joann, is what is floating on the top of my soup bowl," I remark. The Dutchman called it, "High-grade rubber bands." His girlfriend looks decidedly green and dashes out of the food hall. We never see our Dutch friends again.

ДВАДЦАТЬ ОДИН

TWENTY-ONE

JOURNEY TO JAPAN

JIM: WE SAIL INTO THE CALM WATER OF YOKOHAMA harbor about to say farewell to HMS Vomitorium and its "first class" dining delights. As we disembark many questions strike us.

Joann asks two immediate questions we need to answer, "How far are we from Tokyo?" "How do we get there?"

I can think of a couple of others. "Where are we to stay?" "Is Tokyo too far or expensive to take a taxi?" Luckily, Joann's important questions are answered outside the port gates. We can see a train station. We haul our luggage onto the platforms. Sadly, like many American and British people, the Japanese language is not something we studied at school.

We learn quickly that in 1980s Japan there were very few English speakers on hand to assist. Even worse, every platform sign giving information is in Kanji, not English. It is time to talk to the unsuspecting local citizen on the platform. He at least looks sympathetic to our situation. Here is the total of my Japanese:—*Hai*—yes, *Origato*—thank you, and most 'useful' *Metsubushi*. This is a word used when police blow pepper, fine glass, or dust. Confronted by an attacker, a police officer would blow the *metsubushi* in the attacker's eyes, blinding them. I learned this valuable word in martial arts as a blow aimed at the eyes to blind your opponent. I can also count to ten but, now I cannot see how a karate move or reciting one to ten in Japanese will help us get a train to Tokyo.

"I think we are in big trouble, Joann."

I use my first two words with our new friend. By pointing and gesturing, we somehow find the right platform for the local train to Tokyo. As I sit here forty years later, I suspect we did not have valid tickets. The odds of us hitting the jackpot and purchasing a ticket from an automatic ticket machine are pretty low. Nobody asked us to pay so we carried on.

We pass or stop at some stations where all signs are in Japanese Kanji so our anxiety rises. Finally, we pull into a station. Then we see the sign Central Tokyo in English. At this point, we are more than a little anxious and tired. Joann and I do not want another task finding the Best Western hotel or whatever the Japanese equivalent. "That looks like a hotel right there by the station, let's go." The Railway Hotel is not the Best Western or Hilton. We check in and find our room. Joann feels happier, "The room is clean but where is the bathroom?" Another good question Joann, I think. I am sent out on a bathroom scouting party. I learn more new things about Japan. There are two bathrooms on each floor. One toilet is the Japanese squat-over porcelain hole style. Toilet two is a European-style toilet but is a long trek from our room. I bring the good news of my quest back to Joann.

We have both lived in large cities, but Tokyo is fascinating if a little daunting when you don't know the language. It nearly makes you wish for a Russian Intourist guide. The weather is very different. We have gone from Moscow's dry summer climate to Japan's version of a natural sauna with very heavy humidity. The sky is overcast and perspiration oozes from our pores after a few minutes outside. We had a bit of luck finding our way about the city. Taxi drivers somehow made sense of our asking to go to different places. A Moscow friend recommended buying a good short-wave portable radio. On our first city trip, we took a taxi outside our hotel. The driver opens the back doors electronically I confess such gadgets fascinate me. Taxis in Japan were super clean and each we rode in had embroidered seat covers. Joann and I suspect the taxi's cleanliness reflects Japanese culture. The Japanese are fastidious about everything being clean, including the city taxis. We ask the driver to take us to the Akihabara Electric Town district.

As we arrive, I sense Joann has me on a very short leash. I think I have died and gone to electronic heaven. We spent several hours marveling at all the electronic possibilities in the stores. It was not one shop but many on both sides of the street. I love new technology. Neon and sound are everywhere overwhelming our senses.

I could have bought many things but had no room in my suitcase for my clothes. Joann is watching me like a hawk, she knows me too well and my fascination with electronics. What a contrast with the poor electronic offerings in 1980 Moscow. We have sensory overload. The sheer volume (shop size and sound) can be daunting for any tourist in this electronic heaven.

We find the radio we want. I used it for several years in Moscow, Africa, and America. It had an excellent short-wave reception. In Moscow, our wireless gave us a different world view in BBC broadcasts than Radio Moscow. This meant I could listen to British football (soccer as it is called in America). We also got the latest BBC news during the Falklands War when we lived in Zimbabwe. Sadly, a lot of short-wave stations have disappeared because of the internet.

On our second day in Tokyo, we again hail a cab. Our destination was the Ginza shopping district. This turned out to be strictly a shop window gazing expedition. Our teaching salaries in Moscow are good but most of the Ginza goods on display would exhaust our limited travel fund in minutes. We opt for noodles from a street stall for lunch. This avoided the expensive-looking restaurants that always populate high-fashion shopping districts.

The most striking impression in Ginza was the glimpse of 'Japanese salary men'. All dressed in suits, ties loosened, and looking stressed out. We peer into a bar where we see plenty of self-medication going on. I suspect this is their way of combating any salary man's pressure. I know it also has something to do with male business culture that includes drinking with colleagues. Japanese drunks on the street were often looked after by colleagues who could still stand, as they waited for a taxi. Public intoxication was a little different in Moscow. There, the drunks were helped by well-meaning passers-by. Drinking in Moscow could be a solitary activity.

After two days in Tokyo, we find the right station to board the Bullet train to Kyoto. This time we made sure we purchased tickets. We both love train travel. An electronic sign tells us when we get to the top speed of 170 mph. This express trip is not the same as the "express" train travel in the Soviet Union. The carriage is clean and silent. The landscape flies past our carriage's window. There is no familiar click-clack as the train ambles along the rails of the Soviet Union. Two short hours and we arrive at Kyoto Central Station.

Kyoto is the former capital. We had a list of several sites to visit. I also have a couple of other ideas involving purchases and a proposal. Our hotel is a rapid improvement from the Railway Hotel in Tokyo. Each room is small, clean, and has an English-style bathroom. The impression I get is that small is preferable in Japanese culture. This impression is reinforced when I walk down any Japanese street. I tower over most people, yet I am only a very average five foot eleven in height. I now know how the world seems to basketball players and other very tall people.

On the other hand, Joann has found a height-challenged person's heaven. She is the average height for women in Japan at five feet and a bit. She can talk to people face to face and not have to strain to look up as she does elsewhere. Her diminutive stature meant clothes shopping did not include searching for the petite section. I am keen to buy her some clothes in Japan. We rejected the idea of a kimono, beautiful as they are. "Where can I wear it?" I agree with Joann. Instead, she found a two-piece blue silk dress with beautiful orange flowers. Each sale has an elaborate wrapping process and polite formal bowing. I confess I have ulterior motives now Joann is happy with the clothing purchase.

My friend in England sparked my interest in Aikido and Japanese martial arts. He was diligent, unlike me, and became a sixth-dan black belt and a President of the British Aikido Association. Paul gave me a wooden practice sword as a parting gift. I learned enough for the Moscow school's after-school program. A few basic defensive moves impress the Moscow kids who took the class. Again, my friend gave me a couple of instruction books. I taught them how to do rolling break falls. A useful skill I used when being rear-ended in London on my motorcycle. As the saying goes about trapeze artists—'flying through the air with the greatest of ease'. In my case, over the handlebars and a neat rolling break-fall into the gutter. I ached for several days and ruined my jacket, but things could have been much worse.

As I am here in Japan, I have got it in my head to buy a pair of swords. With Joann suitably euphoric and clutching her clothing purchase, we search for a samurai sword shop. It turns out that what Americans call a hardware store is where you can purchase swords. I say more about the transport of this purchase later. Sitting next to kitchen knives and meat cleavers is a selection of swords in a wall cabinet. I make a choice and use our point-and-mime strategy. I walk out of the hardware store with a two samurai sword set and a wooden holder.

Then I blot my copybook by suggesting we go to McDonalds for dinner on the first night in Kyoto. Please pity me! I am not a fan of raw fish, I prefer my fish rectangular, breaded or battered, and always fried. I cannot remember what we ate but it was expensive. Joann has made sure this sin was never forgotten for several years. I was careful not to repeat this sin elsewhere in the future.

Overall, we didn't make many mistakes that foreigners, including us, sometimes encounter when ordering food in a strange land. We did use the same point and pantomime strategy to communicate occasionally in Moscow. Our minimal Japanese meant a lengthy performance when we did order in any Japanese restaurant. Luckily restaurants display plastic replicas of the food on the menu in the front window. We bow politely and point and pantomime for our wait person to follow us to the front window. Joann points to her selection and then I choose mine. There are more *Hai*'s (Yes) and bows as we order.

Joann and I did know some Japanese etiquette. The Anglo-American School shared the building with the Japanese school. The depth of a bow depends on the status of who you are bowing with. We did have a social meeting with the Japanese teaching staff. Talking of etiquette, one Japanese teacher had a tee shirt that said 'fuck you'. The words are artfully printed vertically in a Japanese-like script. He claimed not to understand what his shirt said. It certainly livened the evening when mixed with all those formal bows.

Joann and I found Kyoto to be a wonderful place. Small enough to walk to most sights. As usual, we missed a tour of the Imperial Palace. We forgot to bring our passports from the hotel. Instead, we took a snapshot from the Palace's outer wall. Without a good guide, human, or book, it is easy to miss rules and opening times. When we look at all our photo albums it is easy to see the times, we missed something and in this case a picture of the nondescript palace wall as a reminder of our failure.

The gardens and shrines, Shinto or Buddhist, captured our interest. What a contrast to Russian churches/museums. There are many people in the temples. In one Shinto shrine, we see a very young boy, about five, with his proud grandmother. We were intrigued. This was the first time we saw small shoes that flashed and squeaked as he took a step. This young man was strutting along with Grandma looking on in adoration. She insisted Joann take a photo. The Japanese birthrate is not high children are rare precious gifts. We often recall the squeaky child and his grandmother.

We spent enjoyable hours in the temples and Kyoto's other historic buildings. Joann took lots of photos including one of the ten giant Buddha in Japan. Odd for me, I bought something at the temple gift shop. I purchased what I was informed is a good luck charm. I expected I was going to need some luck later that evening. I think the charm was to provide revenue for the shrine's upkeep. Regardless it was just one of the reminders that customer service and presentation is a high art in Japanese culture. The paper charm is intricately folded inside a red brocade cover and silk tassel.

I kept the charm for many years until water damage in a moving shipment destroyed it. I guess my Japanese luck was gone.

A highlight for me was watching a Zen archer in one of the shrines. The bow is about six feet long. The archer is crouched with feet tucked underneath him. He never looked at the target, he concentrated on the perfect drawing of the bow. He hit the target twice. Martial arts are full of these counterintuitive ideas. For example, when your assailant brandishes a knife, look at their eyes to find out when they are going to attack, never look at the knife. I have only tried it with rubber knives. I have no doubt this counter-intuitive defensive strategy works.

I have a big plan for what I hope is a special evening. We have discovered where the old quarter is in Kyoto. As we walked down the road, the geisha in full kimono dress are on their way to work. It shows the difference in the pre-selfie age. The geisha will stop briefly for a photograph. This does not happen now. Too many foreigners accost and try to embrace the ladies to be included in the picture. I never understand why people need to insert themselves into everything they see. Is it impossible to stand quietly and watch as we did with the Zen archer?

We find a restaurant with a balcony because it is hot and humid even in the evening. Neither of us is keen on air conditioning and inside seating. Joann and I have differing opinions about the balcony we sat at. She claims it was by a moonlit river. I lean more toward a large drainage ditch or canal but with the moon's reflection. Regardless I hope the setting is right for what I plan to do. The restaurant caters to tourists, the menu comes with pictures. We order a tempura selection and Kirin beer. I had thought about asking Joann to marry me all day. The moment seemed right, so I summoned my courage. "Joann, would you like to get married?" I am often accused of being too reserved like many of my English male compatriots. This was one of the best days of my life even after forty-plus years of marriage. She said yes. I was ecstatic, so I didn't know a tiny detail. Joann admitted recently that she had crossed her fingers behind her back. She reasoned she could weasel out of her promise in the future. Joann was allergic to commitment in her younger days. I think I can put the memorable evening down as a good idea. Maybe. Thank you to the American and British Olympic ban for giving us this moment.

We board our first Pan Am plane for the next leg to Los Angeles. Overall, we will only travel on two Pan Am planes despite being the company selling the round-the-world ticket. On our departure from Narita airport, I declare the swords in our luggage at customs. The official wants to see them. I remember my arrival in Moscow where they made me empty my suitcase. I get very anxious. She takes the large sword out and I am horrified when the official touches the blade. This is a real no-no as fingerprints can make the blade rust. I tried to explain but had little success. She was testing to see if I had sharpened the blade. To this day the blades have no cutting edge. Eventually, the swords are replaced in the suitcase. Pan Am stows our luggage in the hold. It shows how the world has changed. In 1980 I transported those swords with me on United Airlines, Pan Am, and British Airways flights, all the way back to Moscow. The swords were either stowed in the hold or on one American domestic United flight kept in the cabin crew's baby stroller storage cubby. As I left the plane a kind steward handed me my swords. "Here are your samurai swords, have a good day."

ДВАДЦАТЬ ДВА

TWENTY-TWO

MISHA BEAR MEETS MICKEY MOUSE

JIM: TEN DAYS IN SOUTHERN CALIFORNIA PASS IN A blur. This is my first landfall in America. I sit alone on a plane to Denver, Colorado, where I review the California highlights. I come from a small family. In 1980 I can count about ten living relatives. I am a little shell-shocked. Joann introduced me to about a hundred people. They are either relatives or friends of the family. I am not great with names so this all seems overwhelming. She warns me that there are even more relatives on the East Coast that I will meet in the future. I detect a slightly evil grin as Joann introduces me to the Italian American horde in California. "Look what you have got yourself in, buddy." is written all over her face.

We stay with her sister and family. Things seem to go well, although I have just been called Chris. It is all very odd—the subject changes after a brief pause. Dody warned me the first morning that they take their coffee strong. I silently agree that it could be an excellent substitute for a paint stripper. "Do you have any tea?' I ask. Yes, is the reply, a teabag is dunked in hot water. I wonder if the teapot is broken. I put some milk and sugar in and raised the cup. Some herbal teas tend to curdle the milk. An undrinkable dairy disaster sits in my cup. I learned that tea in America can consist of odd mixtures of things that were not from a tea bush. I stored this knowledge for future use in America. From now on, I will ask for the original tea leaf type tea, no twigs, and dust for Jim! I store the words Lipton or Red Rose for future reference.

Joann has organized a whirlwind tour of Southern California attractions. At Disneyland, I learned you had to remember that your car is parked in D for Donald Duck, not C for Cinderella or G for Goofy. I had never seen such a huge parking lot. Thank God I remembered we were in D for Donald. Luckily, Hertz put the license plate number on the car key fob, otherwise we could have needed a search party with torches late into the night. The other big revelation is that Americans get in lines, not British queues. The lines snake back and forth with helpful signs telling us we are now thirty, twenty, or ten minutes away from the ride. All this is exhausting in the hot Californian sun for what can be a brief experience at the end of a two-hour wait. This is a great simulation of what people in the Soviet Union do regularly. They line up for more essential things than what Disney provides at the end of those long waits.

We went on a roller coaster inside a dark Space Mountain, an experience I found odd. You cannot see where you are going, meaning you lose the thrill of knowing what is coming up. There was some antique-looking train ride careering around corners and through tunnels. Most memorable for Joann was when she got me on one of her favorite Disney rides, "The Pirates of the Caribbean". We were floating past fierce animatronic pirates, with cannons belching smoke, accompanied by a song, lots of "Yo ho, Yo ho," and not much rum mentioned. Rum and Disney feature in Joann's Disneyland adventures. Disney is PG as I expected.

Getting in long lines was too much as the afternoon wore on. "Look Joann, there is a ride with a small line." This confirmed for Joann that I am slightly mad. Two adults spin gently around in teacups with five-year-olds. Then, I learned what an American earworm is. Disney loves to have you followed with a chorus or two of "It's a Small World After All." Despite the music, I did not get into the full Disney spirit. I strenuously declined to don a pair of mouse ears! I know I am a spoil sport but Joann is known as a premier tease. She would have had photographic evidence of my humiliation for later use.

JOANN: JIM COULDN'T COME TO LOS ANGELES WITH-

out going to Disneyland. As a kid, I went every year, there were always new rides and favorites to ride again. Fantasyland made a huge impression during my younger years, but I never wanted to be Cinderella. I was more impressed with Peter Pan, a child who would never grow up. How many other kids dreamed of flying like a bird? Dolls and princesses were not for me, I wanted adventure and magical worlds like Neverland, Captain Hook, crocodiles, and pirates, how scary and exciting could it get? In Neverland I could play all day with the boys and never have any responsibilities. Well, some things never change.

Disneyland left an indelible stamp on my view of the world. I had no fear of exotic places, people, or animals because I'd already seen the world according to Disney's Jungle Boat Cruise. Anaheim's Mickey Mouse may resemble Moscow's Misha Bear but never the twain shall meet.

So, here we are in Disneyland, having just announced our engagement to my family in Los Angeles. All the most famous and exciting rides required standing in long lines for a few thrills. Fantasyland might have been my favorite as a kid, but Tomorrowland had a new ride. Space Mountain promised a wild roller coaster ride in pitch darkness. The line would take at least an hour, possibly two, it snaked back and forth so you would get to know people's faces as they passed by you, repeatedly. You might even recognize what they were wearing. I for one, worse a snug-fitting grey t-shirt that boldly announced, "Stolen from the Moscow Marine House Bar".

"Did you really steal your t-shirt from the Moscow Marine Bar?" a man queuing behind me asks. Literal thinker that I am, I proclaim that no "I didn't steal my T-shirt. I bought it, I work in Moscow." The man said he didn't think I stole it. I could never tell when people were being facetious. A short conversation becomes longer as Jim now joins in.

While they are talking, I see the familiar face of a guy a few rows back in the bending line. He smiles at me. I smile at him. And I remember back in 7th grade he was the first boy I'd ever kissed. Not one of those tonguey kisses, just two twelve-year-olds' awkward attempt at making out. He doesn't wave, nor do I. Perhaps he's with his wife or other friends. We smile once more in recognition of the rare coincidence that we would be at the same place, on the same day, at the same time. It's what you might call a blast from the past. How funny that out of the tens of thousands of people in Disneyland on that day, you could recognize your first love, kiss, or whatever it was, and he recognized you. What are the chances? And I'm with a lovely man I found by moving 6000 miles away from Los Angeles to Moscow. And he was one person out of the 4.4 billion people in the world in 1980, but I found him, and he found me. Today he'd be one in 8 billion, even more of a crapshoot.

We're now at the front of the line and will enter the vast darkness of Space Mountain. After a three-minute thrill of motion-induced vertigo and disorientation, Jim joked that there was nothing to see in the dark. He was underwhelmed. From his pale pallor and woozy wobble, I think it scared the crap out of him.

Other memories at Disneyland come flooding back as we continue to queue for rides. I don't mention nor reveal my childhood sweetheart to Jim, but something even more poignant from my teenage past. I tell Jim my story about Grad Night at Disneyland, a rite of passage for high school seniors like me. In 1966, Grad Night was an all-night party that lasted from 11:00 pm to 5:00 am. Sixty thousand seniors from thirty-three High Schools descended upon Disneyland. Over five nights, about twelve thousand teenagers each night ran riot in celebration. And for the princely sum of $7.00, we had unlimited use of all rides and attractions with a $1 photo included.

It was the 6th annual Grad Night at Disneyland in 1966 and with that menacing omen of 666, I should have heeded the warning of danger. But I'd already become entangled in those Fantasyland dreams and distortions of reality. It seemed to run in my California blood. "The Number of the Beast is 666", the last in William Blake's Great Red Dragon's paintings, should have forewarned me. Don't be diabolic. I ignored the 666 message and indulged in yet another reckless indiscretion and foolish decision of my youth.

My date for the evening was a 19-year-old past boyfriend of my older sister who'd graduated from the same high school. I often inherited her old hand-me-downs. He didn't want to go when I asked him. Being older, he was much too "cool" to be seen with us high school kids. So, he set up a precondition. He would go, but only if he could drink. Now, this would not be easy since no booze would be sold during the event and minors under twenty-one could not buy alcohol anyway, anywhere. As a deterrent, everyone entering the gates of the Magic Kingdom would be searched. All pockets checked, all purses inspected, and maybe even a quick frisk of suspicious-looking kids. But my date had a plan. He somehow bought the rum, and I could somehow smuggle it in by strapping the flat curved bottle under my clothes. We were partners in crime.

As the song goes on the Pirates of the Caribbean ride, "Yo ho, yo ho, a pirate's life for me." And it was by far my favorite ride in Disneyland, boats riding in the bayou, the 600,000 gallons of splashing water, the sights and sound of pirates, and the animated animals and birds. And "Aye, aye, captain", a good little pirate I will be, setting sail on a swashbuckling voyage with my band of pirates led by Captain Hook. I taped the flask-like curved bottle of rum on my inner thigh, concealed it under my skirt, and secured it firmly between my legs.

After passing muster at the checkpoint with Disney security, I awkwardly waddle on like a penguin. The masking tape is bunching up and now the bottle is slipping down my sweaty little leg. I make it to the first pit stop, the ladies' restroom near the park entrance. Finding an open stall, I yelped in pain as I pulled off the masking tape and placed the bottle into my purse. Walking out, I feel a sticky mess between my thighs. The first punishment for my devilish illicit behavior.

My band of pirates await me and cheer my success, "Argh, Matey." Captain Hook asks "Where be me rum?" Our captain buys us four big colas in wax-coated cups. We find a secluded spot, a rest area surrounded by shrubbery and trees, our hidden pirate cove. There's a large enough bench for all of us pirates—two mateys and two young wenches. Captain says, drink some cola to make room for the rum and we obey his order. He pours each of us a generous shot or two. Like good pirates, we take a few swigs of our rum. But to our surprise, two intruders appear through a break in the trees, walkie-talkies cinched to their belts.

Oh no, they must be the Disney Police! I think and so do the others. In a panic, we quickly stand up and start to walk away, when they issue a command, "Stop, wait up." Foolish kids that were, we tossed our nearly full drinks into the bushes. The smell of rum was incriminating enough and before we could run, our brave Captain surrendered our ship of fools.

Two hours later, we are still in a Mickey and Minnie Mouse holding cell along with other deviants and miscreants. We're called to Donald Duck's desk for a good quacking. "Which one of you carried in the alcohol?" I gulp and fess up. "It was me."

"Oh boy, oh boy, oh boy! But where did you hide it?" The duck garbles. And now I'm really embarrassed. "Between my legs," I whimper. He retorts, "Sufferin soccatash!".

Captain Hook defends his wench. "It's not her fault. I told her to bring in me bottle of rum."

Up comes a big dog with a sloppy walk and baggy clothes. "My name is Captain Goofy, Goofy. Howdy! How ya' doin'? Are ya' havin' fun? You're not drunk, so, I'll let ya' go. Ya' might even have time for some rides."

We never got our photos taken. Just practiced our skills in the arcades and shooting galleries. And, for laughs, we made it to the Pirates of the Caribbean. And I sing along, "Yo ho, yo ho, a pirate's life for me." That song still sticks in my head. An earworm.

I tell Jim my long-winded story and he says, "Booze in your knickers? Bad Joann."

JIM: LIFE WITH JOANN IS NEVER DULL. THE NEXT DAY we were off to Universal Studios, chased by a large fake shark accompanied by the famous Jaws theme music. We drive in a tram past the Psycho motel site on a hill. The Great Hulk entertained us with other film heroes and villains in a large theater. I was amazed at how something up close and fake-looking could be transformed in any film. I saw it as a metaphor for the Soviet Union which up close does not look as good as the propaganda says. When we get home Dody asks "Did you have a good time, Chris? Isn't Universal Studios fun?" Chris aka Jim says it was great.

A new day dawned, and Knotts Berry Farm awaited the English invasion. I am pleased the rides did not have such long lines as Disneyland. We sailed down a steep incline into a water splash in a large plastic log and got soaked. I learned Joann likes roller coasters. This is not good. I have a fear of heights. I looked around, this one was not too high, so I agreed to ride. Although it is not super high, I failed to see that it has a corkscrew in the track that shoves everybody upside down through a loop. The ride goes around a couple of times. I did manage to keep my breakfast down. Maybe it was just the California heat rather than the cold sweat of fear on my fevered brow as we disembarked.

Overall, I enjoyed a wonderful first time in California. I met an old poodle called Buttons whom the family frequently calls Butt-hole. After a few days, I think I am lucky they call me Chris.

My name has always been a problem. My surname Mead meant in school I was "Weedy Mead". I enjoyed that nickname, NOT. My small family agreed with my mother's insistence to call me James. Joann and everybody else call me Jim. My mother's desperate rearguard action was because my grandmother named a series of cats Jim. Mummy was not pleased with this abbreviation of my name. A cat also figured in Dody's family. They had the largest most gentle cat who appropriately is called Mr. Softie.

My future mother-in-law is a superb cook of Italian food. I get brownie points for saying how much I love Italian food. Everyone I met was very welcoming, I despair in learning all those names. Finally, I was put out of my misery. I am told that Chris was Joann's former British boyfriend whom Dody had met. I guess it is one of those instances, where they talk the same and are both English, so it was easy to confuse their names.

Americans I met put up with my heavy London accent, and I realized on the Denver plane that people did not always understand what I said. A couple of years later Dody told me she and Fred, her husband, had a hard time. They could not get coherent meaning from many sentences in rapid London accent, that emerged from my mouth. On the plane, I pledge to myself. I will have to slow down my speech and use American English where possible as I go solo across the country.

When I land in Denver, I will execute a plan I will use elsewhere in America and the UK. Every airport had a Hertz desk that was easy to find. My little red Russian driving license may have some use outside the Soviet Union at least this is my theory. One of Joann's relatives kindly provided me with a Hertz membership card. The routine was simple. Get off the plane and search out the Hertz rental desk. I produce my Russian license (the only car driver's permit I have!) when the Hertz representative asks me for my driving credentials. Brows are furrowed so they cannot read the Cyrillic writing. They had to take my word I was a legal car driver somewhere. The person at Hertz in Denver did ask me why there were no dates on the license. My younger self assures him that Russian licenses are good forever. This left out conveniently that this "forever" is only while I worked in Russia, but why complicate things with that little detail in Colorado? Luckily the license did have my picture even if the Hertz person cannot read the Russian.

I could not believe my luck in Denver when they gave me a brand-new Toyota Supra with 125 miles on the odometer. Thank you, Uncle Dilly, one of the few relative's names that stuck with me from my California trip. That Hertz membership card gave me premium rides! The automatic Toyota sports car was a huge step up from my humble green stick-shift Zhiguli in Moscow.

Denver looks like many cities. I am not impressed enough to spend time there. After all, I am a London city boy, I fancy a trip to the American countryside. I can see the Rocky Mountains and an Interstate seemed to be going toward those mountains. The idea is to keep an eye on my watch and take an exit when four hours have elapsed. I thought this would be a reasonable time for my return ride to Denver airport for an afternoon flight. I take the exit to Colorado Springs and book into my first motel. This Colorado motel has a restaurant, so breakfast and dinner are within easy reach. What I love about American motels is the brochures at the reception. I can find out about possible sights and adventures in the local area. I went trout fishing in a pond and got a horrible sunburn. The next day to avoid more sun I decided on a drive up Pikes Peak. As I stood on the summit, I remembered that I was now as high as Lake

Baikal, in Siberia deep. Siberia is a place I visited last winter on the Trans-Siberian railroad. Early the next morning I drove back to the airport and reluctantly returned my car to Hertz.

My second United flight brings me to O'Hare International in Chicago. No Hertz car this time, Gene, now the ex-principal at the Moscow Anglo-American School, picks me up at the airport. The first night I was taken to a high school basketball game. This time, I am only a spectator. Thankfully, this is not the teacher-student basketball nightmare I had in Moscow. Gene reminds me I will not flatten some unsuspecting student on the court, throw air balls, or have my glasses broken.

I learned another new fact about large American cities like Los Angeles and Chicago, they are spread over a wide area. We drove to Chicago city center for Chicago deep dish pizza. It took over an hour on the expressway to get from the suburb where I stayed. In the case of Los Angeles, it was several years and multiple Westchester visits before I even saw downtown Los Angeles. Fate had it my first trip to downtown LA was to watch the LA Kings play Russia's Red Army hockey team. The Kings won, Go USA!

After a short Chicago visit, I am on the last United flight to Upper New York State. The Hertz rental and my trusty Russian license routine work again. I think my motel is not far from my destination. A walk after dinner was educational. Two young Americans decide to follow me. I suspect they are not looking to be friendly Intourist city guides. Joann could have told me that walking in some American urban areas is a good idea, NOT. It certainly was a sharp contrast to the streets in 1980 Moscow. That city had police everywhere and I never felt threatened as I did that evening. A brisk walk back to my motel room seemed very much in order. I decided a taxi in the morning would get me where I was going. I cannot trust my navigation skills in this part of town. My evening stroll convinced me that stopping and asking for directions when lost is a bad idea.

The reason for this trip is for one of my Moscow responsibilities. I oversee school technology. I have arranged to visit a school district's Audiovisual department. I am given a full tour. They have the equipment I can only dream about in Moscow. My technology storeroom in Moscow is an elephant's graveyard. This is where technology comes to die. Some stored equipment lacks bulbs and other spares that could easily revive them. But most broken equipment deserves a decent funeral rather than accumulating dust. A tasteful funeral I performed several times. In 1979-80 Moscow, I always bought new equipment with enough spare bulbs and other consumables to last a few years. I purchased American equipment, and we ran them on transformers because of the voltage difference. We did not have access to Russian equipment.

After the tour, there is an offer for international schools like mine. In 1980 the offer was to mail videotapes of American children's programs. The red flag was when the offer included programs like Sesame Street.

"Isn't copyright a problem," I ask politely.

I am thinking of Sesame Street which I was told could be sent to Moscow. Cue, thunder and lightning. Count von Count can count numbers, he is counting his royalties! The Count does not like the number Zero. The Count is not free. Cue, more thunder and lightning.

No, I am assured. "After all the videos are going to the Soviet Union and it is for educational use." Russia and the Soviet Union always had a reputation for stealing films, books, and technology. Maybe this American outfit thought as the Soviet Union ignored copyright so could they.

Joann and I return to Moscow together having visited my parents in England. I had fewer relatives to parade for Joann. My mother and Joann got on well, something that continued until my Mum's death. Joann lived in England for four years, it is less of a culture shock for her than America was for me.

Joann will be back teaching Middle School hands-on Science. The teacher's notes say it replicates what scientists do. Joann thinks it should be called "Soppy Science". In practice, Joann spends hours setting up experiments to replicate what scientists did years ago. Soppy is what the kids thought when many of the hours spent on experiments failed to produce the desired result. Kids quickly understood the problem, "Why don't you just tell us the results?" Personally, I enjoyed Soppy Science. I destroyed Joann's lesson with small wooden trucks trundling down an inclined plane. I encouraged the kids to wager on the trucks and mayhem ensued. I thought SAPA science was supposed to be fun? However, I beat a hasty retreat when I saw Joann's thunder-laden look. I'm ready for year two in Moscow with the accidental kindergarten teacher, me, promoted to Grade Six. More living in Russia experiences to look forward to. We were oblivious to the life change about to take place when fate intervened.

ДВАДЦАТЬ ТРИ

TWENTY-THREE

BIG BIRD AND BABA YAGA

JOANN: IN THE FALL, AFTER OUR JOURNEY AROUND the world, I'm no longer the same person I was a year ago. Nor do I know who I will be next year. Know thyself. Yeah, right. Who really understands their biased take on themselves? It's funny how we recall things, no two people have the same perceptions. How Jim sees our world and what went on between us and around us seldom echoed my own sensitivities, or more often, insensitivities. What went on in my brain and what went on in his brain were often poles apart. Some things never change.

I remember a winter night the previous year when eight of us teachers piled into the school van for an evening of skating on the icy walkways of Gorky Park. On most winter nights, the flooded, frozen trails were well-lit. But as it happened, it was the coldest night of the year and all the lights in the sprawling park had been turned off. The winding pathways were shrouded in eerie darkness. The young and fearless of us coursed off in different directions. I paired up with two other women. Together we negotiated our way through an unfamiliar maze, snaking through the frozen blackness of night. Gliding on blades along unfamiliar paths in this foreign, forbidden land was exhilarating.

An hour or more passed when we came across what looked like a statue. On closer inspection, we found a guy anchored in a snowy side-bank. Trying to free his buried skates, he trudged laboriously, struggling towards us, slogging and tromping out of the frozen snow. It was Jim, shivering from the cold. He'd attempted a sport he had never tried in new hockey skates he had never worn before. We flanked and propped him up, then found our way to an Olympic size ice rink where we met up with the others.

No. It was not love at first sight. It's funny how first impressions can be.

I reflect on the summer evening in Kyoto, Japan at a restaurant on the Kamogawa River. Jim says the river was a sewer, but I beg to differ. We dined on a wooden terrace and sat on floor mats under a low table. After eating tempura and drinking Kirin beer, Jim asked me if I would marry him. Surprised by his unexpected question, I thought that, if I said yes, I could somehow get out of it later. I'd never said yes to anyone, although others had asked because I always thought of proposals as entrapment. I was pretty good at getting out of commitments of any kind. So, I crossed my fingers behind my back and said yes.

After traveling 25,000 miles around the world, we are back in Moscow. While standing in the front of my classroom, I thought a rambunctious boy was making a noisy commotion. I scowl at him as a warning but notice that he and the other kids are covered in grey-white chalky dust.

One of the girls pipes up, "Don't look at him, he didn't do anything." Rightly so in his defense. Looking up, I see that chunks of ceiling plaster had come crashing down. Some kids pointed up to the pot-holed ceiling while others brushed debris off their clothes. Those worst affected stood up and shook their heads like wet puppies.

I asked, "Is anyone hurt?" Luckily everyone appeared to be intact. No bodies buried under the rubble or sprawled lifeless on the floor. I look over the kids for signs of blood, then inspect the ceiling for cracks. The girl who chided me volunteered to tell the office staff what happened. She sprints out of the room and down two flights of stairs. Meanwhile, we big kids push our desks to the room's perimeter, hoping the remaining plaster is sufficiently stuck. Our assistant principal arrives, scrutinizes the powdery pile of plaster, and returns with the Russian janitor to clean up the mess.

Hmmm. The sky is falling, or at least a ceiling. Does that mean what I think? Was it an omen for what's to come? Or maybe just a metaphor for what lies ahead. Will my whole world come crumbling down on me?

The kids shelter in the auditorium for the rest of the science lesson. That afternoon, I braved the disaster area and sort through science paraphernalia in the storage room next door to my classroom. A small sturdy woman dressed in stained plasterer attire shows up with a ladder. She's wearing a worn, once-white jumpsuit and an apron full of trowels, plaster knives, a hawk (not a bird), and buckets. On her head rests a pleated puffy bonnet that looks more like a ragged toque blanche, a white chef's hat. By Soviet standards, she quite expertly patched the ceiling. I'm hoping it will last through the school year.

In the fall, I returned to playing Platform tennis, it was too early for Broomball. I sign up for the Russian "Keep-fit" sessions, going "round and round the garden, like a teddy bear". In October, our keep-fit drill sergeant weighs everybody and I've put on two pounds. I'm surprised by the weight gain, no wonder I felt sluggish. And then "I'm late, I'm late, for a very important date." But I don't know why, so I visited a U.S. embassy doctor.

Jim was in the kitchen cooking when I arrived at my apartment. I'd visited the doctor that day for what I thought was a minor problem. But he wanted to do a test. My diagnosis came back quickly, and I was rewarded with a bottle of pills. I pointed to the pills on the kitchen countertop.

"Is this what he prescribed?" Jim asked, without reading the label. "Do you have something?"

"Yeah, I guess you would say that I have something." I couldn't resist a smirk. "Look at this, read it." I pointed to the label on the super-charged multivitamins.

Jim looked confused. It took a while for him to question the significance. "So, what are these for?"

"I'm pregnant," I said, matter-of-fact. I look up to see his reaction. "Those are prenatal vitamins."

He gasped, he squealed, and he cried as he hugged me. It was a cross between happiness and hysteria. I was still in shock over the diagnosis. Pregnant in Moscow as a foreign quasi-diplomat would have its challenges. Mostly, at this point, unforeseen.

JIM: PROBABILITY IS A BITCH! EVERY WEEK, MULTI-

tudes of people buy lottery tickets. Let's call that weekly purchase Event A. Somewhere in the sequence of Event A's, buying tickets, someone will win. Let's call it Event B. When will Event B happen? It could happen anywhere in that sequence of lottery ticket buying. The point of my story is not that random people win lotteries. All ticket buyers hope that Event B (winning) will happen to them, but nobody can say with certainty when it will happen. What comes next is very much Event B.

It is early evening in October, and Joann comes in the door. I am in the kitchen preparing our evening meal. Here comes Jim's stupid question one. "Did you see the doctor?' Stupid because Joann told me at breakfast that she had made an appointment to see the doctor. Joann politely ignored answering my first question. Jim's second dumb question, "Okay, what did the doctor say you have got?" I enquire. Joann produces two plastic pill containers; she rattles them like maracas. There is a hint of a smile that somehow, I miss. Final stupid question by Jim. "What did the doctor give you?"

Joann hands me the pills so I can read the label. The labels read prenatal vitamins. Okay, I am not too quick on the uptake but the light dawns. My Mum, as a family planning nurse, has always told me about the probability of failure of any birth control. It is rare, an Event B, but that probability of a rare event is a bitch if it hits you when not expected. This is not winning the lottery and acquiring extra wealth.

"We are going to have a baby, aren't we?"

Joann nods and she asks, "How do you feel about that?"

Have you noticed how when two people assess how someone feels? An initial reaction is to echo the question. I hope this will give me time to collect my thoughts into something coherent. I not only need to answer, I need to find the right answer. This is an Event B situation, and I need the right answer.

"How do you feel about that?" I blurt out playing for time the echoed question. I am worried because I sense that my answer must be right, so it echoes or reinforces Joann's feelings. This really is an Event B, a thunderbolt neither had expected. I will censor the numerous Event A's that have created the situation. Here is one hint, Event A was not buying lottery tickets!

How does she feel about this? The key question is, do we want to win this particular lottery? I press ahead. "I think it is wonderful, I'm happy." Another rare thing happens to me. I am notorious for keeping my feelings in check. Stiff upper lips are a genetic or cultural trait of all English people. I feel a light trickle of a tear down my cheek. Joann has been watching me like a hawk. "I'm happy too," she says. We held each other and savored that moment of unanimity. Like winning the lottery, sometimes probability can produce a life-changing event.

JOANN: THE EMBASSY DOCTOR SET UP A PROCE-
dure in Finland since my IUD didn't do what it should have done. The embassy

doctor warns me, "Pregnancy for American embassy staff is not advised. If you have problems or if anything happens to you, I can't take care of you. I have no hospital privileges in Moscow." In Moscow, hospitals were always identified by a number, although they might also have a name. So, I'd end up in No. 666.

The doctor is agitated. "I can't even visit you. You'll end up in whatever hospital they put you in. On your own!"

He was frustrated and felt out of control. He had no power to make decisions for his patient's care and worried that he couldn't help me if I had complications. He advised me to have my IUD removed. It was up to me to decide whether or not I wanted my pregnancy terminated in Finland. The clinic would provide whatever I wanted or needed. I realized that, at that moment, my life and Jim's might dramatically change.

JIM: WE HAD PLANNED A HALLOWEEN PARTY AT

Joann's apartment. She will tell the story. I just have a couple of things to say about Halloween or, as Christians call it, All Hallows Eve, the evening before All Saints Day. Christians are really good at commandeering a pagan festival and making it theirs. Pagans had celebrated the end of summer, with the harvest in, firing up a good bonfire and dressing up to ward off ghosts. Our metaphorical harvest is Joann's pregnancy. So, let's have a party.

JOANN: I'D INVITED FRIENDS I KNEW BUT RECOG-

nized only half the people who showed up. Few Russians knew about Halloween, and even fewer celebrated it, but our Moscow friends arrived in fine form. More like a United Nations celebration, there were disparate groups from multiple countries—teachers, diplomats, journalists, photographers, dissident artists, and refuseniks—mostly in disguise. Our invited friends were four Americans, three British, three Canadians, two Australians, two New Zealanders, one Bulgarian, and three Russians. Our Russian friends brought more of their Russian friends and others, anonymous people from who knows where, trickled in. Unrecognizable to me, they could have been anybody. Perhaps some were friends of friends, others were likely spooks and spies, masters in the art of disguise and deception. Were they CIA or KGB? Probably both.

There's a universal mystique around assuming secret identities. No longer yourself, you can role-play. You become your alter ego or a fictitious character, act and perform, and the event is your stage. And everybody just wanted to have fun. There would be no booze for me, I had other things on my mind. Dressed as Big Bird, Sesame Street loomed in my future. I looked like a chicken ready to lay an egg, which I would do in the coming months. My trusty Rollei captures photos of people as they perform, acting in imperfect caricatures. Language barriers do not matter when more spectating than conversing is going on. Let the circus begin!

People dressed up, mostly out of character, and some are parodies of themselves—an authentic-looking Russian czarist hussar, an oriental gentleman and his geisha companion, a naughty French maid, a big pink bunny, a *Beriozka* queen, a sexy black kitten, and an evil black witch. A flasher in a trench coat and a shrouded eastern dancer both stripped down to their underwear. And who were the odd wig-wearing cowboy couple? Not the infamous CIA agents, were they? Our two photographer friends, a hairy bare-chested Russian and a pipe-smoking Bulgarian, were dressed up as caricatures of themselves. Assorted other party animals donned masks and props, but the best was a shirt created by Sasha, Alexander Kalugin. Few people are capable of seeing what images he could see. I guess you would call him a visionary.

Sasha's wife Tamara brought a group of girlfriends, one very pregnant, but none were in costume. Halloween was not a familiar concept to Russians. Sasha had painted his costume, a heavy cotton linen shirt. On the front of the shirt is a bright shining sun with a huge grin and two love birds, all things happy and peaceful. Sasha's black-bearded face is highlighted with yellow, red, and blue streaks. On the back is Baba Yaga, a Russian fairy tale for children. She is scarier than the old evil witch in Hansel and Gretel. Baba Yaga, an ugly pointy-toothed old crone in a fuchsia dress, sits astride a sharp-toothed brown pig going to battle against her enemy, a reptile. Some say it's a political parody of Peter the Great who persecuted old believers. They called him a crocodile. Today, the Ukrainian army goes to battle against their enemy using drones called Baba Yaga to take out expensive T-90M Russian tanks.

Baba Yaga lives in a forest near Baikal where Jim might have seen her on his Siberian journey. Her house is built on four chicken legs, it spins and spins and never stops. Her emotions change with the wind. She can ride through the air, creating tempests as she goes, using her birch broom to sweep away her tracks. I know there will be no birch brooms or broomball tournament for me this winter. No booze party for me wrapping tape on my hooked-stick weapon. Nor would there be visits to the

Joann is Big Bird

Alexander Kalugin in Sunshine Shirt (Front)

Sasha's Baba Yaga Shirt (Back)

banya, the public bath, and beatings with birch branches in steam rooms. I have "a bun in the oven" and Baba Yaga can be a hungry villain, pushing people into her oven for a snack. But maybe she will protect me, as she sometimes does. She's also a guardian of the Water of Life fountain. She can sometimes be nurturing and wise, a babushka. Will she advise me on what to do with my baby? Or not. She's also known to steal, cook, and eat her victims, mostly children and babies!

Oh, Baba Yaga, please don't eat my baby!

Before leaving the party, Sasha literally "gave us the shirt off his back". He said it could be washed, but we never have.

Sasha's friend Sergei is one of the photographers who came to our party. In our bedroom, a nightstand lamp shines light on a black-and-white photo of Sergei's grandfather's attic. What looks like old relics of the past—broken furniture and chairs, strewn papers and books, and an old rocking horse—is a framed photo of Stalin propped up against a world globe. A relic best left discarded.

Sergei was a Jewish dissident "refusenik". Over time he collected friends in high places in various embassies. A year after we left, he married an American exchange student but was still denied an exit visa. He had graduated from the elite Moscow Institute of Physics and Technology and worked in the Soviet defense industry and Russian publishing houses. By 1982 his marriage disappeared and after 50 days on a hunger strike, he nearly disappeared too. For nine years Sergei persisted. A personal set of photographs and portraits prompted Mrs. Hartman, the wife of the United States Ambassador to Moscow (until 1987), to organize a small showing of his work in 1988. (New York Times, March 9, 1988). The next year, with a little help from his friends, he finally got his exit visa.

ДВАДЦАТЬ ЧЕТЫРЕ

TWENTY-FOUR

MARRIED IN MOSCOW?

JIM: **THE PARTY IS OVER IN EVERY SENSE OF THE WORD.**
A short break in the term means we can travel to Finland for several reasons. I am worried about a small procedure that the American doctor in Moscow has said should take place in Finland. The small procedure is the removal of Joann's IUD. Echoes of my Mum quoting percentages of failure with this contraceptive device are in my mind. Probability again raises its ugly head.

JOANN: **MY PREGNANCY WAS SOMETHING WE NOT** only accepted but wanted. We never mentioned our mutual trepidation about that little something that would change our lives. Nor did it matter that we were living in a foreign country that belonged to neither of us.

But first things first. The embassy doctor's first concern was my IUD contraceptive device. At a clinic in Finland, I could have it removed but not without risk. The risk is about a 50:50 chance that the baby will not survive. There are no guarantees in life. So, we took the chance and hoped for the best. We embarked aboard the Red Star Express, the overnight train from Moscow to Helsinki. In a sleeper car for four, we took one side, me in the bottom bunk, Jim on top. Later, we're joined by two burly men traveling to the Arctic Circle to work in oil and gas. They offered us vodka, typical of Russians, but we declined. It was a long night, but they were good company and well-behaved.

At the clinic, the Finnish doctor asked. "Do you want this baby or not? It's your choice." In 1980, women in the U.S. still had the right to choose. When I nodded wide-eyed and said "Yes", he chuckled at my enthusiasm. "But you must stay for three days in Helsinki, just in case there might be complications."

All went as well as we hoped. On Day 3, we decided we would get married. But nothing is ever as easy as it seems. The easy part was buying a wedding band. I still wear it today, a simple bamboo-style gold ring. On a map, we easily found the Courthouse where we could find out how to get married in Finland. Jim asked the secretary at reception our pressing question, showed our passports, and said we worked in Moscow at the diplomatic embassy school. She made a quick phone call.

"Oh, he isn't busy, you can see him."

Not knowing who "he" was, she escorted us to the most ornate office I'd ever set foot in. The chandelier, a hand-carved Victorian sofa, an elegant conference table, and wooden cabinets filled with beautifully embossed law books spoke to the eminence of the office inhabitant, the Supreme Court Justice. After introductions, feeling out of place in our blue jeans and jackets, we asked if we could get married in Finland as soon as possible.

"In Finland, a man does not need to be a resident, you could get married today." He looks at Jim. "But a woman," the friendly judge said as he turned his gaze at me, "must be a resident in Finland for three weeks." So, this dilemma put an end to the conversation. We didn't have three weeks of leisure to spare.

Back in Moscow, we visited the British embassy. No, they had no authority to perform marriages, but some other embassies could. Perhaps the British embassy in Kabul, Afghanistan may help us? Or maybe the embassy in Spain? This was all getting a bit confusing and complicated. There had to be an easier way.

At the U.S. embassy cafeteria, we asked our question to an American preacher while waiting for our "steak-cheese-onion". But no, he had no authority in Moscow to marry us, and in his opinion, he wouldn't marry us if he could because he "didn't think we were suited for each other."

Jim whispered, "Pompous ass."

In Moscow, we had another option. We could get married in a civil ceremony in a "Wedding Palace", usually in a baroque residence. In the Soviet Union, only ceremonies performed in a registry office or Wedding Palace could be "blessed" by the Communist Party. But with a five-month waiting time, I'd look like a party balloon ready to pop.

JIM: WE TAKE THE BIOLOGICAL COIN TOSS; HEADS WE

win a baby, tails we lose. All I know is the coin came up heads and we were now to be a potential family of three not just a couple. Our situation means we must be flexible in the ensuing months.

Teaching, like many occupations, has some obligations to society. The first obligation is, that you are expected to love or like children. This expectation is always there but it can manifest itself in many different and strange ways. Teachers can be motivated by their religion or social beliefs. Teachers may follow a well-known dictum, "Spare the rod and spoil the child." Whatever motivates a teacher, they say it is all for the children's good. The second social obligation is not to have a criminal record. I have been fingerprinted and criminal record checks in several school systems. A third social obligation is that the teacher is a role model for the children (and parents) to look up to. This can be a difficult one. It was true years ago that female teachers in America were expected not to marry. If they did marry, they would lose their teaching jobs. However, like all societal norms, they change over time. Nobody has said anything about the unmarried American teacher, working in Moscow, who is pregnant. But I suspect the foreign community telegraph has been buzzing with opinions.

But now a new challenge has appeared on our problem horizon. How do we get married in a foreign country like Russia? The British and American embassies gave us varied advice on our little dilemma. But we hoped we could somehow fumble to some marriage that would satisfy the Moscow diplomatic rumor mill.

After our Finland trip, I am invited to have lunch with my London Times correspondent friend, Michael, and his wife. This lunch provides an offer for our marriage problem and a resolution of our summer mystery adventure in Nakhodka.

It does not take a genius to see why my friend's wife is making me an offer. She tells me "I have a friend who is a priest in one of the many Christian orthodox sects. It is an accident of history that his church is allowed by the Soviets to preach to Russians in his congregation." She continues. "More to the point, he recently bought an English version of the orthodox wedding ceremony and is keen to try it out. How do you feel about a church wedding? It would be a good idea for you and Joann to have a wedding soon."

This is a woman with her ear adjusted to the community telegraph. We would be foolish not to take the obvious hint. "Let me know after Joann and you have talked. I will set it up and you can meet my friend the priest. Among many languages, he speaks English."

"I will ask Joann when I go home and let you know."

Michael takes over by explaining Joann's mystery detention in Nakhodka that summer. Like all Moscow correspondents, he has sources and likes to piece together any story. He tells me that while Joann was sitting locked in a room and I was pretending everything would be fine on a convenient sofa, the telephone lines to Moscow were busy.

"There were urgent calls to the Soviet Foreign Ministry, the American Embassy, and the British Embassy. Your little trip created a minor diplomatic incident. Luck had it that it was clear that the travel was arranged by the British embassy's Russian local hire staff. She had assumed the two tickets she purchased for you were for two British citizens. She failed to ask who you were traveling with. The Americans had made it clear they knew nothing of any American traveling to Nakhodka. I suspect the error by the Russian staff at the British Embassy meant the Foreign Ministry would not like to bring attention to any Russian mistakes. Joann did not know Americans were only permitted to leave or enter from three places in the Soviet Union: Moscow, Leningrad, and Kiev."

Michael has a big grin which I now share. "Joann didn't have a clue there are only three places in the Soviet Union where Americans can enter or depart." So, I guess we were lucky to get away with it. The same three-city restriction applies to Russians entering and leaving America. The mystery of Joann disappearing and being held for two hours is now solved.

Now, there is a little problem to overcome before we say yes to the Christian orthodox wedding. We planned to have a Soviet Wedding Palace event in the Spring. The advantage is that our marriage would be legal. Pregnancy has changed that plan even if it had been possible in practice. So, our planned Spring wedding is out. We let Michael's wife know we wanted to get married. By the end of November, we'd be "married" in the eyes of the Moscow community. Any marriage would be a good thing as several kids at the school start asking questions as they always do. Why has Joann, their teacher, gained weight? Out of the mouth of babes (comes truth) I believe is the appropriate phrase. We did have to deal with some relatives who had planned to visit in the spring when we married but we can get around that.

JOANN: SO HERE WE WERE ON A FRIDAY, SET TO GET married on Sunday in the Antioch Orthodox church in Moscow. With neither of us particularly religious—me, a lapsed Roman Catholic from Los Angeles, and Jim, a lapsed Anglican from London—neither of us felt conflicted. On Saturday we could not get in touch with any of our friends. Their preparations were a whirlwind of ad hoc efforts by everyone, from flowers to food to finding the way to the church. Their spontaneity and generosity meant there was little that Jim and I had to do, it all just seemed to happen without us. We were merely actors in this story of a most unusual wedding.

Our friends Kareema and Michael arranged the wedding with the Orthodox emissary of the Antioch Church. Under the Soviet Union's separation of church and state, religious wedding ceremonies were not legally valid. But their friend, the orthodox priest, told them his church had been granted diplomatic status as a holdover from Czarist times. The priest usually conducted services in Russian, Arabic, and Greek but also spoke French and English. He had an English translation of the official Orthodox wedding ceremony, printed in America. He had never used it but would be happy to try it out.

The small Orthodox church, adorned with old icons, was now filled with an entourage of friends from the British, American, Canadian, and Australian embassies. The Lebanese priest, draped in a satin brocade robe of emerald green and gold, was flanked by Russian deacons and servers. Our Jordanian friend lent me her wedding gown, a white velvet kaftan. Her English husband was best man. Our bridesmaid is Anne, our Scottish friend. Both held long tapered ceremonial candles that lit up the ceremony. Curious Russian women wandered in to see what was going on. A Bulgarian cameraman, married to a Canadian, took kilometers of film.

The dignified and scholarly priest shifted easily between English, Russian, and Arabic. He directed everyone on what to do. The wedding ceremony and rituals were universal in their messages. The three sips of wine from the shared cup, the mutual exchange beckoned the doubling of joy, the dividing of sorrow. The sharing of hopes. The sharing of dreams.

The priest whispered as he placed two brass and velvet crowns on our heads, "Be

Married in Moscow in 1980

Our Moscow Wedding with Maid of Honor Anne

careful, they are very heavy." I wondered if the weight of the crown signified the gravity of the vows. But then the priest swapped the crowns three times, back and forth between Jim's head and mine. I was struck with fear as we processed around the altar table, afraid my crown would fall off or my white lace scarf would ignite from the burning flame of my bridesmaid's candle. But we made it through the ceremonial first steps of our married life.

Snow is on the ground as we left the church and transitioned to more secular rituals. Following Russian tradition, a baby doll was tied to the front of the car. Dressed in pink, it accurately prophesied the baby girl to come. On the balustrade of Lenin Hills, there were more traditional wedding photographs overlooking the city of Moscow along with other Russian newlyweds. A warm reception with our friends followed with copious toasts of champagne.

A beautifully written, stamped marriage certificate signed by the Antioch Dean in Moscow and the Lebanese Ambassador immortalized our marriage ceremony. But the question now was, were we legally married in the eyes of the Soviet Union? For church weddings to be legal, they must be registered in the country where they are conducted. So, maybe we should try to register ours with the Soviet civil authorities?

Nothing ever goes as expected. No honeymoon was planned so we returned to my apartment. But how could we plan with only two days' notice before our wedding? The night of our wedding was cut short when at 5:00 in the morning, Kate and Tommy knocked at the door. "So, how was your honeymoon?" They chuckled as they greeted me. I'm dressed in my usual blue jeans style. "And where is the groom?" I lead them to our bedroom where Jim lies half-naked in bed. He's trying to find his glasses on the nightstand. Kate and Tommy grin at Jim and tease, "Sorry to sabotage your big night. We'll take good care of Joann."

We didn't want to miss our flight from Moscow to Bucharest, Romania. Four of us staff from the Anglo-American School headed for a planned Eastern Europe International School conference. Nothing ever goes to plan, but when you have no plans, then you really have nothing to lose. A spontaneous wedding, getting married not even one day ago, and I hadn't yet registered the reality of what just happened.

Bucharest was not a place I would have chosen for a honeymoon, even if I had Jim with me. Most of the time, I'm lost in a daze, meetings in the morning, and exploring the city in the afternoon. Bucharest in 1980 was a strict Communist state under the leadership of dictator Nicolae Ceaușescu.

One afternoon, the American head of the international school in Sofia, Bulgaria joined our group as we walked the Bucharest streets lined with poorly constructed Soviet buildings. As usual, I had my little Rollei and hoped for photogenic shots. A long queue of people waiting in line at a store with frozen vegetables captured my interest. For a minute I stopped and framed the image, thinking who in the West would wait for frozen peas? Yes, I knew it was one of those shots that Communist countries didn't want publicized on the other side of the Iron Curtain. Ken, Kate, and Tommy had walked on ahead. Our new American friend, George, paused behind me and pulled out his camera. I walk on, my camera in hand, when I see my friends ahead turn around, they're waving their arms and pointing in my direction. Yelling, "Look behind you at George!" I swing around and see George propped up by two burly, stout Romanian men. They'd taken his camera, grabbed him under his arms, and frog-marched him brusquely away.

Ken, Tommy, and Kate sprint over to where I'm standing. Stunned, but not surprised by what just happened, it's déjà vu all over again. Maybe the thugs thought it would look bad to nab a five-foot foreign woman. I'm feeling guilty, but I didn't fancy another amphibious march. Rivet! We're horrified that George has been abducted by who knows who, taken to who knows where, and for what reason. But I know the reason since I'm the culprit (Bad Joann) who disobeyed the Soviet rule. No taking photographs of people in lines. No revealing shortages of goods, foods, or otherwise. Because, according to the state-controlled media, there are no food supply problems in Romania or anywhere else in the Eastern Bloc. The message is clear. Shoot the contrarian messenger.

So, now what do we do? Contact the U.S. Embassy in Bucharest. Protecting Americans is the job of the Consular Section. History teacher Tommy took the lead and made the call. A few hours went by, with back-and-forth diplomacy between Consular staff and whoever their Romanian contacts were. Hand swatting, arm twisting, and other threats or promises might have been made, but I wouldn't know. Likely George was sequestered away in some small closet. I knew the drill.

Eventually, two U.S. embassy staff, a man and a woman, delivered George to us looking somewhat disheveled from the manhandling by the Romanian secret police. The ruffians must have been tailing us, watching our every move. George opened his camera which was now minus his film. Bewildered and subdued, he seemed relieved. I knew the feeling that comes from an unanticipated detention. My Nakhodka nightmare, still fresh in my mind, left me feeling repentant for his diplomatic disaster. The thugs thought it best to leave the little lady alone. Lucky for them since I would not have gone quietly. I didn't need to be headline news, "American Newlywed Spends Honeymoon in Romanian Jail." A communist prison is no pokey in Disneyland. Forever in Neverland, Bad Joann never learns.

Back in Moscow, the question remained. Are we legally married in the eyes of the Soviet Union? Sometimes the simplest solution is best. Six weeks later, it is Christmas. We flew to Los Angeles. The next morning, we piled into two cars with my family and arrived late-night in Las Vegas. "Should we eat breakfast or get married first?" We asked when we gathered the next morning. Everyone agreed. "Get married."

A quick visit to the justice of the peace was all we needed. The local magistrate stood at a counter wearing a string tie, unlike today where wedding chapels and Elvis themes are the norm. Our marriage certificate recorded in Clark County, Nevada is the legal one. It states our domicile as Moscow, Soviet Union.

ДВАДЦАТЬ ПЯТЬ

TWENTY-FIVE

GOODBYES AND BABY ARRIVALS

JOANN: AS TIME WENT ON, EVERY TIME THE AMERican embassy doctor saw me, my blood pressure ticked upward. More and more alarmed, he was adamant. "You must leave!" The Moscow winter diet didn't help with the lack of fresh fruit and vegetables. But the good doctor supplied me with enormous prenatal vitamins boosted with iron.

Pregnant in Moscow is not for a faint-of-heart foreigner, especially if you have a "condition." My chronic indigestion at six months pregnant only got worse and I continued to devour the British commissary antacids, Rennies. Today's antacids are calcium carbonate, but some early formulas had sodium bicarbonate. My blood pressure continued to soar—too much sodium is not good, especially for a woman carrying a fetus. At seven and a half months pregnant, most airlines don't want you on board, but I wouldn't tell and they didn't ask.

In Moscow, the Russian doctors were sometimes quite good, but they were generally hampered by the lack of medications and even basic sanitation. I remember what Marcia told me about Russian medicine and what happened to her friend. "A grad school buddy of mine went to Saint Petersburg (Leningrad) for a year. He was writing his dissertation. He was the resident director of a study abroad program. Fortunately, he had an associate director who was able to take over for him when his kidney went bad. He woke up one morning with a really terrible pain in his back and took himself to the local *poliklinika*. They asked him a million questions, laid hands on him and felt around for an interminable amount of time and pronounced: it's your kidney; you have X (I can't remember what exactly they diagnosed); the kidney has to come out; we'll set up the surgery.

He said no thanks and hopped onto the next train to Helsinki, Finland. He checked into a beautiful, shiny, new hospital there, with the latest modern equipment. They did a mess of imaging and bloodwork and said: it's your kidney; you have Y; it has to come out; the Russians are a bunch of untrained monkeys, so they got the diagnosis wrong. He said fine, take the kidney. But, no, they couldn't because there was a doctors' strike.

In despair, he got on a plane and went home to Chicago. There, the American doctors did a bunch of tests and said that they weren't sure what was wrong, but the kidney definitely had to come out. He said fine, and they did the surgery. He said that he remembered coming out of the anesthesia and looking up woozily into the eyes of his surgeon, who said four brief words to him: "The Russians were right!" They were pretty good diagnosticians (the Finns notwithstanding), but people had a bad way of dying of infection after surgery since they were lacking in basic disinfectants."

So, now I have a decision to make about staying in Moscow. Did I really want to take more risks with my pregnancy? Throw the dice and hope for a winner? If I stay in Moscow, I'll end up in a local hospital. But from the horror stories I'd heard, it would not be my number one choice. Russian hospitals were not known for their hygiene. A pregnancy story from an Australian Embassy friend really put the frighteners up. She worked at the school as a local hire, her husband was an Australian Embassy naval attaché. Early in her pregnancy she had an emergency and ended up in any one of the many numbered hospitals. The Soviet tradition was to number their hospitals. I'll call it No. 66. She confided, it was a messy miscarriage and "they didn't even bother to clean me." Anyone expecting Western standards of medicine and hygiene found Soviet medicine wanting. Visitors are not allowed, so Russian family and friends would load baskets hung out of windows with hygiene products like soap, clean towels, or bed linens. They might also include a special treat or packs of cigarettes that could be used to bribe hospital staff to change your bed. Socialized medicine did have one big advantage. At least you didn't leave the hospital with a big bill to pay.

I would soon say goodbye to my lovely man Jim. Unlike the friends and lovers you leave behind, there are those you keep and treasure. I hadn't anticipated leaving Moscow pregnant. It wasn't something I thought I wanted— until it just happened. And Jim was the gift that kept on giving. He started a new life for both of us and another life growing.

As a parting celebration, my friends from the school threw a baby shower. There were no brand-name shops for newborn babies, but some ordered unisex clothes from abroad or found locally knit little gems. Others found colorful wooden toys in local stores. The real treasures came from outdoor markets, the rynoks, with beautiful, oversized hand-painted Matryoshka dolls with babies and plaques with intricate illustrated Russian folk tales. Folk art in Moscow can be exquisite—so much better than any machine-made trinkets from the government-owned *beriozka* shops. But the irreplaceable treasures came from the Moscow community—the people I will always remember and the friends who reappeared in our lives so many years later.

JIM: IN THE SPRING OF 1981, THE END OF OUR SECOND

year in Moscow is coming. There is an important goodbye for me. Joann is now over seven months pregnant. I think she finds the growing bump making it increasingly difficult to move. Colleagues at the school helpfully extend an arm and haul Joann up the two flights of stairs.

Our last visit to Sasha and Tamara was memorable for several reasons. In the Summer of 1980, we told our families we were engaged. The idea was for everyone to arrive for the Moscow Wedding Palace ceremony in late March 1981. Fate intervened and our wedding took place much earlier that year without any family. My parents and sister plus Joann's sister and her family were coming for the now non-existent March wedding. They decided that both families would like to meet each other, and the travel was arranged so they could stay in the same Intourist hotel.

Joann is seven months pregnant and is about to leave in early April. I borrowed the school van to ferry seven visitors and Joann to different places. My tiny Zhiguli was not up to the job. Joann had trouble fitting herself behind the steering wheel, so her car stayed at the apartment.

We had a parting gift for Sasha and Tamara. Dody's kids carried two speakers, and the rest of the stereo was spread among the van's passengers. As I drove, my sister told a story about my parents and her. They were locked in their train car from Leningrad to Moscow. "Tourists like us are not allowed to mingle with Russians on the train."

When we reached the apartment block we piled into the elevator. As we ascended, we all kept silent. Sasha and Tamara had enough problems with the authorities and a large group of English speakers would get the neighbors talking. Moscow apartments are tiny, so we had to sit on beds in the front room as we enjoyed their hospitality of *zakuski* dishes. Sasha smiled as he saw my father. He mimics the hammer and chisel performance my father gave the last time they met.

On that last visit with Sasha and Tamara before Joann left Russia, they gave her an antique baby baptismal dress and religious icons with mother and child. They were wrapped up as gifts for our expected baby. How easily they parted with their precious treasures. We were sad to part and wished each other safe travels.

Today, Sasha's wondrous "illegal" paintings, etchings, and drawings decorate our walls. They sharply contrast with our Soviet Realism propaganda posters from the late 1970s. Luckily after the fall of communism and the Soviet Union, in the early 1990s, Sasha's dreams became real. He could buy art materials himself. Even more important, he held several public exhibitions of his work in prestigious art galleries in Europe and the US. After communism, he was allowed to travel and become an artist in residence at a couple of American universities. In 1996 and 1998, Sasha lectured on art and taught American students the art of etching. His graphic etching "Flight to the Monastery" is published on American editions of Bulgakov's novel "The Master and Margarita." The Zimmerli Art Museum at Rutgers, New Jersey holds over twenty of his works in the world's largest collection of Soviet nonconformist art. Grinnell College Museum of Art (Iowa) has a collection of Kalugin's early works. Not to mention the private collections, awards, and exhibits in Moscow where his art is now "legal". We were saddened to hear that Sasha, Alexander Kalugin, died in the Spring of 2023.

It is time for Joann to say goodbye to the school. Joann's doctor has told her she must leave Moscow when she reaches her seventh month of pregnancy. In addition to the variable level of medical care in Moscow, there is a bigger problem. I shall be diplomatic, something that is not always my nature. The Soviet health system was universal, but the quality of care could vary.

Glory to the Soviet People

Several important rules surround your parent's nationalities and where the baby is born. Joann is American and I am British, so our baby will be eligible for American and UK citizenship. We do not know our baby's sex. Sons born in Russia will technically be Russian citizens as well as American and British. Why is this a problem? If our baby is a boy born in the Soviet Union and finds themselves at eighteen in the Soviet Union, in theory, he could be called up to serve in the Soviet military. All males born in Russia are technically expected to serve their conscription. Imagine that a triple national American and Brit might be called up into the Russian military.

This seems to be a complication we do not need to have. In 1980 the Russian troops were serving in Afghanistan and dying in increasing numbers. Maybe that war will be finished but another could happen, so why take the chance? Our son would never be able to travel to Russia while they were of conscription age.

Joann will leave and have our baby in Margate, England. There is a bit of luck. Joann had taught in England for a few years and was given a National Health Identification number. I can only assume the hospital thought we were going to live in England, I was not there to ask. In 1981, the hospitals had a very different way of dealing with people using the health system. In 2023, hospitals have to be immigration officials. This is a task many medical staff resent, and the new stringent checks affect which patients they treat in the free national health system.

We are sitting in Sheremetyevo airport waiting for Joann's flight to Britain to be called. My mother, a former hospital ward sister, and Family Planning clinic nurse has arranged for her to give birth at a local Margate hospital. We said our goodbyes and she went into the departure lounge where I could not see her. As I sit there, I watch people, like most people do in airports. One plane on the tarmac is going to Vienna with its engines fired up. Suddenly, two armed guards frog march an orthodox Jew onto the steps of the plane. "I guess he is getting special treatment, maybe for being late?" I think to myself. I know this is not what is happening to the poor man. Outgoing people, especially Jews, leaving the Soviet Union and possibly emigrating to Israel get this "special" treatment.

Joann sat in the secure departure area and saw more of the old man's harsh treatment. She noticed his carry-on, an old brown leather briefcase, with his well-worn jacket and black fedora. Jewish, likely Hasidic, he wears the distinguishing sidelocks. Joann suspects he was strip-searched or at least interrogated after he was forcibly pulled out of line and taken to one of those favorite little security rooms. Time passed and the flight to Vienna had closed. Joann watched as two guards rushed him back to the gate, suspended by his arms, his feet barely touching the ground. He no longer had his old leather briefcase. He's disheveled and was generally manhandled. It is likely some of his possessions were "confiscated" as they searched through his luggage. At the very last moment, when the man's anxiety is at its highest, he is roughly taken to the aircraft. The plane door shuts, and it is a special Russian "*dosvidanya*" (goodbye) to the Soviet Union for him. It was not "*paka*" the Russian goodbye you use with friends.

At last, I see Joann walk across the tarmac to her waiting plane. This small person waddles alone in a large Finnish puffer coat and those ungainly blue moon boots. She struggles up the stairs and the aircraft door shuts. It will be two months or more before I see the love of my life. Phone calls are scarce. As I wait to see Joann leave, I realize that Joann has had trouble leaving the Soviet Union. The attempt to leave Nakhodka last summer had created a diplomatic incident. I want to make sure she gets on the plane safely. I sat there until I saw her board the plane taxi to the runway.

As I later sit in my empty apartment, I miss the smell of baking. Joann always told me that, unlike any other pregnant woman, she had absolutely no cravings when pregnant. She would tell anyone who asked, "I don't have any urges for pickles and ice cream." In our now over forty years of marriage, I've never had so many Joann-baked offerings as in the months before she left. We would keep the share price of Betty Crocker soaring during her pregnancy. The American commissary only offered pineapple upside-down cake or apple crumble cake. I remember getting either of these baked delights every night for approximately three or four months. However, our long happy marriage is because I have learned what all dutiful spouses say when told "I had no cravings when I was pregnant. Did I?" the correct reply is, "Yes, dear."

JOANN: BEFORE MOSCOW, I HAD TAUGHT IN LONDON,

England for four years in an American School. Luckily, my national health card in the UK was still valid. Jim's mom, a family planning nurse, thought the "teaching" hospital, about a twenty-minute drive from their home, might be the best option for delivering my baby. It was a clinical hospital near the southeast coast of England with Attending physicians, Consultants, residents, and interns. New techniques, methods, and drugs were trialed.

My first doctor's checkup in England echoed my last one in Moscow. I spent little time with Jim's mom and dad before being admitted to the hospital for bed rest. With about six weeks to go before my due date, I knew I'd be in for the long haul. But, luckily for me, I wouldn't end up in Moscow's hospital No. 666. Jim's kind parents looked after me and the national health system took care of my medical needs. Had I flown home to Los Angeles instead, not only would the flight be thirteen hours, but I might not have had medical insurance. Jim would finish his Moscow teaching contract in about eight weeks and we'd, hopefully, be in Jim's family home with our new baby in the beautiful Kent countryside.

As I lay in a hospital bed, in a country not my own, my blood courses through my veins at supersonic speed. Nearby is a Victorian seaside town with littered beaches and rundown arcades. An old rusty Ferris wheel and vintage roller coaster echo its dreary gothic past.

Like ducklings, a group of young interns and residents follow the Attending physician on his morning rounds. I'm the clinical specimen they regularly observe, spoken about but never to. "The American patient", I hear in hushed tones. A few weeks pass before the Attending decides my fate. My difficult pregnancy would not be allowed to take its natural course. "Induction". The physician announces to his ducklings. An induction, not as in a Hall of Fame, nor the magnetic heat of induction. But a birth induction forced by a chemical bombardment, an assault on my body meant to "shock and awe" and my baby subjected to a forced eviction from my womb.

I wake up in a postnatal room where, after delivery, new moms and their babies come and go. The hospital room feels more like a transit lounge after a turbulent flight. Most young moms are hurried on their way, but others are here for a long layover and I'm one of the latter. My baby girl lies in a plastic bassinet at the foot of my bed. She is bruised by forceps but otherwise healthy. Once joined together, we are now two beings on different trajectories.

I stand up to look at her, she's peacefully asleep. But I'm dizzy. My head pounds, it aches, and the room begins to spin. My heart beats hard. My arms and legs tingle. I'm weak and I know I'm not well. I return to my bed and lie back down. Somewhere nearby I hear the voices of nurses talking among themselves.

"Sister, what is the name of the drug given to the new mothers?" a student nurse asks. The nurses call the head nurse "Sister", but she's not a nun. Nor is she somebody's sister. I would never want her to be my sister. This Sister is arrogant, self-righteous, and, like Nurse Ratchet, very cold and bossy. And I could tell she disliked me from the start.

"We gave the mothers Ergometrine. It's being tested. The drug makes the uterus contract, constricts blood vessels…so there should be less bleeding." Sister reads from a textbook, "Ergot is a fungus that infects grain seeds, like rye." Sister checks her watch which hangs pinned to her uniform. "Read your textbook chapter." She sharply demands and departs.

"Ergometrine? Well, that's a mouthful." A young nurse says.

I hear giggles but nothing seems funny to me. I remember my college class, plant pathology, where I first learned about the toxic effects of ergot. The professor told the story of "Saint Anthony's Fire" with its deadly *danse macabre*. People hallucinated, they felt they were in hell.

My dark thoughts bring on a burning sensation. My leg muscles twitch. My blood vessels tighten. My blood speeds on a racecourse, out of control. It needs to slow down. It should have by now. A fiendish demon drives through my veins. A heavy hammer beats at my heart. The thump, thump, thumping gets faster. The whooshing in my head grows louder. And now I know why. It's LSD. It's the lysergic acid found in the ergot they gave me. Timothy Leary would never have prescribed it for expectant mothers.

My heart is pounding, my head is spinning, my brain is reeling, and my blood is surging. And then my blood begins to boil. I know I'm an experimental animal, a lab rat, a mouse, or a guinea pig. And no one has told me. And now I'm angry. I try to stand but I'm weak and shaky. I fall back on the bed, but I struggle to sit up. Two nurses enter the room. One is Sister.

I can hear my voice, I'm nearly screaming. "I feel horrible. It's that drug you gave me! Made my blood pressure surge. Why did you give it to me? Sister, you did this!"

Sister mumbles to the young nurse who then rushes out.

"You must calm down, dear. Lay down." Pushing me, she insists, but I refuse. "It's your fault," I tell her. "You did this….you did it….what are you doing?!"

Sister grabs hold of my arm, I see a long needle. The syringe is full, she stabs my skin and empties the contents. Then everything goes black. How quickly the lights go out and I'm descending into a dark place in a dark time.

I'm lost in a dream, or is it a nightmare? I conjure up images of medieval times. It's the Dark Ages. I'm in a monastery in France with monks from the clinical Order of St. Anthony. They opened a hospital to care for people like me. People with ergotism. They call the illness "St. Anthony's fire" or the "holy fire". They painted the walls red to reflect their patients' burning sensations, racked by fiery visions and diabolic hallucinations. Their convulsions, their seizures, and prickling sensations. Their manic dancing and delusional ranting.

In my nightmare, a monk in a black robe with a blue cross hand-feeds me wheat bread that only the rich can afford. Not the moldy rye bread eaten by the poor. The wheat grain in the bread is free of ergot fungus, unlike the rye. Almost miraculously, within days, I am better. Even in the Dark Ages during periods of war, destruction, and death, some light shines through.

I begin to stir and slowly awaken. I have no idea how long I've been out. The walls of the hospital are green, not red. Green to calm us, not the red that inflames. The lights are too bright for my unadjusted eyes, but a pretty young woman comes into focus. She's in the bed to my left. My baby girl still lies at the foot of my bed. The young mother's baby, a boy with a shock of straight black hair, lies on his belly in his bassinet. The young mother bolts upright in bed, her mouth wide open in fear as she peers at her baby boy.

"My baby's dead!" Her voice is full of dread.

I spring out of bed, sprint a few steps, and stare into the bassinet. The newborn baby lies flat, his head to the side. He looks a bit blue, so I move in closer. I peer at him, carefully looking for signs of life, and I wonder "Is he dead? He's not moving, or is he?" I watch and I watch. And then I see a flutter, his tiny chest moves, and he rises slightly. Relieved, but I'm irritated. I know I'm unwell. My head throbs, I'm spinning. I turn towards the young mom and angrily snap, "Your baby's not dead, he's breathing!"

The vertigo surges, and I collapse back onto my bed. Still riled up, I have little sympathy for the panicked young mother. She seems calmer but looks confused. But I've got my own problems. I'm often delirious during the comings and goings over the next days. Jim's mother visits as I recover and holds her sweet granddaughter. She'd attended the childbirth! They forged a deep bond in years to come.

JIM: SELLING STUFF WAS ONE OF MY PREOCCUPATIONS

as I left the Soviet Union and Joann is in England. I brought a serviceable British stereo system to Moscow. I saw this as how to get a few dollars for my departure. A chance meeting with a Russian recording artist led me to a possible buyer. That evening, I met an American woman who chain-smoked and drank prodigious amounts of espresso. A few weeks later she arrived at my British apartment with her Russian

Goodbye Jim's Green Zhiguli

partner. I learned she was a former student who had married a Russian and stayed. Unlike most foreigners, she had no access to the American embassy services and shops, so buying my stereo for her was a big deal. I remember our meeting as a little sad as she had aged quickly, and her life was not easy.

My two years in the Soviet Union were up and I had to dispose of my faithful Russian car. The "sale" of my Zhiguli involved a road trip of "only" 677 miles. My long Finnish trip was related to the lack of dollars I could bring out of the country. I had a wife and new baby waiting for me in England. We had no new job, so I wanted a small fund to tide us over. The British and Canadian embassies did not offer a service to unload or convert your Russian rubles. In Soviet times the Russian ruble was worthless outside the country. You recall I got my used car because the owners were leaving and wanted some real cash.

My Canadian friend Ken and I discovered that a certain Middle Eastern country would purchase our cars for US dollars. The catch was we had to get the vehicles to Helsinki and make the sale at their embassy. So, after school one Friday we take off heading North. We calculated the trip would take about twelve hours with a rest stop or two along the way and filling up with gas. Luckily this trip was during the Springtime, so the roads were devoid of snow. The road was good in most places and there were frequent truck stops we could use. I vividly remember our last Russian rest stop near the Finnish border among a dense forest. As we looked around this rest stop, to paraphrase Ronald Reagan "Once you have seen one fir tree you have seen them all." We had no idea about crossing the border. Luckily, our diplomatic plates and Russian visas seemed to do the trick.

We knew we were in Finland because instead of tarmac there were cinder roads until we reached the outskirts of Helsinki. Freeze-thaw makes for excellent pothole spelunking on tarmac roads. The cinders stand up better to the freeze-thaw weather conditions. Mid-morning we found the right embassy and parked in the forecourt. Dollars are given and I wave a fond farewell to my trusty green Zhig. At least, I thought, my little car might enjoy some warm climate in the coming years. Taxi to the airport and return to Moscow. I slept on the plane and what remained of the weekend before school on Monday.

JOANN: IT WOULD BE ANOTHER WEEK BEFORE JIM

could leave his teaching job in Moscow. On his first visit, he holds his baby girl, enthralled with her long arms and legs and amused at the furry lanugo that covers her pretty face. He soon took home his wife and new baby daughter.

Summer meant the glorious garden in Jim's family home was in full bloom. I heard something on the local radio news while caring for my newborn. A young mother had walked downstairs with her baby in the middle of the night. She opened the front door, crossed the street, walked out on the sandy beach, and into the dark sea.

Later that day, one of the other mothers called me. We'd met in the hospital transit room. I was shocked, but not completely surprised when she told me, "The young mother and her baby were in the bed next to you."

Eventually, the mother's body washed up on the shore. Her dark-haired baby boy was never found. It was a dark time for some, the loss of a mother, the loss of a baby. She danced to Saint Anthony's sad dance of death, with her baby into the sea. There were glimmers of hope for others, new lives, and brilliant sparks of light. Even in dark times, some things glow. Sometimes even if it is the only hope.

JIM: READERS HAVE PROBABLY GATHERED THAT JOANN has a personal dislike for rules. She does like to set rules for the rest of mankind, especially yours truly. Joann announced her rule that our daughter should not taste chocolate or other sugary treats in her early life. My mother and I look at each other and Mum has a fleeting smile. Our daughter is resting peacefully in Joann's arms. My father suddenly produces a small "chocolate button" just the right size for a two-month-old child to suck. He sits there with chocolate all over his fingers and Gina has the biggest grin, probably a first, on her face. Gina has maintained a love of chocolate to this day.

After forty-plus years of marriage, what is the probability that everything would work out? Probability as I said before can be a bitch but sometimes probability produces some wonderful things.

I have always thought our daughter, Gina, has a slight stubborn streak. Maybe it came from hanging in there because she wanted to be born. Who knows where the stubborn streak comes from? Joann and I insist, like everyone, that we are flexible and never exhibit a stubborn streak. It is other people who are stubborn, never us!

AFTERWORD

JIM: OUR TWO YEARS IN THE SOVIET UNION WERE A life-changing event for both of us. I left England and the culture I was born into. I would never return, except to visit. I will live among strangers and different cultures for the rest of my life. I suspect my introduction to American culture was skewed by my West Coast California wife, Joann. She followed a different path having lived among strangers in England before she arrived in Russia.

As the sage from Monty Python would say, "And now for something completely different." That is my thought as the plane descends to land in Harare, Zimbabwe. We have switched from the snow of Moscow to the heat of Africa. Admittedly it is winter in the Southern Hemisphere; it is only sixty degrees.

Joann, our two-month-old daughter Gina, and I have embarked on a new adventure. Our daughter is asleep as she is already a seasoned air traveler. We flew from London to Los Angeles and back to meet her American relatives when she was five weeks old.

As we make our final descent to Harare, I point out a large fire and smoke we can see out the cabin window. Later I read in the newspaper that an explosion at an ammunition dump had mysteriously caught fire two days before our arrival. I am not worried, but we were sad to miss Bob Marley's Independence concert. Joann and

I feel 'everything will be alright.' We are the "Three Little Birds" as Bob sang, we are ready for a new adventure.

We land and are welcomed along with other passengers by the Deputy Education minister. He tells us he is happy to meet new teachers who were to become citizens of the newly independent country. "Excuse me minister, great to see you but this was advertised as a three-year contract when I interviewed in London."

As a skilled politician he avoids my statement, "How old is the little girl?

Joann replies, "She's just over two months old, minister."

"I think we will be rethinking your assignment, Mr. Mead. We had you teaching in an isolated rural school out in the bush, but with the baby . . ." he leaves things in limbo.

We spent some time in a hotel in Salisbury, a city soon to be renamed Harare. The newly independent government was keen to change many city names from the old colonial regime. A lot of places will have their names changed while we live there. Echoes of the Soviet Union when Leningrad was renamed Saint Petersburg. New governments change names and history like window curtains!

We read articles in the national paper about our group's arrival with photos. The group is a mixture of teachers from England, Australia, and India. We remained oblivious to how the local people saw our group. The white, former Rhodesians thought we were all communists. We have moved thousands of miles and yet some things feel like Moscow. We encounter some curious attitudes from some of our white neighbors and colleagues that require some diplomacy. Joann and I rarely mention our Moscow adventure.

Eventually, I am told we will be in Bulawayo and I will teach Geography in a boys' only secondary school. Bulawayo is in the south and Zimbabwe's second biggest city. We boarded an ancient school bus for several hours to reach our new home.

Like Bob sang. "It's gonna be alright, isn't it?

ABOUT THE AUTHORS

JOANN AND JIM MEAD ARE WRITERS AND AUTHORS. THEIR new book is *Married in Moscow: A Red-hot Memoir in Cold War Times*. Together, they share their unlikely adventures and perilous misadventures as expat teachers in the Soviet Union. For more about their lives during a tumultuous era, back in the USSR, visit their website at www.MarriedinMoscow.com.

Jim Mead was born in Wimbledon (London), England. His interests run the gamut from geography to avant-garde electronic music and, of course, tennis. He writes on ethics, case studies, and philosophy. A PhD in education, he taught every grade from Kindergarten to College.

Joann Mead, a California kid, writes crime and mystery thrillers. Her novels are the *Underlying Crimes* of genetic design. She also writes academic articles about disasters and weapons of mass destruction. Her website is www.UnderlyingCrimes.com. She loves taking photographs, especially illegal ones.

They currently live in East Greenwich, Rhode Island.

Made in the USA
Middletown, DE
12 March 2025